The Lineage of the Gods

Zack Strong

A special THANK YOU to the very talented Jessica Malchus for designing the cover art for this book!

Dedicated to my Eternal Parents and to my goodly earthly parents. I love you!

Contents

Introduction

The world is in commotion. Wars rage, tempers flare, hatred boils, contention festers, immorality billows, doubts chafe, and chaos reigns supreme. At the root of this mischief lie two major causes: 1) Mankind's incorrect ideas about the nature and purposes of God; and 2) the fact that man has forgotten his true identity as a literal child of the Eternal Father. It is my firm belief that if man understood who he is and his correct relationship to Deity, most of the problems humanity faces would vanish like phantoms at the break of dawn.

Man's lineage is glorious! We have a divine pedigree. We come from a royal line that includes God as our Father and Jesus Christ as our Elder Brother. It is soul-stirring to know that we are *literal* children of Almighty God! In the beginning, He formed our spirits and we became His beloved children. We lived with Him, walked with Him, talked with Him, and learned our first lessons in the world of spirits before this earth was created.

We are now here on this beautiful globe to undergo a period of intense testing and growth. We are here to show our Father in Heaven what we are capable of achieving when we are away from home and on our own. Our memories have been temporarily veiled and we only remember glimpses of our pre-earth life as the Holy Spirit reveals them to us and as they are given by prophets who receive revelation on the matter. Through these glorious glimpses, small as they may be, we gain confidence that God knows us individually and that we are truly loved.

This book is designed to peel back the layers to give you a taste of your true identity, God's real nature and Plan for your life, and a sense of your awesome potential as a son or daughter of the Eternal Father. It is also my aim to bear fervent testimony of Jesus Christ. He is our Savior and Redeemer, the King of kings and Lord of lords. I love Him and the Father who sent Him to atone for the sins of the world. I love my Eternal Father and Mother, and my Brother and Savior Jesus Christ. I offer this book, however imperfect it may be, as a witness to the truth that I know in my heart and which I have learned through the whisperings of the Holy Ghost.

One final note before we begin. I do not speak for The Church of Jesus Christ of Latter-day Saints. This is not an official publication of the Church. My thoughts are my own and I also take full responsibility for the arrangement and presentation of the quotes I have used to supplement my testimony. I pray that you will open your heart to receive the truth as the Spirit may communicate it to you. Thank you for taking the time to study this imperative topic and to learn more about who you are and what you mean to God.

Chapter First

Living Intelligences

Dear reader, you lived before your birth here on this planet. You lived for eons of time before being sent to earth by God. You have a personal history stretching back to an immeasurable distance. You simply don't remember it. A figurative veil has been placed over your mind to conceal your past in order to give you an honest opportunity to prove yourself during this brief mortal testing period. When your appointed time here is finished, Almighty God will call you home to receive your just reward for how well, or poorly, you faired in your earthly exams.

Perhaps this doctrine of man's pre-mortal existence is new to you. The concept possibly seems outlandish or unbelievable. Maybe it even smacks of blasphemy or comes across as anti-Christian, mystical, or pagan. Yet, I emphatically testify that it is true. It is an authentic precept of Christianity. I give my personal witness, born of the Holy Spirit, that these things are true and that you have a glorious lineage and spiritual heritage.

The place you lived before your Heavenly Father sent you here is called by various names: The pre-earth life; the pre-existence; the pre-mortal world; the realm of spirits; etc. In a broader sense, sometimes we speak of having lived in Heaven for, as we will discuss, we dwelt with God the Father in this pre-earth state. By all available information, this pre-mortal world was a glorious abode – a place where eternity-shaping events transpired and where the foundation for God's Plan of Salvation for His children was laid and made known to me and you.

How did you and I end up in this pre-earth paradise? Where did we come from? What was the moment of our creation? Or were we created at all? Perhaps the scientific rationale will have to wait until the next life before it can be comprehended. However, what we do know through divine revelation is that *we have existed forever*. This doctrine is difficult – perhaps impossible – for our finite minds to grasp at this stage. Little has been definitively revealed, causing us to live by faith as part of our mortal probation.

Though this doctrine was preached in the beginning to Adam and has been touched upon by ancient seers, it is certainly not popular in modern Christendom. Most Christians believe that God created everything out of nothing. They believe that even man was created out of nothing, that he has no past, and that his first intelligent moments occurred after his mortal birth. The truth, however, is far different. If we stop to put aside our preconceived notions and use logic and let the Holy Spirit and the revelations of God guide us, we will discern the truth about who we are, where we come from, and our true relationship with our Eternal Father.

We once existed as intelligences. What that means precisely has been intentionally kept from us, but will be revealed in the Lord's due time. We do know, however, that in the beginning we had individuality and that each of us was susceptible of advancement, growth, and learning. In fact, we have been learning and progressing from that indefinable period to this very moment.

Just three months prior to his martyrdom, the Prophet Joseph Smith began to peel back the layers of this great mystery and gave us an inkling of knowledge of our true origin. He once remarked that he could reveal "a hundred fold more" than he ever had about "the glories of heaven" if the Saints were prepared to receive it.[1] Though they were not prepared to fully receive this flood of new light, the Prophet gave the Saints a stunning glimpse of the knowledge that awaited them when he explained the following in his King Follett Discourse:

> "Is it logical to say that the intelligence of spirits is immortal, and yet that it has a beginning? The intelligence of spirits had no beginning, neither will it have an end. That is good logic. That which has a beginning may have an end. There never was a time when there were not spirits; for they are [co-eternal] with our Father in heaven.

---

[1] Joseph Smith, *Documentary History of the Church*, Vol. 5, 402, May 21, 1843, https://byustudies.byu.edu/content/volume-5-chapter-21.

". . . I take my ring from my finger and liken it unto the mind of man—the immortal part, because it had no beginning. Suppose you cut it in two; then it has a beginning and an end; but join it again, and it continues one eternal round. So with the spirit of man. As the Lord liveth, if it had a beginning, it will have an end. All the fools and learned and wise men from the beginning of creation, who say that the spirit of man had a beginning, prove that it must have an end; and if that doctrine is true, then the doctrine of annihilation would be true. But if I am right, I might with boldness proclaim from the housetops that God never had the power to create the spirit of man at all. God himself could not create himself.

"Intelligence is eternal and exists upon a self-existent principle. It is a spirit from age to age and there is no creation about it. All the minds and spirits that God ever sent into the world are susceptible of enlargement.

"The first principles of man are self-existent with God. God himself, finding he was in the midst of spirits and glory, because he was more intelligent, saw proper to institute laws whereby the rest could have a privilege to advance like himself. The relationship we have with God places us in a situation to advance in knowledge. He has power to institute laws to instruct the weaker intelligences, that they may be exalted with Himself, so that they might have one glory upon another, and all that knowledge, power, glory, and intelligence, which is requisite in order to save them in the world of spirits."[2]

This is a powerful and revolutionary explanation of man's origin! Let's analyze this important teaching.

The Prophet taught that intelligences, or the "intelligence of spirits," had no beginning. They are eternal, in whatever form "intelligence" takes. This intelligence, of which man consists, has existed for as long as God has

---

[2] Joseph Smith, King Follett Discourse, General Conference, April 7, 1844, https://www.lds.org/ensign/1971/05/the-king-follett-sermon?lang=eng.

existed. God, our Father, found that these intelligences were "susceptible of enlargement." He thereby initiated a Plan for the advancement of these intelligences to become like Himself.

Intelligence is self-existent. It cannot be created and it cannot be destroyed. It is eternal – eternal as God the Father. In one of the most doctrine-filled revelations given to this generation through Joseph Smith, we are informed by the Savior that:

> "Man was also in the beginning with God. Intelligence, or the light of truth, was not created or made, neither indeed can be" (D&C 93:29).

We see that the Prophet's teaching in the King Follett Discourse harmonized with what the Lord has plainly revealed by His own mouth. The intelligences are co-eternal with God and have existed always. Or in other words: "Man was also in the beginning with God."

Commenting on these very truths, President Joseph Fielding Smith gave one explanation why intelligence is eternal and cannot be created. He observed:

> "The Lord revealed to the Prophet Joseph Smith this great truth: That matter is co-eternal with God and always existed. . . .
>
> "If the Lord declares that intelligence, something which we do not fully understand, was co-eternal with him and always existed, there is no argument that we can or should present to contradict it. Why he cannot create intelligence is simply because intelligence, like time and space, always existed, and therefore did not have to be created. However, intelligences spoken of in the Book of Abraham were created, for these are spirit children of God, begotten sons."[3]

Another time, President Smith fielded a question on a similar topic and phrased his teaching this way:

---

[3] Joseph Fielding Smith, *Answers to Gospel Question*, Vol. 3 (Salt Lake City, UT: Deseret Book Company, 1960), 124-125.

"Some of our writers have endeavored to explain what an intelligence is, but to do so is futile, for we have never been given any insight into this matter beyond what the Lord has fragmentarily revealed. We know, however, that there is something called intelligence which always existed. It is the real eternal part of man, which was not created nor made. This intelligence combined with the spirit constitutes a spiritual identity or individual."[4]

In a manner inexplicable to our limited capacity to understand in our present mortal state, God formed the spirit of man in His own image. We were begotten of Him and our Eternal Mother. The intelligences became fully conscious spirit entities when our begotten spirit combined with this eternal intelligence to create an individual son or daughter of God.

This is wherein we were "created" by God. Our spirits, which were begotten by our Eternal Parents, combined with this intelligence we are discussing to create a fully unique spirit identity. As President Smith noted, we know precious little about this process because the Lord simply has not revealed it to us. Considering how we trample other revealed knowledge of dramatically lesser importance, it is no wonder that He has kept this great secret to Himself and is waiting for the Father's children to sufficiently prepare themselves to receive it.

Elder Erastus Snow once described his view of how God "created" us. He explained:

"And when Luke, in giving us the genealogy of Jesus Christ, traces his lineage back through his mother to David, who was the son of Jesse, and so on, he traces his descent until he reaches Abraham, who was the son of Terah, and so on to Noah, who was the son of Lamech; and when he reaches Adam, the first of our race, he says of him, "which was the son of God." Oh, says one, we are told that Adam was created, not born. This is something I am not disposed to dwell upon much at this time. You can think of this as you please, whether he was created or born, or whether a man,

---

[4] Smith, *Answers to Gospel Question*, Vol. 4, 126-127.

because he is born, is not created. I do not understand the term *creation* as meaning something suddenly made out of nothing. I believe man that is born is as much created as the thing which is made in a mold and turned out to dry, which we call an adobie. It matters not whether it takes a few minutes to make it, or a longer period—it is created or made. And the term create I understand to be synonymous with the verb to make, and what is made is created, and what is organized is formed. And when it is written that God formed man in his own image and likeness, it does not describe the time or manner, but simply the fact of having made or created man in his own image."[5]

To Elder Snow, God created man in the same way a craftsman takes pre-existing materials – such as wood, stone, or clay – and forms them into an object such as a table or a vase. We do not see a fallen log and say, "Look, a table!" The wood must be worked and shaped and formed until what is "created" by the craftsman resembles what man recognizes and accepts as a table. Yet, though the labor and expertise of the builder shaped the wood into a table, and he is thus seen as its creator, the wood existed before and did not appear out of nothing. In the same way, God is the literal Father of our spirits, and these spirits, combined through His instrumentality and expertise with pre-existing intelligence, became His "creations," or, more appropriately, His children.

Elder Bruce R. McConkie explained the concepts of intelligence and intelligences this way:

> "Intelligence, or light and truth, is also used as a synonym for spirit element. Scriptures using both terms speak of the self-existent nature of the substance involved. (D&C 93:29; 131:7-8.) Abraham calls the pre-existent spirits "the intelligences that were organized before the world was" (Abra. 3:22) because the intelligences were organized intelligence or in other words the spirit bodies were born from spirit element."

---

[5] Elder Erastus Snow, *Journal of Discourses*, Vol. 19, 323-324, January 20, 1878, http://jod.mrm.org/19/322.

Elder McConkie further observed:

> "Abraham used the name intelligences to apply to the spirit children of the Eternal Father. The intelligence of spirit element became intelligences after the spirits were born as individual entities. (Abra. 3:22-24.) Use of this name designates both the primal element from which the spirit offspring were created and also their inherited capacity to grow in grace, knowledge, power, and intelligence itself, until such intelligences, gaining the fulness of all things, become like their Father, the Supreme Intelligence."[6]

You and I come from intelligence. We are intelligences that combined with "spirit element" from our Father and became truly and literally the spirit children of God. We are His begotten sons and daughters. We inherited from Him a unique "capacity to grow in grace, knowledge, and intelligence itself." We were with God in the beginning, are made of the same substance He is, and possess His extraordinary potential within our very DNA.

In another work, Elder McConkie wrote this of the pre-mortal Christ, part of which applies to us:

> "Though he has now attained unto that exalted state in which he is described as being "from everlasting to everlasting" (D&C 61:1) and "from all eternity to all eternity" (D&C 39:1) – as will eventually be the description and state of all those who gain exaltation (D&C 132:20) – yet, as a conscious identity, he had a beginning. He was born, as were all the spirit children of the Father. God was his Father, as he is of all the rest. For him, as for all men – and he is the Prototype – the eternal spirit element that has neither beginning nor end, and is self-existent by nature, was organized into a spirit body. He was one of "the intelligences that

---

[6] Bruce R. McConkie, *Mormon Doctrine*, 2nd Edition (Salt Lake City, UT: Bookcraft, 1966), 387.

were organized before the world was." (Abr. 3:22.) He was and is the Firstborn of the Father."[7]

Just as Jesus had a "beginning" when His timeless intelligence was fused to a spirit body that was begotten by the Eternal Father and became the very first son of God, so, too, you and I were begotten by the Father and owe our existence as spirits to Him. Our intelligence combined with this spirit element − or spirit body − from the Father to give us our spiritual identity as an irreplaceable son or daughter of the Almighty.

On many occasions, Joseph Smith reiterated this doctrine of the immortality of our spirits. In an 1842 article for the *Times and Seasons*, the Prophet remarked:

> "[T]he spirits of men are eternal . . . they are organized according to that priesthood which is everlasting, "without beginning of days or end of years," − that they all move in their respective spheres, and are governed by the law of God; that when they appear upon the earth they are in a probationary state, and are preparing, if righteous, for a future and greater glory."[8]

President Joseph Fielding Smith also testified of the eternal nature of all things that were organized by the great Elohim:

> "Every creature had a spiritual existence. The spirits of men, beasts, and all animal life, existed before the foundations of the earth were laid, and are living entities."[9]

Another time, President Smith explained:

> "[T]he inhabitants of these worlds created by Jesus Christ, are begotten sons and daughters unto God. Life did not originate

---

[7] Bruce R. McConkie, *The Promised Messiah: The First Coming of Christ* (Salt Lake City, UT: Deseret Book Company, 1978), 46.

[8] Joseph Smith, *Documentary History of the Church*, Vol. 4, 575, April 1, 1842, https://byustudies.byu.edu/content/volume-4-chapter-33.

[9] President Joseph Fielding Smith, in Bruce R. McConkie, ed., *Doctrines of Salvation*, Vol. 1 (Salt Lake City, UT: Bookcraft, 1994),62.

here. We are told by our Father in heaven that man is eternal; that he has always existed, and that all life on this earth came from elsewhere."[10]

All things, even the animals, had an existence prior to the creation of this earth. All of these had immortal spirits which lived in the world of spirits before. These spirits resembled their earthly form and do not change. There they maintained their exclusive gender, form, and individuality. Chief among these spirit creations was man. Immortal man is the child of Eternal God, His glorious progeny.

Since it was spirit that gave our intelligence the vehicle through which to grow and progress, perhaps it is well to ask: What exactly is spirit? As we have seen, the full details have not been revealed. However, we do know that spirit is matter. Spirit is *not* immaterial, as so many of the creeds of Christendom claim. Spirit and intelligence are found in all creations of God. President Brigham Young spoke of this principle often. In one 1856 address, he taught the Saints a little of the function of spirit and matter:

> "I will bring to your minds what I have formerly stated with regard to the spirit's entering the body. Our bodies are composed of visible, tangible matter, as you all understand, you also know that they are born into this world. They then begin to partake of the elements adapted to their organization and growth, increase to manhood, become old, decay, and pass again into the dust. Now in the first place, though I have explained this many times, what we call death is the operation of life, inherent in the matter of which the body is composed, and which causes the decomposition after the spirit has left the body. Were that not the fact, the body, from which has fled the spirit, would remain to all eternity just as it was when the spirit left it, and would not decay.

> "What is commonly called death does not destroy the body, it only causes a separation of spirit and body, but the principle of life, inherent in the native elements, of which the body is

---

[10] Smith, *Doctrines of Salvation*, Vol. 1, 74.

composed, still continues with the particles of that body and causes it to decay, to dissolve itself into the elements of which it was composed, and all of which continue to have life. When the spirit given to man leaves the body, the tabernacle begins to decompose, is that death? No, death only separates the spirit and body, and a principle of life still operates in the untenanted tabernacle, but in a different way, and producing different effects from those observed while it was tenanted by the spirit. There is not a particle of element which is not filled with life, and all space is filled with element; there is no such thing as empty space, though some philosophers contend that there is.

"Life in various proportions, combinations, conditions, &c., fills all matter. Is there life in a tree when it ceases to put forth leaves? You see it standing upright, and when it ceases to bear leaves and fruit you say it is dead, but that is a mistake. It still has life, but that life operates upon the tree in another way, and continues to operate until it resolves it to the native elements. It is life in another condition that begins to operate upon man, upon animal, upon vegetation, and upon minerals when we see the change termed dissolution. There is life in the material of the fleshly tabernacle, independent of the spirit given of God to undergo this probation. There is life in all matter, throughout the vast extent of all the eternities; it is in the rock, the sand, the dust, in water, air, the gases, and, in short, in every description and organization of matter, whether it be solid, liquid, or gaseous, particle operating with particle."[11]

Every "particle of element" in our vast universe is filled with life. There is no "empty space." There is nothing immaterial. Nothing exists in vain. There is, of a truth, "life in all matter" – in the animals, in the earth, and of course in our own human spirits and earthly bodies. We once lived in this realm of spirits and understood the operation of these eternal mechanisms far more extensively than we understand them today.

---

[11] President Brigham Young, *Journal of Discourses*, Vol. 3, 276-277, March 23, 1856, http://jod.mrm.org/3/272.

Fortunately, however, the Lord has sent prophets – choice spirit intelligences – to instruct mankind and prepare us to receive a flood of knowledge and light at some future time.

The beloved apostle, Elder McConkie, touched upon this spirit aspect of our nature when he said:

> "Spirits are eternal beings, men and women created in the image of the Eternal Father, whose offspring they are. Their bodies are made of a more pure and refined substance than that which composes the mortal body. "All spirit is matter," the Prophet said, "but is more fine or pure, and can only be discerned by purer eyes." (D&C 131:7.)"[12]

The type of existence we entered into when intelligence fused with spirit can be seen as an upgrade – an advancement into a state of progression as spirit children of God. These spirit bodies are made of a type of matter. They perfectly resemble our physical bodies but are more pure and refined.

On the topic of spirit substance, the Prophet Joseph Smith wrote:

> "In tracing the thing to the foundation, and looking at it philosophically, we shall find a very material difference between the body and the spirit; the body is supposed to be organized matter, and the spirit, by many, is thought to be immaterial, without substance. With this latter statement we should beg leave to differ, and state that spirit is a substance; that it is material, but that it is more pure, elastic and refined matter than the body; that it existed before the body, can exist in the body; and will exist separate from the body, when the body will be mouldering in the dust; and will in the resurrection, be again united with it."[13]

---

[12] McConkie, *The Promised Messiah*, 47.

[13] Joseph Smith, *Documentary History of the Church*, Vol. 4, 575, April 1, 1842, https://byustudies.byu.edu/content/volume-4-chapter-33.

Our spirits, then, are absolutely *not* immaterial. Nothing, in fact, can be immaterial. Our spirits are a substance of some sort that we do not fully comprehend. A revelation from the Lord teaches:

> "For man is spirit. The elements are eternal, and spirit and element, inseparably connected, receive a fulness of joy" (D&C 93:33).

These spirits from our Eternal Parents fused with our pre-existing intelligence and you and I were "created." When we enter into mortality, these spirits are clothed in a body made of the elements – the "dust of the ground" (Genesis 2:7). Together, this intelligent spirit and the body that houses it can experience "a fulness of joy" such as our Heavenly Father enjoys.

It is an incredible thing to realize whose children we are. This is life-changing knowledge! To know that we are *literal* spirit children of the literal living God should cause a paradigm shift in every mind. It should humble us and also give us confidence to know that we have some portion of divinity within us; that we are as eternal as God; that we have an inherent intelligence within us that can expand and grow indefinitely.

The prophet Brigham Young expressed his tender feelings engendered by this precious knowledge when he taught:

> "This intelligence which is within you and me is from heaven. In gazing upon the intelligence reflected in the countenances of my fellow beings, I gaze upon the image of Him whom I worship—the God I serve. I see His image and a certain amount of His intelligence there. I feel it within myself. My nature shrinks at the divinity we see in others."[14]

When we see our fellow man, we see a glimmer of God. When we deal with our brothers or sisters, we are dealing with beings endowed with godly potential. It is an incredible and humbling thing to realize we are

---

[14] President Brigham Young, *Journal of Discourses*, Vol. 13, 171, May 29, 1870, http://jod.mrm.org/13/170.

associating with heirs of Heaven – and that we ourselves have a largely untouched reserve of divine potential inherent in ourselves.

President Young's statement reminds me of one made by Christian theologian C.S. Lewis. He observed:

> "It is a serious thing to live in a society of possible gods and goddesses, to remember that the dullest and most uninteresting person you talk to may one day be a creature which, if you saw it now, you would be strongly tempted to worship, or else a horror and a corruption such as you now meet, if at all, only in a nightmare. All day long we are, in some degree, helping each other to one or other of these destinations. It is in the light of these overwhelming possibilities, it is with the awe and the circumspection proper to them, that we should conduct all our dealings with one another, all friendships, all loves, all play, all politics. There are no ordinary people. You have never talked to a mere mortal. Nations, cultures, arts, civilizations — these are mortal, and their life is to ours as the life of a gnat. But it is immortals whom we joke with, work with, marry, snub and exploit — immortal horrors or everlasting splendors."[15]

No, we have never seen, talked to, or associated with "mere mortals." Not one of us is "ordinary." We did not originate here on earth and our existence is not attributable to a roll of the cosmic dice or some fateful Big Bang. We are here as part of a greater Plan for our advancement and eventual exaltation in the world of spirits. We are loved and special children of the God of the universe.

Each of us has an untapped reservoir of divinity within us. We are all – even the very weakest and most vicious among us – potential heirs of Almighty God. Our spirits are as immortal and eternal as the Spirit of God. We have a portion of His character, attributes, and potential inside us because *we are His immortal spirit children.*

---

[15] James Jardine, "10 memorable quotes from C.S. Lewis," *Deseret News*, November 19, 2013, accessed July 30, 2018, https://www.deseretnews.com/article/865590913/10-memorable-quotes-from-CS-Lewis.html.

We will now talk a little about different aspects of creation. Jumping back to the King Follett Discourse, we see the Prophet further expounding what is meant by the Bible's opening declaration that: "In the beginning God created the heaven and the earth" (Genesis 1:1). He explained:

> "Now, I ask all who hear me, why the learned men who are preaching salvation, say that God created the heavens and the earth out of nothing? The reason is, that they are unlearned in the things of God, and have not the gift of the Holy Ghost; they account it blasphemy in any one to contradict their idea. If you tell them that God made the world out of something, they will call you a fool. . . .

> "You ask the learned doctors why they say the world was made out of nothing, and they will answer, "Doesn't the Bible say he *created* the world?" And they infer, from the word create, that it must have been made out of nothing. Now, the word create came from the word *baurau,* which does not mean to create out of nothing; it means to organize; the same as a man would organize materials and build a ship. Hence we infer that God had materials to organize the world out of chaos—chaotic matter, which is element, and in which dwells all the glory. Element had an existence from the time He had. The pure principles of element are principles which can never be destroyed; they may be organized and re-organized, but not destroyed. They had no beginning and can have no end."

The Prophet continued:

> ". . . the soul—the mind of man —the immortal spirit. Where did it come from? All learned men and doctors of divinity say that God created it in the beginning; but it is not so: the very idea lessens man in my estimation. I do not believe the doctrine; I know better. Hear it, all ye ends of the world; for God has told me so; and if you don't believe me, it will not make the truth without effect. . . .

> "We say that God Himself is a self-existing being. Who told you so? It is correct enough; but how did it get into your heads? Who

told you that man did not exist in like manner upon the same principles? Man does exist upon the same principles. . . .

"The mind or the intelligence which man possesses is [co-eternal] with God himself. I know that my testimony is true."

This doctrinal clarification of the Bible's intent is logical and it feels right. God is the Creator, yes, but He does *not* create things – let alone His children – out of nothing. Matter or element exists eternally. It can be organized or changed from one form to another, but it cannot be created out of nothing. It also cannot be destroyed or annihilated, though it can have its form or organization manipulated and changed.

This beautiful earth that we live on was not created out of nothing. In fact, we have been taught that this earth is a living entity with its own spirit or intelligence. In Ecclesiastes 1:4, this is hinted at when we are told that "the earth abideth for ever." Anciently, when Enoch had his glorious vision of God, he witnessed the living nature and cognizance of the earth. *The Pearl of Great Price* records:

"And it came to pass that Enoch looked upon the earth; and he heard a voice from the bowels thereof, saying: Wo, wo is me, the mother of men; I am pained, I am weary, because of the wickedness of my children. When shall I rest, and be cleansed from the filthiness which is gone forth out of me? When will my Creator sanctify me, that I may rest, and righteousness for a season abide upon my face?

"And when Enoch heard the earth mourn, he wept, and cried unto the Lord, saying: O Lord, wilt thou not have compassion upon the earth?" (Moses 7:48-49).

Additionally, speaking of the living earth upon which we dwell, modern revelation tells us:

"For after it hath filled the measure of its creation, it shall be crowned with glory, even with the presence of God the Father;

"That bodies who are of the celestial kingdom may possess it forever and ever" (D&C 88:19-20).

Now that we have established the eternal nature of the earth, including the element of spirit or intelligence it possesses, we turn our attention to its physical creation. As noted, the earth was not created out of nothing, but, rather, was created from pre-existing elements of matter. The apostle Orson Pratt once explained:

> "There is not a hint in all the Bible that God created this or any other world out of nothing. The work of creation was to take the materials that existed from all eternity, that never were created or made out of nothing, to take these self-existent materials and organize them into a world. This is called creation. There is, however, a declaration made by many religious people, that "God created all things out of nothing." They even teach it in their Sunday schools; but they have never been able to prove any such thing. It is one of those ideas which have got into the minds of people through the teachings of uninspired men. The ancients— those who lived many centuries before Christ, did not believe this doctrine; but since the days of Christ, and since the days of the great apostasy, they have got up the idea that God made all things out of nothing, and they have incorporated it into their disciplines, catechisms, Sunday schoolbooks, and various works which they have published. The Scriptures say—"In the beginning God created the heavens and the earth." The word "create" does not mean make out of nothing. For instance, when he says—"I created darkness and I created light," what does he do? Does he absolutely form light out of nothing? No, he causes the light that existed from all eternity to shine where darkness existed, and it is light creating light, the same as you, when you attend meeting, lock up your house and blow out the lights. When you return, supposing you say in your own hearts, or to your wife, daughter, or son, "Let there be light." Do you create it out of nothing? No, you look for a match, or for some means by which you can start the light and cause it to be exhibited, where darkness was before. So when God creates light he calls forth and makes to shine that light which has existed from all eternity. We read that God is light. Was there ever a time that God did not exist? No, and if he is light

there never was a time when light did not exist, one being as eternal as the other."[16]

One element of matter is as eternal as the next – and all are as eternal as God. Being the Supreme Intelligence of the universe, however, our Eternal Father saw fit to use His honor, which is His power (D&C 29:36), to prevail upon matter, element, and intelligence to organize and form worlds, and to form man in His own image. This is His joy, His work, and His glory (Moses 1:39).

Another fascinating concept in the divine drama of creation that we mention only momentarily is that it is the Holy Spirit that acts as the energy by which things come to pass and are created, purified, and cleansed. This idea was spoken of by Elder John A. Widtsoe in his fascinating book *Joseph Smith as Scientist*. He wrote:

> "The property of intelligence is to the Holy Spirit what energy is to the gross material of our senses.

> "In one of the generally accepted works of the Church, the energy of nature is actually said to be the workings of the Holy Spirit. The passage reads as follows: "Man observes a universal energy in nature – organization and disorganization succeed each other – the thunders roll through the heavens; the earth trembles and becomes broken by earthquakes; fires consume cities and forests; the waters accumulate, flow over their usual bounds, and cause destruction of life and property; the worlds perform their revolutions in space with a velocity and power incomprehensible to man, and he, covered with a veil of darkness, calls this universal energy, God, when it is the workings of his Spirit, the obedient agent of his power, the wonder-working and life-giving principle in all nature."

> "In short, the writings of the Church clearly indicate that the various forces of nature, the energy of nature, are only

---

[16] Elder Orson Pratt, *Journal of Discourses*, Vol. 16, 315-316, November 22, 1873, http://jod.mrm.org/16/312.

manifestations of the great, pervading force of intelligence. We do not understand the real nature of intelligence any better than we understand the true nature of energy. We only know that by energy or intelligence gross matter is brought within reach of our senses."[17]

Everything is brought to pass, then, by spirit, or intelligence; in particular, by the Holy Spirit of our God. This is the "energy" that pulsates throughout the universe and quickens, cleanses, and prevails upon all matter, spirit, and life.

The title Holy Spirit, in ancient Hebrew and Greek – the languages of the Old and New Testaments – comes from the words meaning breath or wind; *ruach* in Hebrew and *pneuma* in Greek. These not only refer to the Holy Ghost, but to spirit or spirits in general. The scriptures contain many interesting passages that deal with wind or breath. When we understand these as the influence of the Holy Ghost, or as referring to spirit, they make more sense.

I refer to just a few such verses. On the day of Pentecost, for instance, the apostles heard a sound "as of a rushing mighty wind" and "were all filled with the Holy Ghost, and began to speak with other tongues, as the Spirit gave them utterance" (Acts 2:1-4). That occasion was made sacred and momentous because of the presence of the Holy Ghost, this divine breath or wind that rushed upon the apostles.

Ezekiel also recorded:

> "Then said he unto me, Prophesy unto the wind, prophesy, son of man, and say to the wind, Thus saith the Lord God; Come from the four winds, O breath, and breathe upon these slain, that they may live.
>
> "So I prophesied as he commanded me, and the breath came into them, and they lived" (Ezekiel 37:9-10).

---

[17] John A. Widtsoe, *Joseph Smith as Scientist: A Contribution to Mormon Philosophy* (Salt Lake City, UT: The General Board Young Men's Mutual Improvement Associations, 1908), 17.

Lastly, in the book of Moses, we find this teaching about breath and spirit:

> "And I, the Lord God, formed man from the dust of the ground, and breathed into his nostrils the breath of life; and man became a living soul" (Moses 3:7).

Remember, the spirit and body together form a soul (D&C 88:15). Thus, the breath of life is the spirit of life that animated our physical bodies. And the Holy Ghost operates by this same divine power – this breath, wind, spirit, intelligence, and life from God.

Elder Bruce R. McConkie once wrote of this Divine Being:

> "He is the Comforter, Testator, Revelator, Sanctifier, Holy Spirit, Holy Spirit of Promise, Spirit of Truth, Spirit of the Lord, and Messenger of the Father and Son, and his companionship is the greatest gift that mortal man can enjoy. His mission is to perform all of the functions appertaining to the various name-titles which he bears. Because he is a Spirit Personage, he has power – according to the eternal laws ordained by the Father – to perform essential and unique functions for men."[18]

The Holy Ghost performs a myriad of functions and has a somewhat special relationship to man. Through His instrumentality, the Father's and Son's love, light, and influence are carried to the world and into the hearts of individuals. It is His power and influence that is often seen as energy and which moves and influences all things. It is the Holy Spirit who is so personally involved in the process of our conversion to the truth and in the changing of our hearts and natures. We cannot truly come to the Redeemer Jesus Christ without the Holy Ghost enabling us to receive truth, gain testimonies, purge our souls of sin, and become new creatures with new hearts.

One more quotation on the Holy Ghost and His mode of operating seems appropriate before we move forward. President Joseph F. Smith taught:

---

[18] McConkie, Mormon Doctrine, 359.

"The Holy Ghost as a personage of Spirit can no more be omnipresent in person than can the Father or the Son, but by his intelligence, his knowledge, his power and influence, over and through the laws of nature, he is and can be omnipresent throughout all the works of God. It is not the Holy Ghost who in person lighteth every man who is born into the world, but it is the light of Christ, the Spirit of Truth, which proceeds from the source of intelligence, which permeates all nature, which lighteth every man and fills the immensity of space. You may call it the Spirit of God, you may call it the influence of God's intelligence, you may call it the substance of his power, no matter what it is called, it is the spirit of intelligence that permeates the universe and gives to the spirits of men understanding. . . .

". . . The Spirit of God which emanates from Deity may be likened to electricity, or the universal ether . . . which fills the earth and the air, and is everywhere present. It is the power of God, the influence that he exerts throughout all his works by which he can effect his purposes and execute his will, in consonance with the laws of free agency which he has conferred upon man."[19]

These enthralling teachings give us a fragmentary glimpse into the workings of our universe and into the creative process of our great God. Nearly everything hinges upon the concept of intelligence and the existence of living intelligences. The spirit of the Eternal Father operates through all things like the unseen electricity that darts through the air. It is the energy, the force, the presence, the power, the intelligence which "permeates the universe," "lighteth every man," and "fills the immensity of space."

These prophetic teachings have their root in the revealed word of God. In a revelation given to the Prophet Joseph Smith by our resurrected Redeemer, we learn:

---

[19] Joseph F. Smith, *Gospel Doctrine* (Salt Lake City, UT: Deseret Book Company, 1977), 61-62.

"Ye were also in the beginning with the Father; that which is Spirit, even the Spirit of truth. . . .

"The Spirit of truth is of God. I am the Spirit of truth. . . .

"He that keepeth his commandments receiveth truth and light, until he is glorified in truth and knoweth all things.

"Man was also in the beginning with God. Intelligence, or the light of truth, was not created or made, neither indeed can be.

"All truth is independent in that sphere in which God has placed it, to act for itself, as all intelligence also; otherwise there is no existence" (D&C 93:23, 26, 28-30).

We learn from these verses many truths. One of these facts is that truth and intelligence are "independent" and act for themselves. Within the confines of their individual spheres, every intelligence – whether animal, human, or otherwise – is independent and has always been so. Hence, the doctrine of agency is eternal – and one intelligence is as free and independent as the next in its own sphere and within its own limits.

Those intelligences which come to the light and partake of the Spirit of Truth are those which are blessed. We read:

"For intelligence cleaveth unto intelligence; wisdom receiveth wisdom; truth embraceth truth; virtue loveth virtue; light cleaveth unto light" (D&C 88:40).

We can phrase this spiritual law of attraction another way. Those who are intelligent come to the true light, who is Jesus Christ. The light emanates from the Father and the Son through the Holy Ghost. And those who embrace the light embrace the Godhead and share of Their divine nature.

The Savior revealed the origin of light and a portion of its function in the vast universe:

"And the light which shineth, which giveth you light, is through him who enlighteneth your eyes, which is the same light that quickeneth your understandings;

"Which light proceedeth forth from the presence of God to fill the immensity of space –

"The light which is in all things, which giveth life to all things, which is the law by which all things are governed, even the power of God who sitteth upon his throne, who is in the bosom of eternity, who is in the midst of all things. . . .

"He comprehendeth all things, and all things are before him, and all things are round about him; and he is above all things, and in all things, and is through all things, and is round about all things; and all things are by him, and of him, even God, forever and ever.

"And again, verily I say unto you, he hath given a law unto all things, by which they move in their times and their seasons;

"And their courses are fixed, even the courses of the heavens and the earth, which comprehend the earth and all the planets.

"And they give light to each other" (D&C 88:11-13, 41-44).

Light, then, is the manifestation of God's power. It shines forth from His throne. It penetrates and encompasses all things. This light is the everlasting intelligence we are discussing. The planets, and all things, "give light to each other." This, apparently, is how God governs and directs the movement of the planets, the creation of worlds, and all things that He does. The intelligences which "fill the immensity of space" are directed by the light and truth which come from God. They are attracted to the light and intelligence which emanates from Him. They honor and obey His perfect, just commands.

To come to the light, then, in its true sense, means to come to Jesus Christ and His Father. It means to know Them and partake of Their presence. It means to come into harmony with Them and the light which fills space. Those who do this are blessed. Those who come to the eternal light make their abode with God (John 14:21, 23).

By contrast, those intelligences which come under condemnation are those who, though they were in the beginning with God and once partook of His light and truth and affirmed the true nature of all things, now reject the light and the truth because of their agency. In rejecting this intelligence, they reject their very nature, that substance known as intelligence which animates them, and the nature and intelligence of their Father and His Son. They reject the function and order of the universe and despise the honor of God. They set themselves at odds with the light and knowledge that fills space. By rejecting the light, they reject law, order, and true intelligence – even the Supreme Intelligence. Section 93 reads:

> "Behold, here is the agency of man, and here is the condemnation of man; because that which was from the beginning is plainly manifest unto them, and they receive not the light.

> "And every man whose spirit receiveth not the light is under condemnation. . . .

> "The glory of God is intelligence, or, in other words, light and truth.

> "Light and truth forsake that evil one." (D&C 93:31-32, 36-37).

The importance of receiving light and truth, or the divine spirit and godly intelligence, is paramount to eternal progression and happiness. What hangs in the balance of our decision to accept or reject this eternal light emanating from our God was perhaps best described by Jesus when He said: "And ye shall know the truth, and the truth shall make you free" (John 8:32).

If we accept the light, and cleave unto intelligence, we shall be eternally free. By accepting the truth, we accept God – the Supreme Intelligence – and His Son Jesus Christ, who is "the light and the life of the world" (3 Nephi 11:11). If we reject this light, we walk in darkness and march willingly into everlasting captivity. To reject the light is to embrace "that evil one" who is the prince of darkness.

Perhaps, after comprehending this notion of light, truth, and intelligence, we can better understand what Jesus taught when he described the Devil's fallen nature. Of Lucifer – a title ironically denoting "lightbringer" or the "bearer of the light" – the Lord taught:

"He was a murderer from the beginning, and abode not in the truth, because there is no truth in him. When he speaketh a lie, he speaketh of his own: for he is a liar, and the father of it."

The Devil did not cleave unto the light. He did not bring his life into harmony with the plainly manifest truth. He did not accept the overarching intelligence that permeates all things throughout the universe. Instead, he, of his own accord, said he knew better than God. He rejected the very order of the universe. He rejected the intelligence inherent in his own spirit being, and the light from God which animated that spirit. Instead, he embraced chaos and disorder. He embraced darkness, or the absence of God's light, truth, and intelligence. No fate could be worse, particularly for one whose lofty pre-mortal position gave him authority to bear the light (D&C 76:25).

What an indescribable tragedy for a spirit child of the God of Light to reject that very light, truth, and intelligence! Truly, God mourned when He recounted to Enoch how His children hated their own kind and how they, in rejecting their true Father, became the children of Satan and must inevitably suffer:

"The Lord said unto Enoch: Behold these thy brethren; they are the workmanship of mine own hands, and I gave unto them their knowledge, in the day I created them; and in the Garden of Eden, gave I unto man his agency;

"And unto thy brethren have I said, and also given commandment, that they should love one another, and that they should choose me, their Father; but behold, they are without affection, and they hate their own blood;

"And the fire of mine indignation is kindled against them; and in my hot displeasure will I send in the floods upon them, for my fierce anger is kindled against them.

"Behold, I am God; Man of Holiness is my name; Man of Counsel is my name; and Endless and Eternal is my name, also.

"Wherefore, I can stretch forth mine hands and hold all the creations which I have made; and mine eye can pierce them also, and among all the workmanship of mine hands there has not been so great wickedness as among thy brethren.

"But behold, their sins shall be upon the heads of their fathers; Satan shall be their father, and misery shall be their doom; and the whole heavens shall weep over them, even all the workmanship of mind hands; wherefore should not the heavens weep, seeing these shall suffer?" (Moses 7:32-37).

In recalling these scriptures, it becomes plain to see how important it is to use our agency wisely. We must, as intelligences ourselves, cleave unto intelligence. We must embrace the knowledge of our true origin and nature. We must become the "children of light" and embrace the light of our Father and His Son who has ransomed us (Ephesians 5:8; D&C 106:5). If we do not, our fate will be terrible, we will have rejected the light of the universe, and Heaven will weep. Such is the potential, both for good and evil, of the intelligence within our spirits.

At the April 1853 General Conference, Elder Parley P. Pratt discoursed on the "heirship" of the sons and daughters of God. He made a few enlightening remarks about intelligence and intelligences, some of which I repeat here:

"We will go back to the earliest knowledge we have of the existence of intelligences. We learn from the writings of Abraham and others, and from modern revelation, that the intelligences that now inhabit these tabernacles of earth were living, active intelligences in yonder world, while the particles of matter which now compose our outward bodies were yet mingled with their native element; that then our embodied spirits lived, moved, conversed, and exercised an agency. All intelligences which exist possess a degree of independence in their own sphere. For instance, the bee can go at will in search of honey, or remain in the hive. It can visit one flower or another, as independent in its own sphere as God is in His. We find a degree of independence in everything which possesses any degree of intelligence; that thinks, moves, or acts: because the very principle of voluntary action implies an independent will to direct such action.

"Among the intelligences which existed in the beginning, some were more intelligent than others, or, in other words, more noble; and God said to Abraham, "These I will make my rulers!" God said unto Abraham, "Thou art one of them; thou wast chosen before thou wast born."

"Noble! Does He use the word *noble?* Yes; the word noble, or that which signified it, was used in conversation between God and Abraham, and applied to superior intelligences on earth, and which had pre-existed in the heavens. . . .

"Although some eternal intelligences may be superior to others, and although some are more noble, and consequently are elected to fill certain useful and necessary offices for the good of others, yet the greater and the less may both be innocent, and both be justified, and be useful, each in their own capacity; if each magnify their own calling, and act in their own capacity, it is all right.

"It may be inquired, why God made one unequal to another, or inferior in intellect or capacity. To which I reply, that He did not create their intelligence at all. It never was created, being an inherent attribute of the eternal element called spirit, which element composes each individual spirit, and which element exists in an infinitude of degrees in the scale of intellect, in all the varieties manifested in the eternal God, and thence to the lowest agent, which acts by its own will.

"It is a fixed law of nature that the higher intelligence presides over, or has more or less influence over, or control of, that which is less.

"The Lord, in surveying the eternal intelligences which stood before Him, found some more noble or intellectual than others, who were equally innocent. This being so, He exercised the elective franchise upon wise principles, and, like a good and kind father among his children, He chose those for rulers who were

> most capable of benefiting the residue. Among these was our
> noble ancestor, Abraham."[20]

These interesting remarks teach us several important principles and confirm many of the other teachings we have been discussing. According to Elder Pratt, men were once intelligences – "living, active" entities that exercised a degree of agency. Anything with any degree of intelligence exercises agency within its sphere. Each of these intelligences, interestingly enough, had a differing degree of intellect and aptitude.

Elder Pratt taught that inequality of spirits is an eternal verity. No one is created equal – we each enjoy a different level of intelligence or nobility. It is interesting that the word noble and the attribute of nobility are linked to those of superior intelligence. Perhaps those who are nobler are those who are quicker to embrace the light, welcome intelligence and truth into their souls, and exemplify these in their conduct and in their natures.

In modern society, we are fond of saying that everyone is, or should be, "equal." "All men are created equal," trumpets the Declaration of Independence. But is this an eternal verity? Yes, God intends that all of His children be treated equally *under the law* and that protection for our rights and agency be extended equally to all. And all of His children are equally loved. However, equality under the law and being loved by God does not mean equality in character, virtue, intellect, intelligence, wisdom, or judgment. Equality does not mean sameness. No two people are exactly, or equally, alike. No two people think precisely the same. Each is unique. Each will be judged for his own sins. Each stands or falls of his own accord.

I draw one additional excerpt from the discourse of Elder Pratt just cited that is relevant:

> "In the first place, if all men were created alike, if all had the same
> degree of intelligence and purity of disposition, all would be
> equal. But, notwithstanding the declaration of American sages,

---

[20] Elder Parley P. Pratt, *Journal of Discourses*, Vol. 1, 257-258, April 10, 1853, http://jod.mrm.org/1/256.

and of the fathers of our country, to the contrary, it is a fact that all beings are not equal in their intellectual capacity, in their dispositions, and in the gifts and callings of God. It is a fact that some beings are more intelligent than others, and some are endowed with abilities or gifts which others do not possess.

"In organizing and peopling the worlds, it was found necessary to place among the inhabitants some superior intelligences, who were capacitated to teach, to rule, and preside among other intelligences. In short, a variety of gifts, and adaptations to the different arts, sciences, and occupations, was as necessary as the uses and benefits arising therefrom have proved to be. Hence one intelligence is peculiarly adapted to one department of usefulness, and another to another. We read much in the Bible in relation to a choice or *election*, on the part of Deity, towards intelligences in His government on earth, whereby some were chosen to fill stations very different from others. And this election not only affected the individuals thus chosen, but their posterity for long generations, or even forever."

This wonderful man of God went on to explain, as noted earlier, that man existed in the beginning as intelligences. From this early stage, our Holy Father exercised His election and chose "noble and great" spirits who surpassed others in intelligence, nobility, and honor. These He designated, or foreordained, as future rulers, teachers, prophets, and leaders on earth (Alma 13:3-9). The very existence of "noble and great ones" suggest an eternal inequality, yet also testifies that a Supreme Intelligence has organized all things to function at optimum levels for the greatest good of all.

President Joseph Fielding Smith taught this intriguing doctrine of eternal inequality in this manner:

"God gave his children their free agency in the spirit world, by which the individual spirits had the privilege, just as men have here, of choosing the good and rejecting the evil, or partaking of the evil to suffer the consequences of their sins. Because of this, some even there were more faithful than others in keeping the commandments of the Lord. Some were of greater intelligences than others, as we find here, and were honored accordingly. . . .

". . . The spirits of men were not equal. They may have had an equal start, and we know they were all innocent in the beginning; but the right of free agency which was given to them enabled some to outstrip others, and thus, through the eons of immortal existence, to become more intelligent, more faithful, for they were free to act for themselves, to think for themselves, to receive the truth or rebel against it."[21]

Men receive on earth certain rewards for their level of faithfulness and excellence in the world of spirits. Because of their agency, some distinguished themselves while others lagged behind. Some moved at a faster pace than others, and some stopped progressing altogether. Indeed, Lucifer and his followers rebelled and were cursed in that pre-mortal state. Their curse was a total cessation of their upward growth and progression. This is what we know as damnation.

As President Smith testified, our pre-earth deeds follow us into mortality and determine, to a highly significant degree, our lives on earth. It would therefore be beneficial to explore this point of doctrine in more detail. Doing so will help us understand more about ourselves, will engender feelings of humility in our hearts, and will perhaps cause a sweet feeling of gratitude to well up inside us.

Elder Bruce R. McConkie taught this doctrine of eternal inequality, or the law of the harvest, in his brilliant book *A New Witness for the Articles of Faith*. Note his emphasis on chosen lineages and families and the direct correlation to the pre-earth life:

"[I]t is clear that people do not all have the same talent for recognizing truth and believing the doctrines of salvation . . . Why? Why this difference in people?

"To this problem there is no easy answer. Every person stands alone in choosing his beliefs and electing the course he will

---

[21] Smith, *Doctrines of Salvation*, Vol. 1, 58-59.

pursue. No two persons are born with the same talents and capacities; no two are rooted in the same soil of circumstances; each is unique . . . But in the final sense the answer stems back to premortality. We all lived as spirit beings, as children of the Eternal Father, for an infinitely long period of time in the premortal existence. There we developed talents, gifts, and aptitudes; there our capacities and abilities took form; there, by obedience to law, we were endowed with the power, in one degree or another, to believe the truth and follow the promptings of the Spirit. And the talent of greatest worth was that of spirituality, for it enables us to hearken to the Holy Spirit and accept that gospel which prepares us for eternal life.

"Men are not born equal. They enter this life with the talents and capacities developed in preexistence. . . .

"And as it is with the prophets, so is it with all the chosen seed. "God's elect," as Paul calls them (Romans 8:33), are especially endowed at birth with spiritual talents. It is easier for them to believe the gospel than it is for the generality of mankind. Every living soul comes into this world with sufficient talent to believe and be saved, but the Lord's sheep, as a reward for their devotion when they dwelt in his presence, enjoy greater spiritual endowments than their fellows. . . .

". . . Our finite limitations and our lack of knowledge of the innate capacities of all men do not let us envision the complexities of the Lord's system for sending his children to mortality. But we do know one great and eternal principle. We know that the Lord operates through families. He himself lives in the family unit; it is his eternal system of government in heaven and on earth, and he always offers as much of his own system to men as they are willing to receive.

"Adam, our father, the first man, is the presiding high priest over the earth for all ages. The government the Lord gave him was patriarchal . . . the righteous portion of mankind were blessed and governed by a patriarchal theocracy. . . .

""This order was instituted in the days of Adam, and came down by lineage." It was designed "to be handed down from father to son." It came down in succession; it is priesthood government; it is the government of God both on earth and in heaven. And even today, it "rightly belongs to the literal descendants of the chosen seed, to whom the promises were made." (D&C 107:40-41.). . . .

". . . those who believed the gospel and sought salvation remained subject to the patriarchal order revealed and established by the Eternal Patriarch. And into their immediate families the Father of Spirits sent those of his primeval children who, through faith and devotion in preexistence, had earned the right to be born in the households of faith. . . .

". . . The seed of Abraham shall take the gospel and the priesthood to all nations, and those who accept the divine word shall become as though they too were the chosen seed. And also: The literal seed of Abraham's body, his natural descendants, those born with his blood flowing through their veins – though they be scattered and scourged and lost in all nations – yet they have a right to certain blessings. They have a *right* to hear the *gospel*, and if they accept it, to receive the *priesthood*, to have their own family units continue everlastingly so that they with Abraham shall have *eternal life* . . . The Lord operates through families; in general he sends his choice spirits to earth in the lineage of Abraham."[22]

Yes, because each intelligence is independent within its own sphere, some exercised their agency to become more obedient and valiant in the pre-mortal state. These became the "noble and great ones" who were selected as the Lord's earthly servants to preside over and gather other intelligences. They were also chosen to come to earth in specific lineages and families for appointed purposes. In these lineages, they would receive greater blessings as well as greater duties and obligations, while others also reap on earth what they sowed in the pre-earth state.

---

[22] Bruce R. McConkie, *A New Witness for the Articles of Faith* (Salt Lake City, UT: Deseret Book, 1988), 34-37.

Just as Abraham was chosen as an earthly ruler for his pre-mortal nobility and greatness, so, too, those who come into his lineage are chosen because of their pre-earth valiancy. Not only is one's lineage determined by actions in the pre-earth realm, but one's specific family may be chosen and designated as well. All things are eternal to God and one stage of our existence directly impacts the next.

On my part, I feel an overwhelming sense of gratitude to know that I was stalwart enough in my previous stage of progression to earn a chance to live in my family where I could be given a chance to accept the Restored Gospel as well as to enjoy the favorable circumstances that have blessed my life on this Promised Land of America – the Zion of our God. It fills me with a sense of duty and destiny to know that there is a higher purpose for my life and that my mission began long before my birth. It also fills me with a burning desire to do what is right here, and to fulfil the promises I made before so that I can *return* to enjoy the eternities with my family and my Eternal Parents.

All those of the tribes of Israel should feel a similar sense of ecstasy and purpose – especially those who come through the lineages of Joseph. The majority of the members of The Church of Jesus Christ of Latter-day Saints are of the tribe of Ephraim. This is not coincidence. It is not happenstance. It is not insignificant or inconsequential. Being declared an Ephraimite by a patriarch is not a symbolic designation; it is a designation of our literal blood lineage. The omnipotent Creator placed us in our specific lineages for specific reasons and to accomplish specific purposes.

Ephraim was pre-mortally chosen to take the lead in these last days – that is, in the "dispensation of the fulness of times" (Ephesians 1:10) when the Gospel would be restored to earth and the world would be filled with knowledge, inventions, and opportunities that surpass any other era. We were to be the royal vanguard of the Gospel in these last days. It is our sacred duty to gather the remaining Ephraimites from the nations and to prepare to gather the other tribes of Israel and bring them also into the fold of Christ.

A major part of this missionary labor consists of Ephraim's duty to perform salvific work for the hosts of the dead. This work is performed in the holy temples that are beginning to dot the earth. Ephraim, then, must become a more devoted temple-going people if it is to perform its mission. As our current prophet, President Russell M. Nelson, has been repeatedly emphasizing, Heavenly Father's children on both sides of the veil must have the Gospel preached to them. We can rest assured that it is righteous Ephraim – both there and here – who are carrying forward this message of hope. Never has so much been asked of any tribe of Israel as that which has been asked of latter-day Ephraim.

Elder LeGrand Richards taught:

> "We are from Ephraim . . . we are the custodians of [the Lord's] gospel as restored in these latter days."[23]

And President Joseph Fielding Smith stated:

> "The Church today numbers many many thousands and they are of the houses of Israel, principally of the tribe of Ephraim – Ephraim having received the birthright in Israel and the mission to stand at the head, to perform a work for his fellow kinsmen of the other tribes in the dispensation of the fulness of times in which we live."[24]

We who belong to the tribes of Israel – especially those who belong to Ephraim – have a tremendous burden to bear. We are the custodians of the Lord's Gospel – the disciples tasked with taking the truth to the world and gathering our Israelite brothers and sisters. We are a royal generation – a generation chosen in pre-mortality because of our faithfulness to the Lord. Let us be true to our foreordinations and pre-mortal callings, to our special lineage, and to our birthright by faithfully fulfilling that mission the Lord has given to gathered Israel today.

President David O. McKay once took up this topic of pre-mortal distinction and explained how these eternal differences among intelligences

---

[23] Elder LeGrand Richards, "The Gospel to the Jews," General Conference, October, 1956, https://scriptures.byu.edu/#:t354:p4c6.

[24] President Joseph Fielding Smith, *Doctrines of Salvation*, Vol. 3 (Salt Lake City, UT: Bookcraft, 1960), 256-257.

translate into practical terms in our mortal existence and in our earthly lineage. Note how intimately tied together the pre-earth life and mortal life are. President McKay taught:

> "Revelation assures us that [the Father's] plan antedates man's mortal existence, extending back to man's pre-existent state. In that pre-mortal state were "intelligences that were organized before the world was; and among all these were many of the noble and great ones; And God saw these souls that they were good, and he stood in the midst of them, and he said: These I will make my rulers; for he stood among those that were spirits, and he saw that they were good. (Abr. 3:22-3)

> "Manifestly, from this revelation, we may infer two things: first, that there were among those spirits different degrees of intelligence, varying grades of achievement, retarded and advanced spiritual attainment; second, that there were no national distinctions among those spirits such as Americans, Europeans, Asiatics, Australians, etc. Such "bounds of habitation" would have to be "determined" when the spirits entered upon their earthly existence or second estate. . . .

> ". . . Songs of expectant parents come from all parts of the earth, and each little spirit is attracted to the spiritual and mortal parentage for which the spirit has prepared itself.

> "Now if none of these spirits was permitted to enter mortality until they all were good and great and had become leaders, then the diversity of conditions among the children of men as we see them today would certainly seem to indicate discrimination and injustice. But if in their eagerness to take upon themselves bodies, the spirits were willing to come through any lineage for which they were worthy, or to which they were attracted, then they were given the full reward of merit, and were satisfied, yes, and even blessed.

> "Accepting this theory of life, we have a reasonable explanation of existent conditions in the habitations of man. How the law of spiritual attraction works between the spirit and the expectant

parents, has not been revealed, neither can finite mind fully understand. By analogy, however, we can perhaps get a glimpse of what might take place in that spirit world. In physics we refer to the law of attraction wherein some force acting mutually between particles of matter tends to draw them together and to keep them from separating. In chemistry, there is an attractive force exerted between atoms, which causes them to enter into combination. We know, too, that there is an affinity between persons – a spiritual relationship or attraction wherein individuals are either drawn towards others or repelled by others. Might it not be so in the realm of spirit – each individual attracted to the parentage for which it is prepared. Our place in this world would then be determined by our own advancement or condition in the pre-mortal state, just as our place in our future existence will be determined by what we do here in mortality.

"When, therefore, the Creator said to Abraham, and to others of his attainment, "You I will make my rulers," there could exist no feeling of envy or of jealousy among the millions of other spirits, for those who were "good and great" were but receiving their just reward. . . .

"By the operation of some eternal law with which man is yet unfamiliar, spirits come through parentages for which they are worthy – some as Bushmen of Australia, some as Solomon Islanders, some as Americans, as Europeans, as Asiatics, etc., etc., with all the varying degrees of mentality and spirituality manifest in parents of the different races that inhabit the earth.

"Of this we may be sure, each was satisfied and happy to come through the lineage to which he or she was attracted and for which, and only which, he or she was prepared."[25]

If President McKay was correct – and his teaching rests gently and comfortably on my heart and accords with my own internal sense of

---

[25] David O. McKay, in Jerreld Newquist, ed., *Prophets, Principles, and National Survival* (Seattle, Washington: Publishers Press, 1977), 499-501.

justice – then inequality, so-called, is an eternal verity. It is an inevitable fact of existence when agency is present. There is nothing harmful or wrong about it because it is simply the reality. There is no injustice because each reaps what he sows. The law of the harvest is in full effect and we are aware of the justice of it all. Indeed, it is an *essential* part of the Father's Plan that every man possesses a stewardship and be accountable for his own actions.

The Father's magnificent Plan of Salvation went into motion when He found that "he was in the midst of spirits and glory" and "saw proper to institute laws whereby the rest could have a privilege to advance like himself," as the Prophet Joseph Smith taught. God, being greater than all other intelligences, formulated a Plan to clothe those intelligences in spirit. By so doing – by combining spirit with intelligence – they became His *literal* spirit sons and daughters. This could be referred to as a spirit birth. We can perhaps mark that moment as our true spiritual awakening – the real "beginning" of our upward progression as children of God.

Understanding that "man was in the beginning with God" (D&C 93:29), that he was a living intelligence, and that he is an immortal and eternal being, is the first essential step in knowing ourselves. Our eternal journey did not begin with birth on this planet. Our origin was not our mortal conception. From the beginning, we have been living intelligences dwelling in the presence of God and glory.

By understanding something of our nature and the means by which we came into being – which I pray you understand a little more intimately after reading this chapter – we can glimpse the nature of our God. We are formed in His very image, as all children are in the image of their parents. And knowing God, the Savior taught, is eternal life (John 17:3).

Without this priceless knowledge, we are lost. If we do not know God, we do not comprehend light, truth, or intelligence and all is darkness. If we deny God, we deny our nature as His offspring and cannot realize our purpose or potential. Conversely, to acknowledge God and embrace Him *is* to choose light over darkness, good over evil, intelligence over lies. To know ourselves, we *must* know God. And in knowing our Eternal Father, we learn much about ourselves and our true potential.

The Prophet Joseph Smith instructed the Saints in the King Follett Discourse that: "It is the first principle of the gospel to know for a certainty the character of God." To comprehend the nature of God, and thereby understand what we are destined to become if we are faithful, becomes paramount in our individual quest for eternal life.

It is about this glorious God whom we worship, whose children we are, and whose divine potential resides inside our very souls, that we will learn in the next chapter.

Chapter Second

Father and Son

God is your Father. He is my Father. He is the Father of *all* human beings, black or white, Christian or atheist, Greek or Indian, past or present. He is also the Father of our Elder Brother, Jesus of Nazareth. Though Jesus is a God, He is also a Child – the Firstborn in the spirit – of our Father. His Father is the same Personage as *our* Eternal Father. Yes, the Almighty God of the universe, the Creator of worlds without number, the Supreme Intelligence in the galaxy, is our *literal* Father!

What an earth-shattering truth! The Deity who holds all power and who can cause worlds to pass away or come into existence with a single word, is our *Father*. He is not an unknowable Being, an unembodied force, or a detached spirit entity. He is an exalted Man of flesh and bone, a Holy Man with passions, emotions, likes and dislikes, a personality and an identity. And most importantly, He is a Father – the Eternal Father of worlds without number.

Without a sure knowledge of our Parentage, it is impossible to progress very far in spiritual things. We must understand who God is, what type of a Being He is, what His character is, and what our relationship with Him truly looks like. Until we know these things, we will figuratively paddle in circles, never progressing as is our privilege. Until we know who God really is, we cannot even know ourselves and will therefore wander aimlessly onward without purpose, passion, or hope.

During His earthly ministry in the Holy Land, Jesus taught this singular doctrine:

> "And this is life eternal, that they might know thee the only true God, and Jesus Christ, whom thou hast sent" (John 17:3).

While other descriptions could be given of what it takes to achieve eternal life – the "greatest of all the gifts" that our Father in Heaven can bestow upon His children (D&C 14:7) – this one given by the Lord is foundational. According to the Messiah, we must come to *know* God and Jesus Christ in order to qualify for eternal life. So, what does it mean to *know* Them?

The *Merriam-Webster* dictionary defines the verb "to know" as:

"To perceive directly: Have direct recognition;

"To recognize the nature of: Discern;

"To be aware of the truth or factuality of: to be convinced or certain of;

"To have a practical understanding of."[26]

To know God means to see Him for what and who He is. It means to understand His nature, His attributes, and His personality. It means to be convinced of His divinity, perfectness, and supreme power. It means to trust Him implicitly. It means to be able to perceive and distinguish His personal presence. To know our Heavenly Father, and His Son, is to have a practical understanding of who They are, what our relationship to Them is, and what Their great purposes regarding man on this earth entail.

Christians are familiar with the Lord's declaration that at the Judgement Day He will say to the wicked:

"I never knew you: depart from me, ye that work iniquity" (Matthew 7:23).

It is interesting to note that the Prophet Joseph Smith changed this verse in his inspired translation of the Bible. As the Prophet rendered it, the verse reads:

"Ye never knew me; depart from me ye that work iniquity" (JST Matthew 7:33).

"*Ye* never knew me." This small change places the burden squarely upon *us* to truly know, learn about, become acquainted

---

[26] "To Know," *Merriam-Webster, Incorporated*, updated July 23, 2018, accessed August 1, 2018, https://www.merriam-webster.com/dictionary/know.

with, and follow in the footsteps of our Lord and Master Jesus Christ. If *we* do not know Him — His *true* nature — we cannot achieve eternal life. If *we* do not become like Him, do the things He does, and have His image engraved in our countenance (Alma 5:19), we are as salt that has lost its savor and is "cast out . . . to be trodden under foot of men" (3 Nephi 12:13).

Latter-day Saints are taught in the *Lectures on Faith* the necessity of learning the character of God. The reasoning runs in this manner:

> "[C]orrect ideas of the character of God are necessary in order to exercise faith in him unto life and salvation . . . without correct ideas of his character the minds of men could not have sufficient power with God to the exercise of faith necessary to the enjoyment of eternal life . . . correct ideas of his character lay a foundation, as far as his character is concerned, for the exercise of faith, so as to enjoy the fullness of the blessing of the gospel of Jesus Christ, even that of eternal glory."[27]

The scriptures tell us that "without faith it is impossible to please" God (Hebrews 11:6). Thus, if it is true that we must understand God's character *before* we can place full faith in Him, we see the importance and necessity of learning all about Him. The *Lectures on Faith* give one example of how understanding an attribute of God gives us faith in Him. We read:

> "[U]nless God had power over all things, and was able by his power to control all things, and thereby deliver his creatures who put their trust in him from the power of all beings that might seek their destruction, whether in heaven, on earth, or in hell, men could not be saved. But with the idea of the existence of this attribute planted in the mind, men feel as though they had nothing to fear who put their trust in God, believing that he has power to save all who come to him to the very uttermost."[28]

---

[27] *Lectures on Faith* (American Fork, Utah: Covenant Communications, Inc., 2000), 49.

[28] *Lectures on Faith*, 51-52.

While our finite mortal minds do not comprehend all the attributes of God, nor do they comprehend everything God can comprehend, *The Doctrine and Covenants* contains a promise that one day we will comprehend *all* things, including our God. Thus far, however, He has revealed sufficient that we might put our faith in Him. And if we progress in that faith by clinging to and cultivating those attributes that we *do* know, we will one day have the "rest of the story" revealed to us. The revelations teach:

> "[T]he day shall come when you shall comprehend even God, being quickened in him and by him" (D&C 88:49).

> "[M]y voice is Spirit; my Spirit is truth; truth abideth and hath no end; and if it be in you it shall abound.

> "And if your eye be single to my glory, your whole bodies shall be filled with light, and there shall be no darkness in you; and that body which is filled with light comprehendeth all things.

> "Therefore, sanctify yourselves that your minds become single to God, and the days will come that you shall see him; for he will unveil his face unto you, and it shall be in his own time, and in his own way, and according to his own will" (D&C 88:66-68).

What a marvelous promise! We comprehend so little at present. Yet, if we come to Christ and are righteous, we will be sanctified and eventually our entire body will be filled with light, spirit, and truth, and we will be in harmony with God and see Him as He is, and we will comprehend all things.

Yet, we do not presently comprehend all things. We are not yet perfect. But we know that *this* earth life is "the time for men to prepare to meet God" (Alma 34:32). Therefore, we have been given glimpses into the nature of our Heavenly Father. These have come by revelation through prophets. The Lord's Church does *not* claim God is unknowable, but, to the contrary, emphatically declares certain truths about His divine character that are imperative to grasp. Modern prophets have devoted much time to helping man understand all that has been yet revealed about the Almighty's nature. Since it is our work in this chapter to come to know more about our Father, we turn to the words of the prophets who reveal sacred snippets of this great truth.

In his classic talk "The Only True God and Jesus Christ Whom He Hath Sent," Elder Jeffrey R. Holland gave an overview of what Latter-day Saints believe about the nature of the Being they worship. He said:

> "Our first and foremost article of faith in The Church of Jesus Christ of Latter-day Saints is "We believe in God, the Eternal Father, and in His Son, Jesus Christ, and in the Holy Ghost." We believe these three divine persons constituting a single Godhead are united in purpose, in manner, in testimony, in mission. We believe Them to be filled with the same godly sense of mercy and love, justice and grace, patience, forgiveness, and redemption. I think it is accurate to say we believe They are one in every significant and eternal aspect imaginable *except* believing Them to be three persons combined in one substance, a Trinitarian notion never set forth in the scriptures because it is not true."

The Godhead, then, is a unit comprising three divine individuals – God the Father, the Savior Jesus Christ, and the Holy Ghost. They are united in purpose, yet separate in being. Latter-day scripture reveals that:

> "The Father has a body of flesh and bones as tangible as man's; the Son also; but the Holy Ghost has not a body of flesh and bones, but is a personage of Spirit. Were it not so, the Holy Ghost could not dwell in us" (D&C 130:22).

Some may quarrel with the notion that God has a tangible body because the Bible says "God is a spirit" (John 4:24). This, however, is factual. God *is* a spirit Being the same as you and I. Yet, though we have spirits, we also have bodies that house our precious spirits. The fact that the resurrected Lord Jesus possesses a physical body that can be handled, seen, and that can eat food – as abundantly testified of in Luke 24:36-43 – should forever destroy the apostate idea that God is *only* a spirit.

These truths about the corporeal nature of God and His Son sit in direct opposition to the false concept of the mystical, unknowable Trinity so popular throughout the world. Of this "Trinitarian notion" – an idea held in full or in part by most Christian churches today and, though cast in different terminology, by most Eastern religions and their New Age counterparts – Elder Holland said:

> "These various evolutions and iterations of creeds . . . declared the Father, Son, and Holy Ghost to be abstract, absolute, transcendent, immanent, consubstantial, coeternal, and unknowable, without body, parts, or passions and dwelling outside space and time. In such creeds all three members are separate persons, but they are a single being, the oft-noted "mystery of the trinity." They are three distinct persons, yet not three Gods but one. All three persons are incomprehensible, yet it is one God who is incomprehensible.

> "We agree with our critics on at least that point—that such a formulation for divinity is truly incomprehensible . . . How *are* we to trust, love, worship, to say nothing of strive to be like, One who is incomprehensible and unknowable? What of Jesus's prayer to His Father in Heaven that "this is life eternal, that they might *know thee* the only true God, and Jesus Christ, whom *thou* hast sent"?"[29]

A more incomprehensible jumble of contradictions is hard to imagine. The notion of the Trinity is proof positive of a mass apostasy from the true Church established by Christ and directed through His apostles until their martyrdom during the 1st Century A.D. In reality, God's truth is simple and plain. It is easy to understand. It rests easy on the mind. All significant truths can be understood even by children when taught in their original simplicity.

Children in their primary classes are taught that God is their literal Father, that Jesus is His literal Son and their Savior and Elder Brother, and that the Holy Ghost witnesses of Them both. Yes, *all* the saving truths of the Gospel of Jesus Christ can be understood even by children. It was this

---

[29] Elder Jeffrey R. Holland, "The Only True God and Jesus Christ Whom He Hath Sent," General Conference, October, 2007, https://www.lds.org/general-conference/2007/10/the-only-true-god-and-jesus-christ-whom-he-hath-sent?lang=eng.

great plainness that caused Nephi to glory in the Lord's words and in His redemption (2 Nephi 31:3; 2 Nephi 33:6).

The great Thomas Jefferson, my personal hero and a wonderful man who described himself as "a *real Christian*,"[30] once expressed his view that:

> "The Christian priesthood, finding the doctrines of Christ levelled to every understanding, and too plain to need explanation, saw, in the mysticisms of Plato, materials with which they might build up an artificial system which might, from its indistinctness, admit everlasting controversy, give employment for their order, and introduce it to profit, power and pre-eminence. The doctrines which flowed from the lips of Jesus himself are within the comprehension of a child; but thousands of volumes have not yet explained the Platonisms engrafted on them: and for this obvious reason that nonsense can never be explained."[31]

Of the nonsensical and unauthorized additions to Christ's Gospel, and of the Trinitarian fiction specifically, the Sage of Monticello further stated:

> "[W]hen we shall have done away the incomprehensible jargon of the Trinitarian arithmetic, that three are one, and one is three; when we shall have knocked down the artificial scaffolding, reared to mask from view the simple structure of Jesus, when, in short, we shall have unlearned every thing which has been taught since his day, and got back to the pure and simple doctrines he inculcated, we shall then be truly and worthily his disciples: and my opinion is that if nothing had ever been added to what flowed purely from his lips, the whole world would at this day have been Christian."[32]

Yes, the simple doctrines of Jesus, had they been preached in their purity, would have engulfed the world in a flood of light and truth. Instead, they

---

[30] Thomas Jefferson to Charles Thomson, January 9, 1816.

[31] Thomas Jefferson to John Adams, July 5, 1814.

[32] Thomas Jefferson to Timothy Pickering, February 27, 1821.

are obscured by an "artificial scaffolding" – a false mask of incomprehensible philosophizing – and the world consequently crawls about in suffocating darkness because they know not where to find the truth (D&C 123:12; Amos 8:11-12).

In a radio address, President J. Reuben Clark, Jr. chided the world for not accepting the scriptures at face value when they state that God is our Father. After quoting numerous verses from the Bible, this prophetic witness observed:

> "[T]hese words must mean what they say – that man is in the image of God, is God's likeness; that the Only Begotten is in the likeness of the Father, his "express image," and we know man is in the likeness of the Only Begotten for he dwelt amongst us. So God is a person of the same essential form and stature as the Only Begotten and, as his children, he has body, parts, and passions.
>
> "Then why mock God with heresies? Why make him a falsifier by teaching he is something else than what he and what his Son have declared him to be? If God be an essence, immense, nebulous, formless, without body, parts, and passions, as the wisdom of men conceive, why did he not tell us straightforwardly, honestly, explaining:
>
> ""Since you cannot conceive or understand me as I am, I am falsifying by telling you that mine Only Begotten and you, my children, are in my image, in my likeness, and I am having my Only Begotten declare the same falsehood."
>
> "Why did he not so declare? Why? Because this heresy is error, born of Satan, and he is a God of truth.
>
> "God is a person, his Son is in his express image, and man is in his likeness.
>
> "This we must know that we may be on our way to immortality and eternal life."[33]

---

[33] President J. Reuben Clark, Jr., *On the Way to Immortality and Eternal Life* (Salt Lake City, UT: Deseret Book Company, 1950), 16-17.

If we simply believed the Bible, and the other revealed works of God, we would know that God is our Father, that Jesus is His Son, and that we are in every sense of the term children of God. Yet, because we refuse to accept the plain declarations of the Savior and His prophets, we have groped in the dark and stumbled over the Satan-inspired philosophies of men. For generations, the spirit of the Devil has "strongly riveted the creeds of the fathers, who have inherited lies, upon the hearts of the children, and filled the world with confusion, and has been growing stronger and stronger, and is now the very mainspring of all corruption" (D&C 123:7).

Elder Bruce R. McConkie bluntly summed up the retarding effects this "mass of confusion" has had and continues to have on man's progress in these words:

> "To those who are bound to defend the mass of confusion in the creeds of Christendom, the concept that the Father, Son, and the Holy Ghost are not one God is totally incomprehensible. They are baffled by their beliefs, confused by their creeds, unconverted by the incomprehensible. Their only recourse is to glory in the mystery of godliness and to suppose there is something wonderful in worshiping a spirit nothingness that is neither here nor there any more than he exists now or then. The total inability to know God becomes the most basic tenet of their religion and closes the door to that progress which leads to exaltation and Godhood."[34]

All religions and churches close the door to salvation, which is in and through Jesus Christ, when they fail to properly define and identify God and His attributes. Too many people either consciously or inadvertently hide from the personal responsibility of knowing God for themselves by embracing mysterious creeds that allow many interpretations, permit one to travel diverse and even contradictory paths, and hold the individual to lower standards of discipleship. If we do not know our Heavenly Father

---

[34] McConkie, *The Promised Messiah*, 117-118.

and the Christ He has sent, we cut ourselves off from Heaven and wander in darkness.

Today, as Jeremiah described in his day, it is the "pastors" of the people which "scatter the sheep" (Jeremiah 23:1), the false "prophets and priests" who "profane" the word of God and who have "caused my people Israel to err" (Jeremiah 23:11, 13, 15), and the lying leaders of Christendom which speak in their own names but "not out of the mouth of the Lord" (Jeremiah 23:16). These neither know the Lord nor the Father and instead teach the false "wisdom" of men. They are the blind leading the blind (Matthew 15:14) and are "ever learning, and never able to come to the knowledge of the truth" (2 Timothy 3:7).

Elder McConkie also spoke of those who *do* know the true God and Jesus Christ whom He has sent and the exalting influence this pristine knowledge has upon them:

> "To those who are free from creedal chains and who can and do turn to the teachings of the prophets and apostles to whom God revealed himself, there is no problem, no confusion, no uncertainty. To them the oneness of the Godhead is neither unknown nor mysterious. They know that God is their Father and that a father is a parent whose offspring bear the image, bodily and spiritually, of the progenitor. They know that Christ is the Son in the literal and full sense of the word, that he is in the express image of his Father's person, and that having come forth in the resurrection, he now has a glorified body of flesh and bones like that of the Father whose Child he is. Their ability to comprehend even God – as in due course they shall! – becomes the most important doctrine of their religion and opens the door to that eternal progress which enables them to become like him."[35]

Thankfully, with the Restoration of Christ's Gospel, the true nature of God, and man's special relationship to Him, has been revealed once more. The door to eternal progress has been flung wide open. We know whom we worship. We know whose children we are. We know exactly who our

---

[35] McConkie, *The Promised Messiah*, 118.

Father and our God is. And this doctrine is "the most important" in our religion, for only through it do we comprehend Jesus as our Redeemer and recognize the Father who sent Him to save us.

In the same talk previously cited, Elder Holland reiterated in plain terms what God and Jesus have revealed about Their nature. He taught:

> "We declare it is self-evident from the scriptures that the Father, the Son, and the Holy Ghost are separate persons, three divine beings, noting such unequivocal illustrations as the Savior's great Intercessory Prayer just mentioned, His baptism at the hands of John, the experience on the Mount of Transfiguration, and the martyrdom of Stephen—to name just four.

> "With these New Testament sources and more ringing in our ears, it may be redundant to ask what Jesus meant when He said, "The Son can do nothing of himself, but what he seeth the Father do." On another occasion He said, "I came down from heaven, not to do mine own will, but the will of him that sent me." Of His antagonists He said, "[They have] . . . seen and hated both me and my Father." And there is, of course, that always deferential subordination to His Father that had Jesus say, "Why callest thou me good? there is none good but one, that is, God." "My father is greater than I."

> "To whom was Jesus pleading so fervently all those years, including in such anguished cries as "O my Father, if it be possible, let this cup pass from me" and "My God, my God, why hast thou forsaken me"? To acknowledge the scriptural evidence that otherwise perfectly united members of the Godhead are nevertheless separate and distinct beings is not to be guilty of polytheism; it is, rather, part of the great revelation Jesus came to deliver concerning the nature of divine beings. Perhaps the

Apostle Paul said it best: "Christ Jesus . . . being in the form of God, thought it not robbery to be equal with God.""[36]

We steal no truth, power, pre-eminence, or glory away from God when we declare that He and the Son and the Holy Ghost are three separate Persons. That these Beings are three separate Gods united under the Father as one Godhead is self-evident. Even the first chapter of the book of Genesis in the Bible hints at the separate and distinct nature of the Godhead. We read:

"And God said, Let us make man in our image, after our likeness. . . .

"So God created man in his own image, in the image of God created he him; male and female created he them" (Genesis 1:26-27).

There are certain words here that are very important to note. Why did God say, "Let US make man in OUR image, after OUR likeness," if there was not more than one Being – Himself – in existence? Who was He talking to when He said "us" and "our"? And we are dealing with both males and females. Are females created in *His* image? Yes, they are His children, but they are created in the image of His eternal companion, our Mother in Heaven. God is *not* genderless, androgynous, or a split male-female personality. He is a Holy Man, our Father, with the exalted and glorified body of a Man. Logic forces us to admit that more than one individual is being referred to in these earliest of Bible verses.

Modern prophets have confirmed, for instance, that we also have Mother in Heaven. President Spencer W. Kimball spoke of our Eternal Mother and man's creation when He said:

"God made man in his own image and certainly he made woman in the image of his wife-partner."[37]

---

[36] Elder Jeffrey R. Holland, "The Only True God and Jesus Christ Whom He Hath Sent," General Conference, October, 2007, https://www.lds.org/general-conference/2007/10/the-only-true-god-and-jesus-christ-whom-he-hath-sent?lang=eng.

Yes, we have a literal Mother in Heaven just like we have a literal Father in Heaven! She was integral in the creative process. For reasons best known to Him, our Father has chosen to not reveal much about our Eternal Mother. Suffice it to say, our Heavenly Father has a wife and that She has been by His side in the most significant aspects of the Creation and in the begetting of Their spirit children.

To restate the salient points thus far noted, members of The Church of Jesus Christ of Latter-day Saints understand that God, His Son Jesus Christ, and the Holy Ghost are three distinct and separate Beings. They are three divine individuals with their own unique identities. In the beginning, these Beings formed what we call the Godhead. Unlike the bizarre notion of a three-in-one, unknowable, mysterious Trinity, the Godhead refers simply to three *separate* Gods – the Father, the Son, and the Holy Spirit – working together to achieve the all-important purpose of saving and exalting mankind.

These three Personages have combined Their talents to perform specific missions in order to "bring to pass the immortality and eternal life of man" (Moses 1:39). Each performs work the other cannot. The Father, as an exalted Being, cannot lay down His body for a sacrifice; but the Son can, and has done so to ransom mankind. The Son cannot dwell within us the same way the unembodied Holy Spirit can, and it is the Holy Ghost whose presence we are invited to receive after baptism. Jesus Christ and the rest of mankind would not exist as spirit beings capable of progressing if it were not for the Father creating our spirits. And so forth.

The divine members of Godhead work in perfect harmony of mind, under the Headship of the Eternal Father, to accomplish Their objective and to instruct and guide the lesser intelligences to become like Them. A witness of the separate and individual nature of the members of the Godhead is in fact contained in *all* the standard works of the Church precisely because it is so fundamentally important to understand.

---

[37] President Spencer W. Kimball, in Edward L. Kimball, ed., *The Teachings of Spencer W. Kimball* (Salt Lake City, UT: Bookcraft, 1994), 25.

The resurrected Lord gave this description of the Godhead's close, interworking relationship when He taught the Nephites:

> "And this is my doctrine, and it is the doctrine which the Father hath given unto me; and I bear record of the Father, and the Father beareth record of me, and the Holy Ghost beareth record of the Father and me; and I bear record that the Father Commandeth all men, everywhere, to repent and believe in me. . . .
>
> ". . . and whoso believeth in me believeth in the Father also; and unto him will the Father bear record of me, for he will visit him with fire and with the Holy Ghost.
>
> "And thus will the Father bear record of me, and the Holy Ghost will bear record unto him of the Father and me; for the Father, and I, and the Holy Ghost are one" (3 Nephi 11:32, 35-36).

Each member of this godly unit serves a different function, and all harmonize with each other. The doctrine of Christ which says that all men should believe in Him comes from the Father, and the Father bears record of the Son. And the Son bears record of His Father's commandments and doctrine and is the perfect example of them in action. And the Holy Ghost bears record of the Father and Son, purifies hearts, and sanctifies individuals that they might, through Christ's redemption, enter Their presence. Together, then, They bring men into Their presence by assisting us in *knowing* the Godhead, which constitutes eternal life (John 17:3).

The Prophet Joseph Smith gave a wonderful description of the roles each of these Gods performs in accomplishing Their holy ends. He taught:

> "Everlasting covenant was made between three personages before the organization of this earth, and relates to their dispensation of things to men on the earth; these personages, according to Abraham's record, are called God the first, the

Creator; God the second, the Redeemer; and God the third the witness or Testator."[38]

God the first, or the Creator and Supreme Intelligence, is our Heavenly Father. God the second, the Redeemer, is the Holy Son, Jesus Christ, known also pre-mortally as Jehovah. And God the third, the Testator, the Revelator, is the Holy Ghost whose special mission is to bear witness of the Father and the Son and use His influence that fills the immensity of space to bring about God's commands. In the beginning, these three Beings formed a sacred covenant, as noted, to bring about the immortality and eternal life of the Father's children (Moses 1:39).

What kind of religion do we have if we acknowledge the separate nature of the Godhead? A 1960 course of study for the Priesthood titled *Apostasy to Restoration* and written by Elder T. Edgar Lyon spoke of the notion of polytheism versus monotheism. It spoke also of the exclusivity of Christ's Gospel and its unapologetic assertion that only through Christ can man be saved. I draw out this important reference:

> "The Christian can hardly be said to have embraced a monotheistic religion, as he believed in an eternal Father, in this Father's divine Son, and in a personage of spirit called the Holy Ghost or Holy Spirit. But polytheistic, in the sense that the term is used to refer to the contemporary paganism, he certainly was not. To him, there was one supreme God, the Eternal Father. Christ had been a manifestation of this Supreme Being in the flesh, but since His resurrection, had ascended to heaven and was in the presence of the Father. Here there was no disharmony, competition, or divergent goals. It was a belief in a supreme triumvirate that had no competitors. Through the atonement of Christ, a plan of salvation had been offered, and it likewise was an exclusive plan. It was not just an additional way to gain salvation. The Christian announced that it was the only way to acquire salvation in the eternal worlds. To have accepted a place as a legal religion would have made the Christian recognize the others as

---

[38] Joseph Fielding Smith, ed., *Teachings of the Prophet Joseph Smith* (American Fork, Utah: Covenant Communications, Inc., 2002), 194.

equal potentials for the securing of eternal life and would have made the Christian godhead nothing more than an additional god in competition with many others of lower standards and sometimes questionable morals. His attitude toward his Father in Heaven and his faith in the Risen Lord and Savior provided the foundation for the Roman government's opposition. Christianity became an illicit, outlawed and "underground" religion."[39]

In all ages of time, those with a correct understanding of the nature of God have been persecuted by those who accept a loose, ecumenical idea of God and salvation. Because the early Christian disciples refused to agree that salvation could be found in other gods – whether through Mithra, Tammuz, Baal, or Zeus – or on other spiritual paths – be it through Kabbalism, the Eleusinian mysteries, or some other pagan conception – they were persecuted and hated wherever they went. Because they declared that God is a personal Being with a body of flesh and bones, that His Son was also an embodied Deity, that the Holy Ghost was separate from both of These, and that *only* through these Beings could exaltation come, the Christians were persecuted and driven underground.

Today, true Christians are figuratively crucified by those who reject the correct conception of God (and, in parts of the world, many still face physical violence and even death for their beliefs). Christians believe in a Supreme Triumvirate and that each of its members is a personal Being with a unique identity. Faith in the Savior Jesus Christ is the only means of accessing the power of the Godhead. It is an "exclusive plan." It is not just one of many spiritual paths a person may take – it is the *only* path that leads to eternal life.

When we stand up for these glorious truths, we become "reformers of error" and thus open ourselves up to persecution and the "torches of

---

[39] T. Edgar Lyon, *Apostasy to Restoration* (Salt Lake City, UT: Deseret Book Company, 1960), 53.

martyrdom," both figurative and literal, of those who know not God.[40] Yet, stand we must, because that is what truth requires.

President Boyd K. Packer once discoursed on the nature of the Godhead. He emphasized the separate character of each member of that body and explained that, by default, Christians must accept a plurality of Gods:

> "What is in error, then, when we use the term *Godhood* to describe the ultimate destiny of mankind? We may now be young in our progression—juvenile, even infantile, compared with Him. Nevertheless, in the eternities to come, if we are worthy, we may be like unto Him, enter His presence, "see as [we] are seen, and know as [we] are known," and receive a "fulness." (D&C 76:94.)

> "This doctrine is not at variance with the scriptures. Nevertheless, it is easy to understand why some Christians reject it, because it introduces the possibility that man may achieve Godhood. . . .

> "The acceptance of this truth does not mean accepting the multiple gods of mythology nor the polytheism of the pagans, which was so roundly condemned by Isaiah and the other prophets.

> "There is *one* God, the Father of all. This we accept as fundamental doctrine.

> "There is only *one* Redeemer, Mediator, Savior. This we know.

> "There is *one* Holy Ghost, a personage of spirit, who completes the Godhead.

> "I have emphasized the word *one,* in each sentence, but I have used it three times. Three is plural.

> "Paul used the plural *many* and the singular *one* in the same verse:

---

[40] Thomas Jefferson to James Ogilvie, August 4, 1811.

""For though there be that are called gods, whether in heaven or in earth, (as there be gods many, and lords many,)

""But to us there is but one God, the Father." (1 Cor. 8:5–6.)

"Anyone who believes and teaches of God the Father, and accepts the divinity of Christ, and of the Holy Ghost, teaches a plurality of Gods."[41]

The Bible is full of this doctrine. From Genesis through the New Testament, the members of the Godhead are distinguished as *three separate, divine individuals* – three Gods united in purpose. Even in the story of Jesus' baptism is this truth taught when we witness Jesus standing in the water, the Father's voice sounding from Heaven, and the Holy Ghost descending in the sign of the dove (Matthew 3:16-17). Unless we claim Jesus was a master ventriloquist, we must admit the separate nature of the members of the Godhead. Accepting such a truth opens up the soul to further light and knowledge from Heaven.

In this chapter, our focus is on God the first, the Creator, our Father, the Supreme Intelligence of the cosmos. Most of what can be said of the Father, however, can be said of the Son, Jesus Christ. This is true as regards Their personalities, attributes, talents, thought processes, perfection, behavior, character, and mission. Jesus is the great revealer, in the flesh, of who and what the Father is and stands for. In our Savior, we have the best example and picture of what our Father is truly like. Thus, we will analyze the Son's attributes to come to a better knowledge of the Father, for, in the words of our Savior: "If ye had known me, ye should have known my Father also" (John 14:7).

In the first place, it should be noted that we are created in the Son's image just as much as the Father's. Abinadi testified "that Christ was the God, the Father of all things, and said that he should take upon him the image of man, and it should be the image after which man was created in the beginning" (Mosiah 7:27). Moreover, Christ was the Firstborn and

[41] President Boyd K. Packer, "The Pattern of Our Parentage," General Conference, October, 1984, https://www.lds.org/general-conference/1984/10/the-pattern-of-our-parentage?lang=eng.

Eldest of the Father's children. Because of His station as Firstborn and, indeed, as a God Himself, the Son can teach, and has taught, that we are created in His image.

During his encounter with the Adversary, Moses testified that he received the following knowledge from God:

> "Get thee hence, Satan; deceive me not; for God said unto me: Thou art after the similitude of mine Only Begotten" (Moses 1:16).

Man is in the similitude of the Son of God. We are sons of God, too, and bear the features of our Savior and our Father. We are members of the same eternal family of God that inhabits worlds without number.

Additionally, the antemortal Messiah, when He appeared to the Brother of Jared, taught this reality:

> "Seest thou that ye are created after mine own image? Yea, even all men were created in the beginning after mine own image.
>
> "Behold, this body, which ye now behold, is the body of my spirit; and man have I created after the body of my spirit; and even as I appear unto thee to be in the spirit will I appear unto my people in the flesh" (Ether 3:15-16).

Moroni, who compiled this incredible account, then added an editorial comment:

> "Jesus showed himself unto this man in the spirit, even after the manner and in the likeness of the same body even as he showed himself unto the Nephites. . . .
>
> ". . . and all this, that this man might know that he was God" (Ether 3:17-18).

We thus learn that man is created in the image of Jesus as Jesus is created in the image of the Father. The perfection of the Son is such that He can say we are created in His likeness. Before His mortal existence, the Lord Jehovah lived as a spirit that exactly resembled His later mortal body. That is, the mortal Messiah physically resembled the pre-mortal Messiah. So much so, in fact, that the Brother of Jared believed Christ's spirit body *was* flesh and bone. Just as Jesus' body resembled its inward spirit, so, too, do our mortal bodies resemble the pre-existent spirits inside them. And all of us share the genes and DNA of our Eternal Father and resemble Him as children resemble their parents.

The purpose of this glorious visitation was so that the Brother of Jared might *know* God's true nature. The Lord revealed Himself to this great man so that his knowledge of the Being he worshipped would be perfect. The most effective way for the Lord to reveal the Father was to show Himself to the Brother of Jared, for He represents the Father in every way. Like this blessed man, we must also come to know God – the *real* Him.

In our discovering the Father by studying the Son, we next mention the fact that Jesus is a Creator like His Father. He learned His creative skills from His Father under His divine tutelage, just as we learned our first lessons in pre-mortality from Him as well. The scriptures testify that our Elder Brother Jesus worked with the Father to create worlds for the Father's spirit children. An ancient revelation divulged in modern times through the instrumentality of the Prophet Joseph Smith teaches:

> "And behold, the glory of the Lord was upon Moses, so that Moses stood in the presence of God, and talked with him face to face. And the Lord God said unto Moses: For mine own purpose have I made these things. Here is wisdom and it remaineth with me.

> "And by the word of my power, have I created them, which is mine Only Begotten Son, who is full of grace and truth,

> "And worlds without number have I created; and I also created them for mine own purpose; and by the Son I created them, which is mine Only Begotten" (Moses 1:31-33).

A modern revelation given through the Prophet Joseph Smith further tutors us concerning Christ:

> "That by him, and through him, and of him, the world are and were created, and the inhabitants thereof are begotten sons and daughters of God" (D&C 76:24).

And these two revelations naturally harmonize with what John wrote in his testimony of the Savior, whom he calls "the Word":

> "All things were made by him; and without him was not any thing made that was made" (John 1:3).

We thus note that our God is a Creator – a divine Architect, Designer, and Builder. He is an Organizer of galaxies, worlds, and earths. The Son dutifully follows in His footsteps, creating this earth and others too numerous to count. We thereby learn that several divine entities – each separate in substance, person, and individuality from one another – worked together in the creative drama that brought about this earth and the people upon it. Yes, worlds without number were created by Jesus Christ under the direction of His Father and through the instrumentality of that power which emanates from His throne.

Jesus Christ is also referred to at times as our "Father." This is true in a spiritual or religious sense. We become His spiritual children when we are truly converted, cleansed from sin, and born again into the Gospel fold. King Benjamin taught that "because of the covenant . . . ye shall be called the children of Christ, his sons, and his daughters; for behold, this day he hath spiritually begotten you; for ye say that your hearts are changed through faith on his name; therefore, ye are born of him and have become his sons and his daughters" (Mosiah 5:7).

Whereas the Father *literally* begot us, Christ *spiritually* begets us when we become converted to His Gospel. As the One who redeemed and atoned for us, He becomes symbolically our Father *in the spirit*, or in a Gospel sense. However, God the Father is our *literal* Father – the Father of our immortal spirits. He is also the literal Father of Jesus, His Eldest Son. He is the only Being I will refer to in this work as Father, unless specifically designated otherwise. Yet, from these things we can learn that the Father's work, as the Son's, is the redemption of the family of God. This is a family affair from start to finish. And we can learn also that the Son has again exemplified the Father's nature as a *Father* by adopting this title of reverence.

As a divine Son, the Lord learned all that He knows from that Being we all call Father. In the mighty King Follett Discourse, the Prophet Joseph Smith taught us something of our Father's origin and, in so doing, revealed perhaps the greatest secret of them all – a mystery we scarcely comprehend. Yet, it is a truth we must grasp, at least in its rudiments, if we are to know ourselves and understand how to approach God and how to progress to perfection like Him, as we have been commanded (Matthew 5:48; 3 Nephi 12:48).

The Seer taught the Saints of the Son's upward progression in His quest to become like His Father. He progressed, we will see, *by doing those same things His Father did.* And it should be noted that we must also climb ever upward following the example of the Son, who did only that which His Father had done before Him (John 5:19). The Prophet revealed:

> "I will go back to the beginning before the world was, to show what kind of a being God is. What sort of a being was God in the beginning? . . . .

> "God himself was once as we are now, and is an exalted man, and sits enthroned in yonder heavens! That is the great secret. If the veil were rent today, and the great God who holds this world in its orbit, and who upholds all worlds and all things by His power, was to make himself visible—I say, if you were to see him today, you would see him like a man in form—like yourselves in all the person, image, and very form as a man; for Adam was created in the very fashion, image and likeness of God, and received instruction from, and walked, talked and conversed with Him, as one man talks and communes with another. . . .

> ". . . These ideas are incomprehensible to some, but they are simple. It is the first principle of the gospel to know for a certainty the character of God, and to know that we may converse with Him as one man converses with another, and that He was once a man like us; yea, that God himself, the Father of us all, dwelt on an earth, the same as Jesus Christ Himself did. . . .

> "The scriptures inform us that Jesus said, as the Father hath power in himself, even so hath the Son power—to do what? Why, what the Father did. The answer is obvious—in a manner to lay down his body and take it up again. Jesus, what are you going to

do? To lay down my life as my Father did, and take it up again. Do you believe it? If you do not believe it you do not believe the Bible. The scriptures say it, and I defy all the learning and wisdom and all the combined powers of earth and hell together to refute it. Here, then, is eternal life—to know the only wise and true God; and you have got to learn how to be gods yourselves, and to be kings and priests to God, the same as all gods have done before you, namely, by going from one small degree to another, and from a small capacity to a great one; from grace to grace, from exaltation to exaltation, until you attain to the resurrection of the dead, and are able to dwell in everlasting burnings, and to sit in glory, as do those who sit enthroned in everlasting power. . . .

". . . What did Jesus do? Why, I do the things I saw my Father do when worlds came rolling into existence. My Father worked out His kingdom with fear and trembling, and I must do the same; and when I get my kingdom, I shall present it to My Father, so that He may obtain kingdom upon kingdom, and it will exalt Him in glory. He will then take a higher exaltation, and I will take His place, and thereby become exalted myself. So that Jesus treads in the tracks of His Father, and inherits what God did before; and God is thus glorified and exalted in the salvation and exaltation of all His children. It is plain beyond disputation, and you thus learn some of the first principles of the gospel, about which so much hath been said.

"When you climb up a ladder, you must begin at the bottom, and ascend step by step, until you arrive at the top; and so it is with the principles of the gospel—you must begin with the first, and go on until you learn all the principles of exaltation. But it will be a great while after you have passed through the veil before you will have learned them. It is not all to be comprehended in this world; it will be a great work to learn our salvation and exaltation even beyond the grave."[42]

---

[42] Joseph Smith, King Follett Discourse, General Conference, April 7, 1844, https://www.lds.org/ensign/1971/04/the-king-follett-sermon?lang=eng.

What an incredible teaching! *God was once as we are now!* Man is not only in the physical image of God, but we are so very much like Him in other distinct ways, including in our humanity. There is nothing we experience that He does not comprehend through firsthand familiarity as an exalted Man. As we sojourn on this earth, He once sojourned on an earth. As we are attempting to live by eternal laws, so He, too, has brought Himself into conformity with them and is qualified to lead and direct.

In His ministry, Jesus testified: "The Son can do nothing of himself, but what he seeth the Father do; for what things soever he doeth, these also doeth the Son likewise" (John 5:19). As the Prophet Joseph Smith said, Jesus climbed the ladder from the bottom to the top by following in His Father's footsteps. There was no other way. The Father has gone before all and was then the only One qualified to mark the path.

Jesus, "though he were a Son, yet learned he obedience by the things which he suffered" (Hebrew 5:8). The Lord "received not of the fulness at first, but continued from grace to grace, until he received a fulness" (D&C 93:12). The Son of God, even Jesus Christ, achieved His exaltation by perfectly traversing the path set before Him by the Father. In so doing, He not only delivered His own individual soul and gained exaltation and eternal lives, but delivered the souls of all those who have ever or will ever believe on His name and enter, by ordinances, into His fold.

Like the Savior did, we must take it one step at a time, growing continuously, until we eventually achieve perfection and exaltation. This is the only possible path and the one that all the gods before us have trod. In the *Millennial Star*, Elder Daniel H. Wells once wrote:

> "God is a being of agency and He has passed along the path He wishes us to tread, and has attained to His exaltation just as He wishes us to attain to ours."[43]

---

[43] Milton R. Hunter, *The Gospel Through the Ages* (Salt Lake City, UT: Stevens and Wallis, Inc., 1945), 105.

Agency is an eternal principle. Agency correctly used is willful action in conformity to law. By living obediently and in perfect harmony with eternal laws, one acquires honor, which honor and nobility and virtue is their power (D&C 29:36). This is what our Father did. It is what the Savior has done. And it is what we are commanded to do.

Do we ever picture God as once a Man like us – an individual working out His salvation? Some believe the idea lessens Him and brings Him down to our level. Yet, perhaps the idea raises us upward and shows that we truly have divine potential, just like our Father. If He can do it, we can do it; especially with His expert guidance. He knows from personal experience how to lead His children right. The evidence of this is Jesus Christ who became perfected and exalted by following the Father's Plan with exactness.

More than one General Authority has taught the idea that God was once like us and traveled a similarly upward trajectory. From these teachings, we know that, like Him, we must "climb up a ladder" comprised of eternal law, make and keep sacred covenants, and receive saving ordinances. We must "begin with the first [principles of the Gospel], and go on until [we] learn all the principles of exaltation," as Brother Joseph explained.

Understanding that our Eternal Father has gone through this process and is now an Exalted Man, a Man of Holiness, *the* God of the universe, should strike us with awe and give us the confidence and desire to follow Him. Who does not feel inspired by such a thought? Who does not feel a greater yearning in his soul to push forward and live the Gospel so that he might also achieve exaltation and become like his Father?

President Brigham Young taught of Heavenly Father's origin and exaltation and testified that we, too, can become like Him and receive the rewards of His Kingdom:

> "If we could see our heavenly Father, we should see a being similar to our earthly parent, with this difference, our Father in heaven is exalted and glorified. He has received His thrones, His principalities and powers, and He sits as a governor, as a monarch, and overrules kingdoms, thrones, and dominions that have been bequeathed to Him, and such as we anticipate

receiving. While He was in the flesh, as we are, He was as we are. But it is now written of Him that our God is as a consuming fire, that He dwells in everlasting burnings, and this is why sin cannot be where He is."[44]

Do we "anticipate receiving" all that our Father has? Is this something we eagerly look forward to or does the thought not even enter our minds? Do we square our shoulders and push forward in excited anticipation or do we give ear to the Devil's lies designed to discourage us and trick us into thinking man is too far below God to ever be worthy of Him? We must have the correct idea fixed in our mind if we are to overcome Satan; namely, that though we are in a fallen world, God is our Father and has commanded us to become like Him and to follow our Elder Brother back to our Heavenly Home.

Unless we are working towards this goal of becoming like the Father, we will never achieve it. Unless we truly believe that we are the literal offspring of God, we will never find the motivation necessary to become like Him and purify our lives in holiness. Think of the glorious promises that await us if we remain faithful to the counsel of our loving Father! The Lord has revealed:

> "For he that receiveth my servants receiveth me;
>
> "And he that receiveth me receiveth my Father;
>
> "And he that receiveth my Father receiveth my Father's kingdom; therefore all that my Father hath shall be given unto him" (D&C 84:36-38).

In order to receive "all that [the] Father hath," we must accept the Lord's servants, His prophets. These prophets reveal Christ and the doctrines of His Gospel. We must also come to *know* the Lord and receive Him and be cleansed by His blood. If we truly receive the Savior, we automatically receive the Father because the Father and Son are one in purpose and mission, attributes and character. Once these principles are accepted,

---

[44] President Brigham Young, *Journal of Discourses*, Vol. 4, September 21, 1856, https://jod.mrm.org/4/51.

these truths learned, and holy ordinances received under proper authority, we qualify to receive all that the Father has.

President Brigham Young has described our mortal struggles as part of an eternal process that has always and will always play out among those seeking exaltation. He said:

> "It is written, "Prove all things; hold fast that which is good." Refuse evil, choose good, hate iniquity, love truth. All this our fathers have done before us; I do not particularly mean father Adam, or his Father; I do not particularly mean Abraham, or Moses, the Prophets, or Apostles, but I mean our fathers who have been exalted for millions of years previous to Adam's time. They have all passed through the same ordeals we are now passing through, and have searched all things, even to the depths of hell."[45]

Our Father, as one of those exalted Beings, has suffered the same as we have and has proved Himself and has become our God – the Father of worlds. It is our privilege to follow in His divine footsteps and rise in similar fashion.

In an incredible sermon, Elder Orson Hyde taught even more about God's firsthand experience as a mortal Man. He testified that the Father is in a position to help us through all challenges because He has walked the path before. Elder Hyde witnessed:

> "Remember that God, our heavenly Father, was perhaps once a child, and mortal like we ourselves, and rose step by step in the scale of progress, in the school of advancement; has moved forward and overcome, until He has arrived at the point where He now is. "Is this really possible?" Why, my dear friends, how would you like to be governed by a ruler who had not been through all the vicissitudes of life that are common to mortals? If he had not suffered, how could he sympathize with the distress of others? If

---

[45] President Brigham Young, *Journal of Discourses*, Vol. 9, 243, March 6, 1862, http://jod.mrm.org/9/242.

he himself had not endured the same, how could he sympathize and be touched with the feelings of our infirmities? He could not, unless he himself had passed through the same ordeal, and overcome step by step. If this is the case, it accounts for the reason why we do not see Him—He is too pure a being to show himself to the eyes of mortals; He has overcome, and goes no more out, but He is the temple of my God, and is a pillar there.

"What is a pillar? It is that power which supports the superstructure which bears up the edifice; and if that should be removed from its place, the edifice is in danger of falling. Hence, our heavenly Father ascended to a throne of power; He has passed through scenes of tribulation, as the Saints in all ages have, and are still passing through; and having overcome, and ascended His throne, He can look down upon those who are following in the same track, and can realize the nature of their infirmities, troubles, and difficulties, like the aged father who looks upon his race, upon the smallest child; and when he sees them grappling with difficulties, his heart is touched with compassion. Why? Because he has felt the same, been in the same situation, and he knows how to administer just chastisement, mingled with the kindest feelings of a father's heart. So with our heavenly Father; when He sees we are going astray, He stretches forth His chastening hand, at the same time He realizes the difficulties with which we have to contend, because he has felt the same; but having overcome, He goes no more out.

"When the world was lost in wretchedness and woe, what did He do? Did He come here Himself? No. But, says he, I will send my son to be my agent, the one who is the nearest to my person, that is bone of my bone, and flesh of my flesh; I will send my son, and I will say, he that heareth him, heareth me. Go then, my son. He came, and how did he look? He looked just like his Father, and just as they treated him they treated his Father in heaven. For inasmuch as they did it unto him, they did it unto his Father. He was the agent, the representative, chosen and sent of God for the purpose."[46]

Our Heavenly Father understands mortality better than we think — and not merely from an intellectual perspective, but from an experiential point of view. He has walked before us down the pain-filled path of morality and knows our struggles and weaknesses. I have often thought that it would help me to know more about the weaknesses and struggles our prophets have gone through and overcome. Yet, how much more incredible to comprehend that the very God of Heaven wrestled in the flesh with the same trials and came off conqueror!

We are all enrolled in this school of advancement, yet most of us have not taken our studies very seriously. Some of us have skipped these lessons altogether. But if we ever want to be like our Father in Heaven, we must dedicate ourselves to learning those same lessons that He learned through His own personal experience. Our Exemplar on the path is, of course, the Savior Jesus Christ. This is because Jesus reveals, exemplifies, follows, obeys, and glorifies our Father who has gone before all and stands at the head of His family.

The Savior's mortal journey, in all its perfection, best shows us what our Father once was, what He has had to do to achieve exaltation, and what He has consequently become. In the Son's journey from mortal birth to earthly ministry to His atoning sacrifice for mankind to His eventual resurrection and exaltation above, the Father's own upward track to greater and greater exaltations and Kingdoms is revealed. When we thus understand this small speck of truth regarding our Father's nature, we learn that we *can* approach Him and talk with Him as one man talks with another — for He is a Holy and Exalted Man just like Jesus whose mortal feet walked the dusty roads of Palestine.

President Spencer W. Kimball once went into great detail about the attributes of our Savior, and, by parallel, of our Father. He described some of them this way:

---

[46] Elder Orson Hyde, *Journal of Discourses*, Vol. 1, 123-124, October 6, 1853, http://jod.mrm.org/1/121.

"To be like Christ! What an ambitious goal! What a lofty ideal! The Savior had a pleasing personality, he was kind, he was pleasant, he was understanding, he never went off on tangents, he was perfectly balanced. No eccentricities could be found in his life. Here was no ostentation and show, but he was real and humble and genuine. He made no play for popularity. He made no compromises to gain favor. He did the right thing always, regardless of how it might appeal to men. He drew all good people to him as a magnet. . . .

"To be like him, then, one must resist evil. One must fortify one's self by keeping away from temptation, out of the devil's area. One must control desire, harness passion, bridle every urge, and keep away from the approach of error. Total cleanliness in thought and action is required if one is to be Christlike. . . .

""What manner of men ought ye to be?" The answer comes: "Even as I am." It means a life of courage. Jesus was bold in defense of truth, even against great odds of numbers in the temple when he discussed the scriptures with the great and the mighty. He was courageous when he flailed the Pharisees and Sadducees, when he with uncompromising boldness lashed out against their wickedness, their hypocrisies, their deceitfulness. He, unarmed, unprotected, called them to repentance of their sins, convicted them of their weaknesses. He walked into the camps of his enemies fearlessly to do that which needed doing. He chastised the wicked but always had compassion for the righteous and the downtrodden and the humble. He attacked the sins of the times fearlessly. He urged mercy from creditor to debtor. He insisted on the payment of debts. He decried the divorce evil. He chastened the rich who collected usury and who ground his heel upon the poor."

President Kimball mentioned numerous additional characteristics exemplified by Christ, including kindness, unselfishness, devoutness, loving nature, obedient, wise, possessing keen intellect, service-oriented, cleanliness, etc. He then said that Jesus "had all virtues at their best" and had "no peer except his Father, God." Jesus has marked the way before us. He has shown us, in perfection, what type of a Man our Father is, what type of works our Father does, and what type of a glorious personality our Father has.[47]

That humble Man of Nazareth was and is our example in all things, our Lord and our King. Yet, He was also a Child. We note the following once more for emphasis. Paul told us:

> "Though he were a Son, yet learned he obedience by the things which he suffered;
>
> "And being made perfect, he became the author of eternal salvation unto all them that obey him" (Hebrews 5:8-9).

And from John we learn that Jesus:

> "received not of the fulness at the first, but received grace for grace;
>
> "And he received not of the fulness at first, but continued from grace to grace, until he received a fulness;
>
> "And thus he was called the Son of God, because he received not the fulness at the first" (D&C 93:12-14).

The Son reverently deferred to His Father, taught His Father's commandments, did His Father's will, and marked the path we all might take to return to our Father. Like Jesus, we are the very children of God. Like Him, we have divine potential inherited through our Father's lineage. His divine DNA, His glorious genes, His sacred Spirit flows through our spirits!

The holy word of God confirms the doctrine that man is a *child* of God with all the attributes, as yet in an undeveloped state, of our Father. Paul the Apostle taught:

> "The Spirit itself beareth witness with our spirit, that we are the children of God:

---

[47] President Kimball, *The Teachings of Spencer W. Kimball*, 13-15.

"And if children, then heirs; heirs of God, and joint-heirs with Christ; if so be that we suffer with *him,* that we may be also glorified together" (Romans 8:16-17).

Though the truth that we are "children of God" and "heirs of God" seems unmistakably plain and logical as Paul explained it here, most mainstream Christians protest and say that these verses only refer to those who accept Christ and are *spiritually* born again as figurative sons and daughters of the Lord. Fortunately, prophets both ancient and modern have testified that we are the *actual* children of God and that He has not used the title "Father" in vain.

Anciently, for instance, the prophet Malachi rhetorically asked:

"Have we not all one father? hath not one God created us?" (Malachi 2:10).

And from the New Testament, we hear John similarly testifying of our Father and His children:

"Behold, what manner of love the Father hath bestowed upon us, that we should be called the sons of God. . . .

"Beloved, now are we the sons of God, and it doth not yet appear what we shall be: but we know that, when he shall appear, we shall be like him; for we shall see him as he is" (1 John 3:1-2).

The Apostle Paul also told the Greeks who worshipped the "Unknown God" that that Being was actually their Father and that they were His children. Said he:

"For in him we live, and move, and have our being; as certain also of your own poets have said, For we are also his offspring.

". . . we are the offspring of God" (Acts 17:28-29).

Why call our Creator "Father" if He is not truly our Father? Why did Paul call us "children of God" and "heirs" if we are just His creations and have no familial relationship to Him? Why did he teach the Greeks that they were the "offspring of God"? Why did John testify that we are "the sons of God" and that when we shall see Him "we shall be like him" if indeed that is not true and we have no potential to be like Him? And why did Christ, in His bitterest agony in Gethsemane, cry out "Abba," which, in its most familiar sense, means Papa, if the Father was not literally His Father (Mark 14:36)? Through the Restoration of the Gospel, our intimate Parent-child relationship with our Eternal Father is revealed in all its uplifting splendor.

My favorite statement ever given expressing our relationship with God comes from Elder Delbert L. Stapley of the Quorum of the Twelve Apostles. The title of this work is taken from his statement. Though I have always inherently known that God is my Father, Elder Stapley's words added a dimension of comprehension that has brought me much joy and confidence. And so I share it with you in hopes that you too will feel the grandeur of your heritage and potential. This great apostle affirmed:

> "Regardless of man's claims to the contrary, God is still God; Christ is His son – His Only Begotten Son in the flesh. He is in the express image of His Father's person, and is our Redeemer, Savior, Lord, and King. The scriptures teach us that we are descended from the lineage of the Gods; therefore, we are created in their likeness and image, in both spirit and body, and we are endowed with like character traits, qualities, and powers. We are not the product of evolution from some lower organism of life as man speculates and would have us believe."[48]

We are descended from the lineage of the Gods! What could be more stirring and motivating than to know that God, the Master of the Universe, is our Father and that we are *literally* descended from Him? And what's more, we are not only His literal children, but we possess "like character traits, qualities, and powers" as our Father. We did not evolve from a lower lifeform – we descended from on high where our Father reigns in glory! We are members of the family of God.

---

[48] Elder Delbert L. Stapley, May 5, 1964, in R. Wayne Shute, ed., *His Servants Speak: Excerpts from Devotional Addresses given at Brigham Young University by General Authorities of The Church of Jesus Christ of Latter-day Saints* (Salt Lake City, UT: Bookcraft, 1967), 23.

In 1910, the Church published a manual of study for the priests. It contained a quote from Elder B.H. Roberts who used similar language to Elder Stapley's comment about man's origin:

> "Man has descended from God: In fact, he is of the same race as the Gods. His descent has not been from a lower form of life, but from the Highest Form of Life; in other words, man is, in the most literal sense, a child of God. This is not only true of the spirit of man, but of his body also."[49]

The language of the two statements is nearly identical, and the principle is the same: Man is descended from God. We are of the lineage of the Gods. We are of the same race and species of God and all those who have achieved their exaltation in the eternal worlds. We did not ascend from below, but descended from above. We must look to the stars, not the slime, for our true origin and destiny.

President Lorenzo Snow also taught frequently about our relationship to our Eternal Father. In 1901, he testified of the truth the Spirit had revealed to him:

> "Now, I have told you what Father Smith said to me, that I should become as great as I could want to be, even as great as God Himself. About two years and a half after, in Nauvoo, I asked Elder Sherwood to explain a certain passage of scripture; and while he was endeavoring to give an explanation, the Spirit of God fell upon me to a marked extent, and the Lord revealed to me, just as plainly as the sun at noonday, this principle, which I put in a couplet: "As man now is, God once was; As God now is, man may be." That fulfilled Father Smith's declaration. Nothing was ever revealed more distinctly than that was to me. Of course, now that it is so well known that it may not appear such a wonderful

---

[49] "Overview of the Plan of Salvation," accessed August 29, 2018, http://emp.byui.edu/huffr/Overview%20of%20the%20Plan%20of%20Salvation.htm; and "1910 Message: Was there a 1910 First Presidency Message that taught that man may have evolved?" Joseph Smith Foundation, May 30, 2018, accessed August 29, 2018, http://josephsmithfoundation.org/faqs/10-1910-message-was-there-a-1910-first-presidency-message-that-taught-that-man-may-have-evolved/#cite_note-7.

manifestation; but when I received it, the knowledge was marvelous to me. This principle, in substance, is found also in the scriptures. The Lord said to John, as recorded in the third chapter of his Revelation: "To him that overcometh will I grant to sit with me in my throne, even as I also overcame, and am set down with my Father in his throne."""[50]

What "marvelous" knowledge this is indeed! It is precious to my soul and I bear witness of its authenticity. As God now is, man may be! While astounding to some, it is perfectly logical if we are truly the Father's children. I testify fervently that we are and that we scarcely fathom the potential we possess because of our Parentage.

The prophets in all the holy scriptures, and in all dispensations of time, also testify of this resplendent reality. In this, the Dispensation of the Fulness of Times, the Lord has revealed this truth once more in its purity. The Holy Ghost has rested upon the minds and hearts of the Lord's chosen seers and they have in turn shared their convictions with us.

On another occasion, President Snow remarked:

> "Through a continual course of progression, our Heavenly Father has received exaltation and glory, and He points us out the same path; and inasmuch as He is clothed with power, authority, and glory, He says, "Walk ye up and come in possession of the same glory and happiness that I possess."""[51]

Because our Father resides in an exalted state, He is in a position to help us progress to where He is. His hand reaches down to lift us up and partake of His power, greatness, and glory. He is always with us. He is always beckoning. He is always willing and able to bring us into His loving embrace. And His Son, having achieved His exaltation, is in the trenches beside us, lifting us, urging us, helping us, and gradually nudging us forward to the Father.

---

[50] President Lorenzo Snow, in Clyde J. Williams, ed., *The Teachings of Lorenzo Snow* (Salt Lake City, UT: Bookcraft, 1984), 2.

[51] Snow, *The Teachings of Lorenzo Snow*, 3-4.

A third time, this wonderful prophet revealed more about our divine potential as children of the Almighty:

> "I believe that we are the sons and daughters of God, and that He has bestowed upon us the capacity for infinite wisdom and knowledge, because He has given us a portion of Himself. We are told that we were made in His own image, and we find that there is a character of immortality in the soul of man. There is a spiritual organism within this tabernacle, and that spiritual organism has a divinity in itself, though perhaps in an infantile state; but it has within itself the capability of improving and advancing, as the infant that receives sustenance from its mother. Though the infant may be very ignorant, yet there are possibilities in it that by passing through the various ordeals of childhood to maturity enable it to rise to a superiority that is perfectly marvelous, compared with its infantile ignorance. Why and how is it that this is accomplished? Because it possesses the susceptibilities and the capabilities of its father. So in regard to ourselves. There is a divinity within ourselves that is immortal and never dies. Thousands and thousands of years hence we will be ourselves, and nobody else, so far as our individuality is concerned. That never dies from all eternity to all eternity."[52]

Though spiritual infants at present, we have a "spiritual organism" in our bodies that is susceptible of infinite growth and enlargement. Our spirits are immortal. They possess an inherent and pre-existent intelligence that craves knowledge and advancement. And because these intelligences have been clothed with spirit element from our Father, they have a boundless capacity and potential. We truly have divinity within us.

Finally, President Snow proclaimed:

> "We were born in the image of God our Father; He begot us like unto Himself. There is the nature of deity in the composition of our spiritual organization; in our spiritual birth our Father transmitted to us the capabilities, powers and faculties which He

---

[52] President Lorenzo Snow, General Conference, April 10, 1898, 63.

Himself possessed – as much so as the child on its mother's bosom possesses, although in an undeveloped state, the faculties, powers, and susceptibilities of its parent."[53]

As the Prophet Joseph said, this doctrine tastes good. It feels right. It fills the heart with gladness. We are the literal children of a literal God. As such, we are entitled – if we follow the same course our Father and Savior have walked before us – to progress as He has progressed and become what He has become. Every ounce of strength, majesty, and potential that our Father has He transmitted to us when He clothed our intelligence with a spirit formed in His likeness.

As a baby chick will naturally grow and become a chicken, and as a baby boy or girl will progress to become every bit the man or woman their earthly parents were, so, too, can each of us, by virtue of our godly lineage, become like our Eternal Father and Mother. Nothing is more natural and logical than this. And nothing could be more wonderful, impressive, and satisfying than to be like God – the very children of Deity! And the fact is we are already like Him in so many ways because He is our literal Father and has shared His divine DNA with us!

President Brigham Young once testified of how precious and valuable life is and why we must not waste a single second, but continually forge a life worthy of exaltation with the Gods above:

"When we look upon the human face we look upon the image of our Father and God; there is a divinity in each person male and female; there is the heavenly, there is the divine and with this is amalgamated the human, the earthly, the weaker portions of our nature, and it is the human that shrinks in the presence of the divine, and this accounts for our manfearing spirit. . . .

"I am now looking upon beings who are expressly created to inhabit the celestial kingdom of our Father and God. They are the children of God, the brethren and sisters of Jesus Christ, of the same family and descent. My best efforts are too feeble to

---

[53] Snow, *The Teachings of Lorenzo Snow*, 4.

portray before you the worth of the life we now possess. Probably there is not a single person upon the earth that properly magnifies his life to the fullest extent, or, as it was designed he should, to prepare him to dwell with God and holy angels. Many passages of Scripture can be produced showing how the ancients complained of the folly and wickedness of mankind, but they never undervalued life. The first life must be magnified as a preparatory step to the enjoyment of the second. Those immortal and glorified beings that inherit higher spheres understood this principle, have magnified their mortal existence and passed on to immortality, to possess exaltations in eternal life. We ought not to speak lightly of and undervalue the life we now enjoy, but so dispose of each passing day that the hours and minutes are spent in doing good, or at least doing no harm, in making ourselves useful, in improving our talents and abilities to do more good, cultivating the principle of kindness to every being pertaining to our earthly sphere, learning their uses and how to apply them to produce the greatest possible amount of good; learning to conduct ourselves towards our families and friends in a way to win the love and confidence of the good, and overcome every ungovernable passion by a constant practice of cool judgment and deliberate thoughts.

"I feel continually to say God bless the people. God bless the brethren who go on Missions to preach the Gospel, and those who are already in their fields of labor. I desire to see righteousness prevail, this is my whole delight; I have no other business on hand; I wish to have no other. I have no other joy or affection for anything, only the perfection of the kingdom of God, and to see righteousness reign triumphantly. I delight to see my brethren and sisters live in a way to promote that life which will never end. Instead of preparing to die, prepare to live in the midst of all the exaltations of the Gods. I do not mean to leave this world, God being my helper, until sin and iniquity are banished from it, and the reign of everlasting righteousness is introduced, and Jesus Christ comes and reigns king of nations as he does king of Saints, and the earth with all the Saints that dwell upon it are brought into the presence of the Father and Son, there to dwell forever."[54]

Because we are the children of the Most High, we know that each day on earth is priceless. We know that we are preparing to meet God; and not only to meet Him, but to be like Him. This is the destiny of all those, if faithful, in whose spirits teem the genes of Almighty God.

President Ezra Taft Benson also bore witness of our spiritual lineage. He stated:

> "We believe God to be the personal Heavenly Father to all mankind, that all mortal beings are literally His spirit offspring. We worship God as a personal, all-knowing, all-powerful being, endowed with all the attributes of perfection. As God's literal offspring, we believe man to be His only creation blessed with His image and His likeness."[55]

We are His literal offspring – His choicest creations. We are God's only creations which have the full potential that He has and which bear His divine image and likeness. We are His precious children. He loves us. He wants us to succeed. He wants us to become like Him.

Sometimes we forget who we are. We forget that we have divine Parents in Heaven. Our true identity is often covered by a barrage of false labels and names. The Adversary wants us to belittle ourselves and ignore our lineage. He does not want us to know that we are of the lineage of the Gods!

President Gordon B. Hinckley, ever the optimist, taught:

> "Don't waste your time feeling sorry for yourself. Don't belittle yourself. Never forget that you are a child of God. You have a divine birthright. Something of the very nature of God is within

---

[54] President Brigham Young, *Journal of Discourses*, Vol. 9, 291-292, April 27, 1862, http://jod.mrm.org/9/290.

[55] Ezra Taft Benson, *This Nation Shall Endure* (Salt Lake City, UT: Deseret Book Company, 1979), 126.

you. The Psalmist sang, "I have said, Ye are gods; and all of you are children of the most High." (Ps. 82:6.)

"I think that David must have been sitting under the stars thinking of this great potential when he wrote:

""What is man, that thou art mindful of him? and the son of man, that thou visitest him?

""For thou hast made him a little lower than the angels, and hast crowned him with glory and honour.

""Thou madest him to have dominion over the works of thy hands; thou hast put all things under his feet." (Ps. 8:4–6.)

"Each person has the potential for great things. Said the Lord through revelation, "Be thou humble; and the Lord thy God will lead thee by the hand, and give thee answer to thy prayers." (D&C 112:10.) What a marvelous promise that is, and so applicable to our personal development."[56]

We each have a tremendous potential because of our lineage. We should never belittle ourselves – that is precisely what the Adversary wants us to do. Rather, we should remember how mindful the Lord is of us and that He has promised to lead us by the hand and aid us every step of the way on our march to the Celestial Kingdom.

Another time, President Hinckley affirmed:

"We sing, "I am a child of God" (*Hymns,* no. 301). That isn't just a figment, a poetic figment—that is the living truth. There is something of divinity within each of us that needs cultivation, that needs to come to the surface, that needs to find expression. You fathers and mothers, teach your children that they are, in a very literal way, sons and daughters of God. There is no greater truth

---

[56] President Gordon B. Hinckley, "Strengthening Each Other," *Ensign,* February, 1985, https://www.lds.org/ensign/1985/02/strengthening-each-other?lang=eng.

in all the world than that—to think that we have something of divinity in us."[57]

There is *no greater truth in all the world* than to know we have a portion of God's divinity inside of us. Knowing our divine lineage is an anecdote to depression, a cure for lack of confidence, and a spiritual B12 shot designed to uplift, enlighten, and gladden the soul.

If a man or woman, boy or girl, remembers that he or she is a child of a King, an heir of God, a god-in-the-making, what could he or she not accomplish? What lies could the Devil effectively hurl at a person who understands his true origin, nature, Parentage, and destiny? Such knowledge is a shining armor that deflects Satan's shafts in the whirlwind. It is imperative that we understand for ourselves, and that we teach our children, the great truth that we are sons and daughters of the Most High God.

In a few sweet words, President Benson expressed what it means to be God's literal offspring:

> "As God's offspring, we have His attributes in us. We are gods in embryo, and thus have an unlimited potential for progress and attainment."[58]

Gods in embryo – what a concept! We have "His attributes in us." We have a spark of divinity within our own souls just waiting to be ignited. Once the fuse is lit, we have an "unlimited potential for progress and attainment" – an eternity of growth, development, and spiritual stretching.

In the same train of thought, President Benson again emphasized:

---

[57] President Gordon B. Hinckley, *Teachings of Presidents of the Church: Gordon B. Hinckley* (The Church of Jesus Christ of Latter-day Saints, 2016), 77.

[58] President Ezra Taft Benson, *The Teachings of Ezra Taft Benson* (Salt Lake City, UT: Bookcraft, 1988), 21.

"Our doctrine of God is clear. He is our Heavenly and Eternal Father. We are His literal children. Through righteous living according to His plan we can see God and become like Him."[59]

Yes, we may become like God. And in ourselves, we can see something of God, too. We can sense His traits and attributes in our fellow man. In the noble and great ones – the prophets and righteous men of the earth – we can see these attributes in greater development. And, of course, in our Savior we have the greatest example of what man can become through obedience to Gospel law.

This doctrine is not new, though it had been lost for centuries and was restored in modern times. But in truth, the ancients knew they may become gods if they obeyed the Lord's law. In Psalms, we encounter this candid declaration:

"I have said, Ye *are* gods; and all of you *are* children of the most High" (Psalms 82:6).

Most Christians ignore the psalmist's statement. When forced to acknowledge it, they brush it off as inconsequential, twist its meaning, or claim that it is one of the many "unknowable" mysteries of the Gospel. They infer that we cannot take the scriptures at face value, yet they turn around and claim the Bible is infallible and perfect. If it is the inspired word of God, then this teaching is true.

I testify that the psalmist said what he meant and meant what he said. His statement was straightforward and plain to the understanding of all men: We are the *children* of the Most High. And as children, we are logically and naturally heirs of all that our Eternal Father has and is. Hence the statement, "Ye are gods." The Lord would not permit such a declaration to pollute the holy scriptures if it was not true.

To wit, during His ministry the mortal Messiah referenced and confirmed the accuracy of this ancient statement. When accosted by the unbelieving Jews concerning His station as the Son of God, Jesus referred to these ancient words. The record details the conversation this way:

---

[59] Benson, *The Teachings of Ezra Taft Benson*, 4-5.

"[Jesus said] I and my Father are one.

"Then the Jews took up stones again to stone him.

"Jesus answered them, Many good works have I shewed you from my Father; for which of those works do ye stone me?

"The Jews answered him, saying, For a good work we stone thee not; but for blasphemy; and because that thou, being a man, makest thyself God.

"Jesus answered them, Is it not written in your law, I said, Ye are gods?

"If he called them gods, unto whom the word of God came, and the scripture cannot be broken;

"Say ye of him, whom the Father hath sanctified, and sent into the world, Thou blasphemest; because I said, I am the Son of God?" (John 10:30-36).

We see here that the Savior Himself taught that men can be gods. He said it was a part of the Gospel law which He, as the pre-mortal Jehovah, had given to Israel. This law "cannot be broken" no matter how viciously it is denounced by modern Christian priests.

We are gods in embryo – children of the Most High. He is our Father, we are His sons and daughters. Jesus was the pre-eminent Son and, as we read elsewhere, "thought it not robbery to be equal with God" (Philippians 2:6). Yes, the very Messiah taught and confirmed what the ancient psalmist wrote; namely, that we are the children of God and may become gods ourselves if we follow Him, keep His commandments, and adopt His attributes.

Elder Jeffrey R. Holland taught of the importance of recognizing God's attributes, as imperfect as we presently exemplify them, in ourselves. In the context of discussing the procreative power, which he called a sacrament, Elder Holland remarked:

"[I]f our definition of sacrament is that act of claiming and sharing and exercising God's own inestimable power, then I know of virtually *no* other divine privilege so routinely given to us all—women or men, ordained or unordained, Latter-day Saint or non-Latter-day Saint—than the miraculous and majestic power of transmitting life, the unspeakable, unfathomable, unbroken power of procreation. There are those special moments in your lives when the other, more formal ordinances of the gospel—the sacraments, if you will—allow you to feel the grace and grandeur of God's power. Many are one-time experiences (such as our own confirmation or our own marriage), and some are repeatable (such as administering to the sick or doing ordinance work for others in the temple). But I know of nothing so earth-shatteringly powerful and yet so universally and unstintingly given to us as the God-given power available in every one of us from our early teen years on to create a human body, that wonder of all wonders, a genetically and spiritually unique being never seen before in the history of the world and never to be duplicated again in all the ages of eternity—a child, *your* child—with eyes and ears and fingers and toes and a future of unspeakable grandeur.

"Imagine that, if you will. Veritable teenagers—and all of us for many decades thereafter—carrying daily, hourly, minute-to-minute, virtually every waking and sleeping moment of our lives, the power and the chemistry and the eternally transmitted seeds of life to grant someone else her second estate, someone else his next level of development in the divine plan of salvation. I submit to you that no power, priesthood or otherwise, is given by God so universally to so many with virtually no control over its use except *self-control.* And I submit to you that *you will never be more like God at any other time in this life than when you are expressing that particular power.* Of all the titles he has chosen for himself, Father is the one he declares, and Creation is his watchword—especially human creation, creation in his image. His glory isn't a mountain, as stunning as mountains are. It isn't in sea or sky or snow or sunrise, as beautiful as they all are. It isn't in art or technology, be that a concerto or computer. No, his glory—and his grief—is in his children. You and I, we are his prized possessions, and we are the earthly evidence, however inadequate, of what he truly is. Human life—that is the greatest of God's powers, the most mysterious and magnificent chemistry of it all—and you and I have been given it, but under the most serious and sacred of restrictions. You and I who can make neither mountain nor moonlight, not one raindrop nor a single rose—yet we have this greater gift in an absolutely unlimited way. And the only control placed on us is self-control—self-control born of respect for the divine sacramental power it is.

"Surely God's trust in us to respect this future-forming gift is awesomely staggering. We who may not be able to repair a bicycle nor assemble an average jigsaw puzzle—yet with all our weaknesses and imperfections, we carry this procreative power that makes us very much like God in at least one grand and majestic way."[60]

The Eternal Father's glory, His ultimate handiwork, the most magnificent manifestation of who and what He is, is us – His children. We are the "earthly evidence, however inadequate, of what he truly is." We bear His image in our very bodies and in our immortal spirits. We are His offspring in every sense of the word.

As His offspring, we have His same attributes and powers and we use them every day. We exercise the most earth-shattering power in the cosmos when we follow our Father's example and engage in the sacred process of creating life. We truly are His children and, even though most do not realize it, we are following in His footsteps in joining with Him to create tabernacles – earthly temples – to house His spirit children. Yes, we are "very much like God in at least one grand and majestic way."

Because we have this unspeakable power, Satan has focused the crosshairs of his demonic assault upon this procreative power. Through fornication, adultery, self-defilement, pornography, lustful thoughts, and lewd speech, the Evil One seeks to bring us down by causing us to misuse,

---

[60] Elder Jeffrey R. Holland, "Souls, Symbols, and Sacraments," BYU Devotional, January 12, 1988, https://speeches.byu.edu/talks/jeffrey-r-holland_souls-symbols-sacraments/.

abuse, and treat lightly this power. Lucifer is jealous of our ability to have and create bodies. It was the power both to create bodies, the spirits to inhabit those bodies, that he craved so cravenly that he rebelled against the Father and Son. This power of "eternal lives" – or the ability to create offspring eternally – is the greatest power in eternity (D&C 132:19, 24, 55; D&C 131:1-4). It is that authority which Lucifer selfishly sought for his own and which, consequently, he and his followers have been denied.

Speaking of the great importance of our bodies, and the purposes for which we inhabit them, President Brigham Young said:

> "Our mortal bodies are all important to us; without them we never can be glorified in the eternities that will be. We are in this state of being for the express purpose of obtaining habitations for our spirits to dwell in, that they may become personages of tabernacle. . . .

> "Brother Kimball quoted a saying of Joseph the Prophet, that he would not worship a God who had not a Father; and I do not know that he would if he had not a mother; the one would be as absurd as the other. If he had a Father, he was made in his likeness. And if he is our Father we are made after his image and likeness. He once possessed a body, as we now do; and our bodies are as much to us, as his body to him. Every iota of this organization is necessary to secure for us an exaltation with the Gods. . . .

> "We have received these bodies for an exaltation, to be crowned with those who have been crowned with crowns of glory and eternal life. . . .

> "If we live in these bodies as we should we shall be prepared to receive all the glory he has for the faithful. Let us continue the warfare, fight the good fight of faith, sanctify our hearts before the Lord, and day by day perform the labor he has for us to do, and we shall be accounted worthy to receive our exaltation."[61]

---

[61] President Brigham Young, *Journal of Discourses*, Vol. 9, 286-287, 289, February 23, 1862, http://jod.mrm.org/9/286.

Bodies were granted to man that he might, through self-mastery, become worthy to receive an inheritance with the Gods up above. They are essential to eternal progression. If we use them properly, we will be exalted in the end.

Though mankind almost universally misuses their great gifts and has forgotten who they really are, they are nonetheless the children of God with glorious potential. Through repentance, faith on the Lord, and righteous living, any man or woman on earth can rise in stature to become like God. This potential is embedded in their DNA and cannot be erased – it can only be stifled and suppressed by one's own sinful actions. To overcome our challenges and break through the lies that bind us down, we must remember who we are and what we mean to Heavenly Father.

President Spencer W. Kimball agreed that man is the high-water mark of God's greatness – the evidence of His power and omnipotence:

> "Man is the masterpiece – in all the creations of God nothing even approaches him."[62]

No, nothing is like man, because man is in the express image of Almighty God! We are His children, heirs of His Kingdom, the living embodiment of His excellence and perfection. And the Redeemer Jesus Christ is *the* jewel among gems.

A third prophet has confirmed that man is the greatest of all God's workmanship. In *Doctrines of Salvation*, President Joseph Fielding Smith taught:

> "Man is the greatest of all the creations of God. He is his offspring. We are all his children. It was made known through the Prophet Joseph Smith and Sidney Rigdon, who saw it in vision, that the inhabitants of this earth and other worlds are begotten sons and daughters unto God. That ought to put an end – so far as Latter-day Saints are concerned – to all this nonsense prevailing in the world regarding the origin of man.

---

[62] Kimball, *The Teachings of Spencer W. Kimball*, 30.

"Man, I say, as the offspring of God, is the greatest of all his creations. He is greater than the moon, the sun, and the stars, which are the work of the fingers of God, and are made for the benefit of man. It is man's place to rule, and stand at the head of all other dominions, powers, creations, and beings, which the Lord our God has created."[63]

Because of our direct lineage – our divine lineage – we have the opportunity and duty to "stand at the head of all other dominions, powers, creations, and beings" in the universe because we are greater than all. All of these were created by God, and we are the heirs of God our Father. From Him, we have received endowments of power, personality, and potential that surpass anything known to mortal man. We should never wonder who we truly are because it has been sufficiently revealed that we are the offspring of God, His sons and daughters! We did not evolve from below. We are not animals. We are human beings, sons and daughters of divinity – the children of light.

Moreover, God is happiest of all when He is creating and when He is helping His children advance toward godhood and eternal life. Elder Jeffrey R. Holland taught in General Conference that:

"of all the titles God has chosen for Himself, *Father* is the one He favors most, and *creation* is His watchword—especially human creation, creation in His image. You and I have been given something of that godliness, *but under the most serious and sacred of restrictions.*"[64]

The Almighty knows that knowledge and power hoarded are knowledge and power wasted. He therefore shares all that He has and is with His children, as quickly as they are prepared to receive it (D&C 124:41). Yes, He places limits and restrictions on us while we are in our spiritual infancy, just as a mortal father puts training wheels on his child's bike to help him navigate the new experience of bike riding and protect him from

---

[63] Smith, *Doctrines of Salvation*, Vol. 1, 62-263.

[64] Elder Jeffrey R. Holland, "Personal Purity," General Conference, October, 1988, https://www.lds.org/general-conference/1998/10/personal-purity?lang=eng&_r=1.

unnecessary falls. Nonetheless, the Father shares what He knows and gives us line upon line as fast as we are able to receive it (2 Nephi 28:30).

As a Father, He wants His children to be safe, healthy, clean, upright, and happy. He wants us to be full human beings and not short-changed in any respect. He wants our lives to bear sweet fruit. Elder Sterling W. Sill taught:

> "God does not want us to be dull, negative, unattractive or unlearned. He has said, "No man can be saved in ignorance." Ignorance is probably the most potent factor by which we set up our own limitations. God is not pleased when we live little, dwarfed and stunted lives. Jesus wants us to produce."[65]

Yes, God wants each of us to become informed, alert, active, creative, curious, adventurous, aspiring, industrious, hearty, virtuous, noble, honorable, clean, jubilant, peaceful, and versed in all good things. He wants us to have the abundant life (John 10:10). He wants all those in His family circle to enjoy the opulence and radiance of eternity with Him. He has given us every opportunity to, as our Savior did, pull ourselves upward to Him and become like Him in deed, thought, and character. He has so arranged things that, if we choose, we may "feast upon his love . . . forever" (Jacob 3:2).

In His unmatched wisdom, God has organized our universe in such a way so as to give His children the best chance of advancement possible. Nothing has been overlooked or left to chance. The laws of the universe are on our side. President Benson taught:

> "Mormon philosophy, based on the revelations of God, assures us that our Heavenly Father is the supreme scientist of the universe. He is the supreme authority of the humanities. God is the supreme authority on politics, on economics, on sociology. He is the master teacher, with a glorious plan based on freedom of choice, for the building of godlike men and women. He stands

---

[65] Sterling W. Sill, *The Law of the Harvest* (Salt Lake City, UT: Bookcraft, Inc., 1963), 170.

today ready to help us reach out and tap that great unseen power as we heed the counsel of His living mouthpiece, a true prophet of God."[66]

Our God has planned meticulously. He has foreseen every phase of earth life, knows every science and discipline, and has instituted the earthly laws, governments, and institutions necessary for man to achieve happiness and eventual exaltation. He truly is the "supreme authority" on all matters – particularly those related to His precious children. If His children have faith in Him, He will lead them correctly until they return back to Him.

President George Q. Cannon also spoke of our affectionate relationship to our Heavenly Parent and how this knowledge buoys us, makes us happy, and gives us confidence. He said:

> "There was a period when we, with Jesus and others, basked in the light of the presence of God and enjoyed His smiles. We are the children of God, and as His children there is no attribute we ascribe to Him that we do not possess, though they may be dormant or in embryo. The mission of the Gospel is to develop these powers and make us like our Heavenly Parent. I know this is true, and such knowledge makes me feel happy.

> "God in His infinite mercy has revealed to us a great truth. It is a truth that, when understood by us, gives us a new light to our existence and inspires us with the most exalted hopes. That truth is that God is our Father, and we are His children. What a tender relationship! What a feeling of nearness it creates within us! What? God my Father? Am I indeed His son? Am I indeed His daughter? Do I belong to the family of God? Is this literally true? The answer is, "Yes." God has revealed it, that we are literally His children, His offspring, that we are just as much His children as

---

[66] Benson, *The Teachings of Ezra Taft Benson*, 5.

our offspring are our children, that He begot us, and that we existed with Him in the family relationship as His children."[67]

I fully concur that this knowledge makes one happy. I know that it increases my desire to go to my Father in prayer. It gives me confidence that my prayers will be answered. Did not Jesus teach that the Father, being good, hears and answers the prayers of His children (Matthew 7:7-11)? If I am a son of my Eternal Father, then I can approach Him and commune with Him with a confident expectation that He will hear me. I have had too many experiences with answered prayers – prayers answered in direct and powerful fashion – to deny this great principle. I know I am a loved and known son of God.

Yes, we are the family of God, and He, being the Patriarch of this family, leads, protects, provides, inspires, teaches, and chastens in righteousness. He looks out for His children and "doeth not anything save it be for the benefit of the world; for he loveth the world" (2 Nephi 26:24). We can therefore answer with absolute confidence President Cannon's question: "Am I indeed His son? Am I indeed His daughter?"

We *are* the sons and daughters of our Eternal Parents. And because of this inborn connection, we can know something of our Father's personality traits and behavior when we see the conduct of those who have the Holy Spirit with them. President Heber C. Kimball gave this colorful statement about the character and attributes of our dear Father and how he personally felt when overcome by the Father's influence. He testified:

> "Often when I have been in the presence of brother Brigham, we would feel such a buoyant spirit that when we began to talk we could not express our feelings, and so, "Hallelujah," says Brigham, "Glory to God," says I. I feel it and say it.
>
> "Some of the brethren kind of turn their noses on one side at me when I make such expressions, but they would not do it if they

---

[67] Jerreld Newquist, ed., *Gospel Truth: Discourses and Writings of President George Q. Cannon*, Vol. 1 (Salt Lake City, UT: Deseret Book Company, 1974), 3.

knew God. Such ones do not even know brothers Brigham and Heber; if they did they would not turn a wry face at us. I am perfectly satisfied that my Father and my God is a cheerful, pleasant, lively, and good-natured Being. Why? Because I am cheerful, pleasant, lively, and good-natured when I have His Spirit. That is one reason why I know; and another is—the Lord said, through Joseph Smith, "I delight in a glad heart and a cheerful countenance." That arises from the perfection of His attributes; He is a jovial, lively person, and a beautiful man."[68]

Our Father is a beautiful Man – a perfect, lovely, good-natured, and jovial Person. What a beautiful description of the most beautiful Being in the universe.

Those times that I have felt His presence strongly have turned into times of great joy and thanksgiving. We must learn, like Presidents Young and Kimball, to embrace the Lord's Spirit and glory in His perfections. We must learn to shout praises to God and let our souls gush with gratitude and love for Him. We are here on earth to be tested and part of that test is to see the good in the bad and to cry "Hallelujah" when God blesses us with His beautiful presence and cheerful Spirit. Or, as the Savior instructed, "be of good cheer" (John 16:33).

Our Eternal Father's character is not only beautiful, but everlastingly perfect. His senses of mercy and justice are flawlessly balanced and He is seamlessly kind, good, and loving. The Prophet Joseph Smith taught the following:

"Our Heavenly Father is more liberal in his views, and boundless in his mercies and blessings, than we are ready to believe or receive; and, at the same time, is more terrible to the workers of iniquity, more awful in the executions of his punishments, and

---

[68] President Heber C. Kimball, *Journal of Discourses*, Vol. 4, 222, February 8, 1857, http://jod.mrm.org/4/221.

more ready to detect every false way, than we are apt to suppose him to be."[69]

Like any good Father, our Eternal Father is also a teacher and instructor. He teaches through example and the history of His dealings with mankind testify to his liberality and mercy. He blesses us daily with life, sends rain and light upon the earth, and preserves us in difficult circumstances when we turn to Him. He forgives us in His infinite mercy when we desire it and He gives us answers to our prayers when we seek them. He is also a Father who disciplines and corrects when such is necessary. He does so, however, out of a pure love and a desire for our betterment (D&C 95:1). His goal is to see us progress and become like Him as fast as we are prepared to do so.

President Spencer W. Kimball spoke many times on the Fatherhood of God and our family relationship with Him. On one such occasion, he reminded us to turn to Him that we might pass our tests with flying colors:

> "My brothers and sisters, we're away from home. We're off to school. Our lessons will not be easy. The way we react to them, the way we conquer and accomplish and live will determine our rewards, and they will be permanent and eternal."[70]

We are as children away from their parents at a long day of school. But when the school bell rings, we will return home to our Father and Mother, report card in hand. Will our Parents be pleased at the marks on our report card?

President Kimball additionally taught:

> "Man can transform himself and he must. Man has in himself the seeds of godhood, which can germinate and grow and develop. As the acorn becomes the oak, the mortal man becomes a god. It is

---

[69] Joseph Smith, *Documentary History of the Church*, Vol. 5, 136, August 27, 1842, https://byustudies.byu.edu/content/volume-5-chapter-7.

[70] Kimball, *The Teachings of Spencer W. Kimball*, 28.

within his power to lift himself by his very bootstraps from the plane on which he finds himself to the plane on which he should be. It may be a long, hard lift with many obstacles, but it is a real possibility."[71]

Yes, godhood "is a real possibility." However, it requires us to follow in the footsteps of our Savior Jesus Christ, as He followed in the footsteps of our great God. No matter how hard it may be, we have the potential and opportunity because inside of us are "the seeds of godhood" transmitted to us in our spirits by our literal Father in Heaven.

We have every chance and opportunity to use our agency to obey the Lord's commands which will make us "joint-heirs" with Him. President Kimball said:

> "We are not like the animal which can change little and lives largely by instinct. Being the real offspring of God, we can, if we are normal, fashion our own lives and make them productive, beautiful, godlike."[72]

If we were mere creatures, upright animals with no divine origin and no eternal Parentage, we would be wholly justified in not progressing very far. However, the truth is that we are "the real offspring of God." Therefore, we *can* change and grow and become godlike. We can eventually be perfect as our God has commanded us to be. We can, because of our lineage, be like God.

President Kimball certainly believed that perfection is possible. He told the Saints:

> "I would emphasize that the teachings of Christ that we should become perfect were not mere rhetoric. He meant literally that it is the right of mankind to become like the Father and like the Son,

---

[71] Kimball, *The Teachings of Spencer W. Kimball*, 28.

[72] Kimball, *The Teachings of Spencer W. Kimball*, 27.

having overcome human weaknesses and developed attributes of divinity."[73]

No, it is not rhetoric. The Lord spoke the truth for He was and is the Spirit of Truth (D&C 93:26). It is the destiny of man to be perfected and develop his innate attributes, inherited from his Father, until he rises to the station of a god. We each have divinity within us. We each have a holy potential. And until we truly understand this, we cannot fully respect, love, and understand our fellow man, or, for that matter, ourselves.

In the April 1951 General Conference, President Stephen L. Richards referred to our divine lineage and the influence this lineage has upon us. He taught:

> "I believe that man has divine attributes emanating from divine lineage. The Spirit of the Father is distributed through the Universe, and influences all life and all things.
>
> "There is a spirit in man which, within the limitations of his contacts in life, radiates from him and touches the lives and things about him. This spirit may be called personality. Whatever it is called, it exists and it is a potent force. When once set in motion it cannot well be controlled, but fortunately it is within our power to determine the characteristics which go into the structure of our lives and thus determine the influences and radiations which come from us. Our living will mold these characteristics into our lives."

Just as the influence of our Father's Spirit fills the immensity of space, so, too, can we radiate that same spirit in our own lives and with those we come in contact with. We act as conduits for good or for evil and this energy we project outward. We have the potential and privilege to use our influence for good and to assist the Father in His grand design of exalting His children. The conduct of our lives "mold these characteristics" and determine how much influence the Father can have through us.

---

[73] Kimball, *The Teachings of Spencer W. Kimball*, 26.

President Richards proceeded to give some fascinating thoughts about our kinship with our Eternal Father and how crucial to world peace and societal happiness this knowledge really is. He remarked:

> "We are all His spirit children in antemortal life. We come to earth "to be tabernacled in the flesh." In earth life we are, in large measure, the creatures of our environment, but we never entirely lose our spiritual investitures. . . .
>
> ". . . It is doubtful, my brethren and sisters in the family of our Eternal Parent, that anything is more important and vital to peaceful association in the world than a recognition and acceptance of this kinship in the spirits of men.
>
> "Herein lies a solid, understandable foundation for the spiritual brotherhood of the world. It has always seemed to me most difficult to establish fraternity without paternity. Surely those who acknowledge the Omnipotent God to be the Creator of the Universe, should find no difficulty in according to Him His place of distinction as the Father of all men—"Our Father who is in heaven" (Matt. 6:9). How else could He be "Our Father" except as the progenitor of our spirits, the begetter of that part of us which is deathless and immortal?
>
> "How regrettable it is that man, seemingly oblivious to this honorable and sacred relationship, should profane His holy name and blaspheme Christ. Do you think that a son can damn his father and love him?
>
> "Some may say this procreation of spirits is too realistic, involving an assumption of personality in the Father inconsonant with the ethereal nature sometimes ascribed to Him. Don't you think, my friends, that we can safely rely on the recorded words of His Son, our elder brother, and the prophets in the interpretation of this all-important relationship of man to God? To those acquainted with the Scriptures there is no need for quotations, they are filled with references to the veritable fatherhood of God and support for a divine personality which, in terms of human understanding,

can be conceived only as one in whose image we are created (Gen. 1:26).

"It is doubtful if there are any people in the world today who retard more seriously the progress of humanity in finding solutions for the world's problems, particularly the one of living together in peace, than those who deny and teach denial of the personality of God and His fatherhood of the spirits of men.

"By so doing, they rob brotherhood of its firmest prop, they rob man of the dignity of a noble lineage, and they take from him the most impelling incentives to live to be worthy of his inheritance and to come back again into the eternal presence of the author of his life. I do not see how it is possible for men of religion to do much for this sorry world unless they can establish and re-establish this fundamental doctrine of the veritable fatherhood of God."[74]

The knowledge that God is our Father and we are His children is the greatest knowledge in eternity. It is ennobling to know of this "sacred relationship." More than sacred, our relationship with our Eternal Father is "all-important." Without it, man is nothing (Moses 1:9-11).

To rob man of his familial connection to Deity and, thus, "of the dignity of a noble lineage," is to denigrate, belittle, and insult him. Nothing can "retard more seriously the progress of humanity" than to steal from man the knowledge that he is the *literal* offspring of God. To deny, conceal, or mutilate this truth is to plunge the human race into hopelessness and confusion.

President Brigham Young taught that this world was created as a sphere of testing in which man could come, receive a body, undergo trials, and, through faithful living, achieve exaltation. He said that knowing all peoples on earth are connected by blood to God is crucial to the efficient operation of earth life. He taught:

---

[74] President Stephen L. Richards, "Kinship of Spirits," General Conference, April, 1951, http://scriptures.byu.edu/#:t200:p530.

"The whole object of the creation of this world is to exalt the intelligences that are placed upon it, that they may live, endure, and increase forever and ever. We are not here to quarrel and contend about the things of this world, but we are here to subdue and beautify it. Let every man and woman worship their God with all their heart. Let them pay their devotions and sacrifices to him, the Supreme, and the Author of their existence. Do all the good you can to your fellow creatures. You are flesh of my flesh and bone of my bone. God has created of one blood all the nations and kingdoms of men that dwell upon all the face of the earth: black, white, copper-colored, or whatever their color, customs, or religion, they have all sprung from the same origin; the blood of all is from the same element."[75]

Though there are inherent differences in the races, and though certain lineages and races have been blessed in greater proportion than others and possess different faculties and responsibilities, it is nonetheless true that all people, of all races and nationalities, are members of God's family. All have His blood flowing in their veins. All are descendants of Adam and Eve and are related. If we are to bring this boisterous world into harmony, all must realize they are brothers and sisters and share the same Heavenly Father.

Knowing that we are all brothers and sisters and that our universal Father is the God of Heaven is the one sure truth that could bring about peace and fraternity on a global scale. Only this knowledge can produce the "spiritual brotherhood of the world" which President Richards envisioned. If we knew our Father and recognized Him as our divine Parent, we would know that we are brothers and sisters. Imagine the peaceful and friendly feelings which would well up in our hearts for one another, regardless of nationality, creed, or race. It is only when we realize this connection to the divine that we can become, as we have been commanded, "one."

One of the reasons it is so imperative to "flood the earth with the Book of Mormon," as President Ezra Taft Benson charged us with doing, is

---

[75] President Brigham Young, *Journal of Discourses*, Vol. 7, 290, October 9, 1859, http://jod.mrm.org/7/282.

because "a man would get nearer to God by abiding by its precepts, than by any other book."[76] If man needs any one thing, he desperately needs to get closer to God. We must remember our relationship to Him. We must remember that we are His children and that He is our Father. If anything can stop the tide of wickedness and perversion sweeping the globe, it is this knowledge of our true nature as literal offspring of God; it is the knowledge that "we are descended from the lineage of the Gods."

Another thing man needs to learn to do is to pray; in other words, to commune, speak, counsel, and talk with God as one person speaks with another. Prayer in its true form is a lost art. It has been replaced with rote, lifeless repetitions on the one hand and with nothing on the other. Prayer is the vital lifeline between man and God.

When I was on my mission in Russia, we taught a man who knew nothing of God. He did not even know how to pray. We taught him to speak with his Heavenly Father as he would his earthly father because he was a child of God. I was privileged to be there when this man prayed for the first time in his life. The first words out of his mouth were, translated into English, "Good afternoon, Father." I count that experience as one of the best of my mission. It was gratifying to hear someone, in such a childlike and faith-filled manner, say "good afternoon" to Heavenly Father. And why shouldn't he? He is a son of his Father in Heaven. So, too, are we children of the Almighty and have every right to approach Him in the same childlike, familiar, familial way.

We are witnessing rising levels of depression, anxiety, confusion, and self-deprecation in our society and throughout the world. The consolation, knowledge, and power that prayer provides could be a healing balm to soothe humanity's pain. President Ezra Taft Benson recommended prayer as a national healing balm. He wrote:

"There is great safety in a nation on its knees.

---

[76] Joseph Smith, *The Book of Mormon: Another Testament of Jesus Christ*, Introduction page.

"What assurance it would give of the much-needed blessings of the Lord if the American people, and people everywhere, could be found daily – night and morning – on their knees expressing gratitude for blessings already received, acknowledging our dependence upon God, and seeking his divine guidance.

"The spectacle of a nation praying is more awe-inspiring, more powerful, than the explosion of an atomic bomb. The force of prayer is greater than any possible combination of man-controlled powers, because "prayer is man's greatest means of tapping the resources of God.""[77]

Satan could have no power over this earth if its people were found on their knees praying as children to their Father. As the saying goes, Satan trembles when he sees the weakest Saint on his knees. The powers of hell would be shaken forever if we understood we are the children of light and petitioned the Lord of Light for mercy and assistance.

Yet, because man lacks the fundamental knowledge of his relationship with His Eternal Father, he is unable to adequately apply this soothing spiritual ointment. In the truest sense, it is impossible to correctly commune with God in prayer unless we know that we are approaching our literal Father. Prayer is the lifeblood of a Saint; we must pray. Yet, unless we know to whom we are praying, we cannot expect our prayers to be effective.

Elder Richard L. Evans taught this important principle about prayer:

"[T]he kind of prayer that really enables a man to walk serenely through all of the hazards and uncertainties of life with unwavering confidence and assurance is that prayer in which a man knows that he is talking to his Father in Heaven as literally as if he were talking to his father on earth. Until one can do this

---

[77] Ezra Taft Benson, *God, Family, Country: Our Three Great Loyalties* (Salt Lake City, UT: Deseret Book Company, 1975), 365.

there is much that he does not and cannot understand about prayer."[78]

If we are to spiritually survive this mortal life and pass our grueling exams, we must know how to communicate with our Father in Heaven. Just knowing that He is really our Father makes all the difference and enables a man to approach God with "unwavering confidence and assurance" that his petitions will be heard. Until we learn to speak with God as a child speaks with its father, our prayers will avail very little.

Knowing how to prayerfully commune with our God and how to have spiritual brotherhood with our fellow man are imperative if we are to make a paradise of this earth. That this is so important is self-evident when we know President Joseph Fielding Smith explained that:

> "Mortality is the testing or proving ground for exaltation to find out who among the children of God are worthy to become Gods themselves."[79]

If we want to be like our Father in the eternal worlds, we must learn to approach Him in this mortal state. If we are to become gods like our Father and Savior, we must know Their true nature and also see as we are seen (D&C 76:94). These grand promises can only be fulfilled through gaining firsthand knowledge of God and His Son. We thus must exert all our effort to learn of Them, to learn how we relate to Them, and to learn how we might approach and commune with Them.

In 1885, Bishop Orson F. Whitney described our relationship with our God and His tender feelings for us. He spoke of the universal and everlasting nature of this teaching, as well as the narrow, but rewarding, path which leads to eternal life. He taught:

> "I have always been taught to regard our Father in heaven as the source of all intelligence, and that wherever intelligence is

---

[78] Richard L. Evans, *This Day . . . And Always* (New York: Harper & Brothers Publishers, 1942), 84.

[79] Smith, *Doctrines of Salvation*, Vol. 1, 69.

manifested throughout the earth, among His creatures, it has its primal origin in Him who is the fountain of life and light; and that if men are qualified to perform any great or good work, it must necessarily be by reason of the power from God which rests upon them. The Latter-day Saints take this view of the relationship of God with mankind; that He is not simply the Father, or creator of a part of the human race, or a portion of earth's creatures, but He is the creator of all things—the maker of the earth, the maker of heaven, and that the children of men are the sons and daughters of one common parentage; that He feels for them all the day long; that He has their welfare constantly in view, and He makes no movement, so far as His children upon this earth are concerned, but He does it for their salvation and their good here and hereafter.

". . . For, while we acknowledge that God is the Father of the human race, and interested in the salvation of all, we do maintain that our mission as a part of the human family is peculiar, separate and distinct from the missions which have been given to others. God is the author of many plans and purposes, but all his plans, all his purposes and designs converge to one point, have one focus, whether He uses the Christian world, the heathen world, or even this little handful of Latter-day Saints; no matter whom He uses to accomplish His ends, these purposes blend and have but one grand object. They are like rivers or streams of different kinds and sizes flowing towards one ocean into which they all must empty. . . .

"We are placed in this world measurably in the dark. We no longer see our Father face to face. While it is true that we once did; that we once stood in His presence, seeing as we are seen, knowing, according to our intelligence, as we are known; the curtain has dropped, we have changed our abode, we have taken upon ourselves flesh; the veil of forgetfulness intervenes between this life and that, and we are left, as Paul expresses it, to "see through a glass darkly," to "know in part and to prophesy in part;" to see only to a limited extent, the end from the beginning. We do not comprehend things in their fullness. But we have the promise, if we will receive and live by every word that proceeds from the mouth of God, wisely using the intelligence, the opportunities, the advantages, and the possessions which He continually bestows upon us—the time will come, in the eternal course of events, when our minds will be cleared from every cloud, the past will recur to memory, the future will be an open vision, and we will behold things as they are, and the past, present and future will be one eternal day, as it is in the eyes of God our Father, who knows neither past, present or future; whose course is one eternal round; who creates, who saves, redeems and glorifies the workmanship of His hands, in which He Himself is glorified.

"The earth upon which we dwell is only one among the many creations of God. The stars that glitter in the heavens at night and give light unto the earth are His creations, redeemed worlds, perhaps, or worlds that are passing through the course of their redemption, being saved, purified, glorified and exalted by obedience to the principles of truth which we are now struggling to obey. Thus is the work of our Father made perpetual, and as fast as one world and its inhabitants are disposed of, He will roll another into existence, He will create another earth, He will people it with His offspring, the offspring of the Gods in eternity, and they will pass through probations such as we are now passing through, that they may prove their integrity by their works; that they may give an assurance to the Almighty that they are worthy to be exalted through obedience to those principles, that unchangeable plan of salvation which has been revealed to us.

"It is one of the grandest attributes of Deity that He saves and exalts the human family upon just and eternal principles; that He gives to no man, or no woman that which they have not been willing to work for, which they have not deserved, which they have not expanded themselves to receive by putting in practice the principles He reveals, against all opposition, facing the wrath and scorn of the world—the world which cannot give a just cause, a reasonable pretext for the opposition it has ever manifested to the truths of heaven. It is a characteristic of our Father, a principle of His divine economy to exact from every soul a fitting proof of its worthiness to attain the exaltation to which it aspires. There are no heights that may not be surmounted, but they must be reached in the way that God has ordained. Man may think to accomplish his salvation by carrying out the selfish desires of his own heart; but when he fails to take God into consideration, his Creator, and the framer of the laws whereby we mount unto exaltation and eternal life, he knocks the ladder from under him whereby he might climb to that glorious state.

"The exclusiveness which the Latter-day Saints exhibit is this: they maintain that the Lord has but one way to save the human race; that the term "everlasting gospel" is not a misnomer, but means exactly what it says, and that it is eternal as its maker or framer is eternal. It can no more change than He can change. A man must obey the same principles now that were obeyed two thousand years ago, or six thousand years ago, or millions of ages ago, in order to attain the presence of His Father and God. There is but one way, one plan of life and salvation, and there need be but one; for God, being an economist, does not create that which is superfluous; and there can be, in the very nature of things, only one true plan of eternal life, for if there were two they must necessarily differ, since no two things can be exactly alike, and if one of these two things is perfect that which differs from it, must be imperfect. Of a necessity God is the author of perfection; His works are not deficient in any respect; and what He ordains for the salvation of man is the only way for man to be saved."[80]

What a beautiful witness of the truth. What a powerful testimony of the fact that our Father reaches out to us "all the day long" and has our welfare "constantly in view." As we have noted, our Father's purpose is "to bring to pass the immortality and eternal life of man" (Moses 1:39). Everything is calculated to achieve this purpose. Our Father does not want

---

[80] Bishop Orson F. Whitney, *Journal of Discourses*, Vol. 26, 194-197, April 19, 1885, http://jod.mrm.org/26/194.

to lose a single one of His children. Yet, we have our agency. We must choose to obey and follow our Elder Brother or we cannot return to the Father.

The Gospel laws are not arbitrary. They were not hastily thought-up or suddenly invented. They are not implemented unfairly or in a biased manner. Nephi testified:

> "He doeth not anything save it be for the benefit of the world; for he loveth the world, even that he layeth down his own life that he may draw all men unto him. Wherefore, he Commandeth none that they shall not partake of his salvation.

> "Behold, doth he cry unto any, saying: Depart from me? Behold, I say unto you, Nay; but he saith: Come unto me all ye ends of the earth, buy milk and honey, without money and without price. . . .

> "Hath he commanded any that they should not partake of his salvation? Behold I say unto you, Nay; but he hath given it free for all men; and he hath commanded his people that they should persuade all men to repentance.

> "Behold, hath the Lord commanded that they should not partake of his goodness? Behold I say unto you, Nay; but all men are privileged the one like unto the other, and none are forbidden" (2 Nephi 26:24-25, 27-28).

God's Gospel is "everlasting" and "is eternal as its maker or framer is eternal." God cannot change or alter His laws. They are fixed and unending. And Jesus, the Redeemer of all mankind, has invited all to come unto Him, receive of His goodness, partake of His love and mercy, and enjoy salvation with Him and His Father.

In order to progress upward, one must obey the same laws today as men in times past had to obey. Our Lord is our Exemplar. He obeyed each law in order to fulfill all righteousness and thereby "showeth unto the children of men that, according to the flesh he humbleth himself before the Father, and witnesseth unto the Father that he would be obedient unto him in keeping his commandments" (2 Nephi 31:7).

We find motivation to keep the commandments when we realize that because God is our Father and that He is eager to help His children. When we know this, we know that His commandments are not restrictive, oppressive, or limiting. They are, in reality, empowering. They are guardrails helping us stay on the path that leads to eternal life and never-ending happiness.

We find additional strength in knowing that Jesus is our Brother and that since we are expected to be like Him, we have been granted the tools by which to succeed. If we succeed, we become "joint-heirs" with Him in the eternal worlds (Romans 8:17). If we are expected – yes, even commanded – to be perfect like He and the Father, then we can expect that divine assistance will be forthcoming. Knowing that God is our Eternal Father and that He loves us as a son or daughter makes all the difference in the world in determining our level of commitment to the principles of life and exaltation.

Eternal life, as we have seen in this chapter, consists in knowing that God is our Father, that Jesus is His Son, and that the Holy Ghost bears witness of Them in Their divine roles as Father and Son, Creator and Redeemer. It also consists in understanding and imitating, to the best of our finite ability, Their attributes and perfections and in comprehending the relationship we have with Them. This knowledge is crucial. It is vital. It is absolutely imperative.

The Prophet Joseph Smith taught us this great truth:

> "If you wish to go where God is, you must be like God, or possess the principles which God possesses. . . .
>
> "As far as we degenerate from God, we descend to the devil and lose knowledge, and without knowledge we cannot be saved. . . .
>
> "A man is saved no faster than he gets knowledge for if he does not get knowledge, he will be brought into captivity by some evil power in the other world, as evil spirits will have more

knowledge, and consequently more power than many men who are on the earth."[81]

If we are to progress to godhood, thus fulfilling the end of our creation, we must possess knowledge. We must learn of God and, as the Savior, submit ourselves to Him and *do* His will. We must *know* God the Father and His Son Jesus, which is eternal life.

And this brings us to the final key to *knowing* God that we will discuss. With all of this *knowing*, we must also be *doing*. President David O. McKay taught simply:

> "Eternal life is the result of knowledge, and knowledge is obtained by doing the will of God."[82]

As the Savior humbled Himself in all things and showed to the world that He would be obedient to the Father's commands, so, too, must we humble ourselves. And we can do so with confidence knowing that "he that shall humble himself shall be exalted" (Matthew 23:12).

Let us then behave as good children of our Father. Let us walk in His footsteps, as exemplified by our Elder Brother. Let us remember who we are and where we stand in relation to God – our Father, our Friend, the Supreme Intelligence of the galaxy. Let us remember that we are, truly, of "the lineage of the Gods" and stand stalwart forever more in that knowledge which saves.

---

[81] Joseph Smith, *Documentary History of the Church*, Vol. 4, 588, April 10, 1842, https://byustudies.byu.edu/content/volume-4-chapter-34.

[82] David O. McKay, *Gospel Ideals: Selections from the Discourses of David O. McKay* (Salt Lake City, UT: Improvement Era, 1953), 8.

Chapter Third

Pre-Mortality and the Father's Plan

My soul loves the doctrine of pre-mortality! I believe it is the lynchpin to understanding our identity and the purpose of this mortal life. Everything we have discussed thus far deals directly with our existence as intelligences and spirits in this pre-mortal realm. This chapter will also focus on pre-mortality and will discuss the first lessons we learned while there, foremost among which was gaining knowledge of the Father's Plan of Salvation for His children.

It is an essential aspect of Christ's Gospel to know for certain that we lived before our birth on earth. Indeed, it is fundamental if we are to know who we are and whose children we are. Without the knowledge of a previous existence wherein we were raised to spiritual maturity in the presence of our Eternal Father, learned to exercise free will, chose to follow the Savior, were instructed in the principles of the everlasting Gospel, and were prepared for our testing period in morality, life would indeed be a mysterious, unfair, cruel, and seemingly arbitrary thing.

That you and I lived before this life is one of the greatest truths in eternity. It is also one of the least accepted truths in the world today; at least, by Christians. I know of only one Christian denomination that teaches that human beings lived before this life in the presence of God their Father, and that He is the literal Father of their spirits. Various world religions teach the incorrect doctrine of reincarnation and, thus, the concept of past lives. And several strains of New Age philosophy, Eastern mysticism, and even Freemasonry teach that men lived before – even on different planets and stars. However, the doctrine of pre-mortal life as taught by The Church of Jesus Christ of Latter-day Saints is a very different concept from these incorrect teachings. A closer comparison of these teachings will be given in chapter five.

The orthodox Christian may wonder where this doctrine of pre-mortality is to be found in his Bible. If it is in the Bible, why hasn't his preacher, pastor, bishop, or minister ever delivered a sermon on this concept? I assure the reader that this teaching *is* contained in the Bible. However, it is more plainly delineated by modern revelation and the teachings of contemporary prophets. We will use both modern and Biblical passages to confirm this precept.

In the Old Testament book of Ecclesiastes, the prophet tells us that when man dies, his spirit shall return to God. His wording reads:

> "Then shall the dust return to the earth as it was: and the spirit shall return unto God who gave it" (Ecclesiastes 12:7).

This clearly states that our bodies, the "dust," shall return back to the earth when we die. Our spirits, however, will *return* to that God who sent them to earth. How can something *return* to a place it has never before been? And if God "gave it," He must have clearly had it beforehand. This is simple, but sound, logic.

The Pearl of Great Price provides us with perhaps the clearest assurances that we lived before this life. One passage about the creation of our earth and life upon it explains:

> "For I, the Lord God, created all things, of which I have spoken, spiritually, before they were naturally upon the face of the earth . . . And I, the Lord God, had created all the children of men; and not yet a man to till the ground; for in heaven created I them; and there was not yet flesh upon the earth, neither in the water, neither in the air; . . . .

> "And I, the Lord God, formed man from the dust of the ground, and breathed into his nostrils the breath of life; and man became a living soul, the first flesh upon the earth, the first man also; nevertheless, all things were before created; but spiritually were they created and made according to my word" (Moses 3:5, 7).

We each had a *spiritual* existence prior to our birth into mortality. The animals and all things that exist were created before in the world of spirits. This accords with the verse from Ecclesiastes which testifies that man's spirit will *return* to the God who gave it when his mission here on earth is complete.

When Jesus and His disciples came across a man born blind, the disciples asked the Lord this curious question:

> "Master, who did sin, this man, or his parents, that he was born blind?" (John 9:2).

How could this man have sinned *before* he was born if indeed he had not existed previously? It seems evident that the Twelve Apostles believed that man existed, and could even sin, *prior* to his mortal birth. And Jesus apparently confirms the doctrine of an antemortal existence when He responded that neither this man nor his parents had sinned.

The Apostle Paul also mentioned our pre-earth life. He said that the Lord "hath chosen us in him before the foundation of the world" (Ephesians 1:4). How could the Lord choose us *before* the foundation of the world if man did not exist until his mortal birth? The theologians and priests attempt to pick this and other verses apart, searching for hidden mysteries that do not exist. They twist and mangle until the meaning of a verse fits the individual's personal beliefs, instead of the individual expanding his heart to accept the truth. Often, a verse has a very simple meaning that needs no extra over-thinking and only requires that the reader take the prophetic statement in good faith.

The prophet Jacob noted this corrupting tendency among the ancient Jews when he said:

> "The Jews were a stiffnecked people; and they despised the words of plainness, and killed the prophets, and sought for things that they could not understand. Wherefore, because of their blindness, which blindness came by looking beyond the mark, they must needs fall" (Jacob 4:14).

Are we not the same as these ancient peoples? So often we look for mysteries when we ought to understand plainness. We argue about definitions and miss the principles. Paul, a man of great secular learning himself, understood this tendency and warned:

> "Neither give heed to fables and endless genealogies, which minister questions, rather than godly edifying" (1 Timothy 1:4).

Discounting simple declarations such as "the spirit shall return unto God" produces unnecessary questions that lead people astray and cause them to look beyond the mark. It happens so frequently that I have come to believe that some people often *want* to be confused. They *want* there to be mysteries too great to understand and too incomprehensible to grasp. If they do not understand, then they cannot be held accountable and less is required of them. I believe this is a "natural man" tendency that we must learn to shave off of our character (Mosiah 3:19).

The scriptural evidence of our pre-mortal existence is everywhere to be seen if only we learn to see with the eyes of our spirit. In Proverbs chapter 8, wise Solomon wrote a beautiful passage regarding man's pre-earth origin. He elucidated:

> "The Lord possessed me in the beginning of his way, before the works of old.
>
> "I was set up from everlasting, from the beginning, or ever the earth was.
>
> "When there were no depths, I was brought forth; when there were no fountains abounding with water.
>
> "Before the mountains were settled, before the hills was I brought forth:
>
> "While as yet he had not made the earth, nor the fields, nor the highest part of the dust of the world.
>
> "When he prepared the heavens, I was there: when he set a compass upon the face of the depth:
>
> "When he established the clouds above: When he strengthened the fountains of the deep:

"When he gave to the sea his decree, that the waters should not pass his commandment: when he appointed the foundations of the earth:

"Then I was by him, as one brought up with him: and I was daily his delight, rejoicing always before him;

"Rejoicing in the habitable part of his earth; and my delights were with the sons of men" (Proverbs 8:22-31).

These verses are so plain that they don't need much explanation. However, to recapitulate, Solomon said that man was "set up from everlasting, from the beginning" before the earth was. Before there was an earth with its majestic mountains and unconquerable seas, man "was brought forth" as the greatest creation of Deity. As the Lord constructed the Heavens and the planets, "I was there," said Solomon. "Then I was by him" as He went about His pre-earth organizing of the elements into a world. Yes, the "sons of men" were daily with God rejoicing as He created an earth for them to inhabit.

Can anyone deny this powerful testimony of the truth? Can anyone deny, after reading these things, that the Bible bears witness of pre-mortality? Can anyone deny Solomon's plain assurance that when God created the foundations of the earth "then I was by him"? How can a Christian familiar with these teachings doubt man's pre-earth existence? I testify that man *did* live before this earth came into being, as the Bible attests.

In a remarkably similar vein, we read these curious lines in the book of Job in the Old Testament:

"Then the Lord answered Job out of the whirlwind, and said. . . .

"Where wast thou when I laid the foundations of the earth? . . . .

"When the morning stars sang together, and all the sons of God shouted for joy?" (Job 38:1, 4, 7).

Indeed, where was Job, and where were all of us, when God was laying the foundations for this earth? Was Job with Solomon and the rest of the sons of God as He laid the foundations of this earth? The Lord Himself rhetorically answered in the affirmative that as He created this earth the "morning stars sang together, and all the sons of God shouted for joy." "Morning stars" is a figurative expression referring to those who were in the beginning with God. It can also denote the distinguished spirits such as the "noble and great ones" seen by Abraham.

Even more plainly, however, the text declares that the "sons of God" shouted for joy when the foundations of the earth were laid. The *"sons of God"* refers to His children. And how could they have shouted for joy, or sang together, if they did not exist? Clearly, we – the Father's children – not only existed, but we had intelligence and cognizance and were able to sing and shout and experience joy *before* the earth was created. The witness of Solomon and Job harmonize perfectly on this great truth.

In Revelation 2:28 and 22:16, the Savior Jesus Christ is referred to by the title "the morning star." The context of Revelation 22:16 makes it plain that this distinction refers to the Lord:

> "I Jesus have sent mine angel to testify unto you these things in the churches. I am the root and the offspring of David, and the bright and morning star."

Jesus is *the* morning star. In other words, He is *the* Firstborn of the Father in the beginning and *the* pre-eminent Spirit. Other scriptural passages confirm this point, such as Romans 8:29, Isaiah 41:4, Psalms 89:27, and D&C 93:21. The other "morning stars" of Job's account are the rest of the Father's children – me and you. We were also, as the revelations state, in the beginning with the Father (D&C 93:29).

In Revelation 12:4, the Apostle John also refers to the pre-mortal spirits of Heavenly Father as "the stars of Heaven." Satan, we are told, "drew the third part of the stars of heaven" away after him. Revelation chapter twelve is one of the greatest proofs of the pre-earth existence and War in Heaven in all of holy writ. A few verses from that chapter will benefit our understanding:

> "And there appeared another wonder in heaven; and behold a great red dragon, having seven heads and ten horns, and seven crowns upon his heads.

"And his tail drew the third part of the stars of heaven, and did cast them to the earth: and the dragon stood before the woman which was ready to be delivered, for to devour her child as soon as it was born. . . .

"And there was war in heaven: Michael and his angels fought against the dragon; and the dragon fought and his angels,

"And prevailed not; neither was their place found any more in heaven.

"And the great dragon was cast out, and the old serpent, called the Devil, and Satan, which deceiveth the whole world: he was cast out into the earth, and his angels were cast out with him" (Revelation 12:3-4, 7-9).

The dragon here depicted is Satan. Satan and "his angels" started a "war in heaven." He was opposed by Michael, whom we know through the Prophet Joseph Smith was Adam, and "his angels." Adam, therefore, and the righteous two-thirds of the "stars of heaven," or sons of God, fought against Satan, pre-mortally called Lucifer, and his followers.

The word angel here is at times taken too literally. In Christendom, most people think angels are a race of beings separate from humans. This is not so. Angels *are* the children of God. When we realize this, we realize that God's children were present during this momentous War in Heaven.

What happened to the rebellious one-third who followed Satan? The dragon's tail "drew the third part of the starts of heaven, and did cast them to the earth." Because they followed Satan, who is the dragon, a "third part" of Heavenly Father's children rebelled and were, as a consequence, cast down to the earth. It is these wicked spirits, led by Satan, who tempt and terrorize mankind. They are not demons or djinn of some otherworldly species of creation. They are merely rebellious children of God – our fallen brothers and sisters. Just as man can fall and reject the Lord in mortality, so, too, did they have their agency in the pre-earth life.

We also had our agency. Those of us who have been privileged to come into mortality – yes, every one of us – once chose the Father's Plan.

Knowing that we once chose God should bolster our resolve to choose Him again here. Knowing that we conquered Satan once before ought to give us the faith to do so again. Let us now make the same choice we made pre-mortally and reject Lucifer's lies in favor of the Father's Plan.

This imagery of stars representing children of God, as well as the incredible account of the War in Heaven, is recorded in other places in the Bible, too. Isaiah, for instance, tells of Lucifer's treachery. Isaiah chapter 14 tells the tale. Three verses from that powerful passage are cited here:

> "How are thou fallen from heaven, O Lucifer, a son of the morning! how art thou cut down to the ground, which didst weaken the nations!

> "For thou hast said in thine heart, I will ascend into heaven, I will exalt my throne above the stars of God: I will sit also upon the mount of the congregation, in the sides of the north:

> "I will ascend above the heights of the clouds; I will be like the most High" (Isaiah 14:12-14).

"Son of the morning" refers to the fact that Lucifer was one of the earliest created of God's children. He was, as we have noted, an angel in authority in the pre-mortal realm (D&C 76:25). In his pride, Lucifer sought to exalt his throne above the Father's children and to "be like the most High." In other words, Satan wanted to rule over everyone – over all the "stars of God" – as their God. His lust was for power. He wanted to be worshipped, honored, and adored. Today, he also wants to be recognized as God, though he is a fallen and miserable man.

In a revelation to Joseph Smith, the Lord revealed this about the War in Heaven:

> "And this we saw also, and bear record, that an angel of God who was in authority in the presence of God, who rebelled against the Only Begotten Son whom the Father loved and who was in the bosom of the Father, was thrust down from the presence of God and the Son,

"And was called Perdition, for the heavens wept over him – he was Lucifer, a son of the morning.

"And we beheld, and lo, he is fallen! is fallen, even a son of the morning!

"And while we were yet in the Spirit, the Lord commanded us that we should write the vision; for we beheld Satan, that old serpent, even the devil, who rebelled against God, and sought to take the kingdom of our God and his Christ –

"Wherefore, he maketh war with the saints of God, and encompasseth them round about" (D&C 76:25-29).

Again we note that Lucifer was called a "son of the morning" and was with God in the beginning, as we all were.

Those who were rebellious in the pre-earth state are said to have not kept their "first estate." "First estate" merely means the pre-earth, former, or first stage of eternal progression. The disciple named Jude used this term when he testified:

"And the angels which kept not their first estate, but left their own habitation, he hath reserved in everlasting chains under darkness unto the judgment of the great day" (Jude 1:6).

When read in the context of John's record concerning the War in Heaven where "the dragon" and "his angels" rebelled and were cast out, it becomes obvious that "first estate" is synonymous with the pre-mortal realm. The English word "estate" was taken from the Greek word which can also mean "domain," "dominion," "principality," "appointed sphere," "responsibility," and "original rank."[83] This is made even clearer in latter-day revelation.

In Abraham's record translated by the Prophet Joseph Smith, we read:

---

[83] Alexander L. Baugh, "First Estate," *The Encyclopedia of Mormonism*, last modified May 27, 2011, accessed August 9, 2018, http://eom.byu.edu/index.php/First_Estate.

> "And they who keep their first estate shall be added upon; and they who keep not their first estate shall not have glory in the same kingdom with those who keep their first estate; and they who keep their second estate shall have glory added upon their heads for ever and ever.

> "And the Lord said: Whom shall I send? And one answered like unto the Son of Man: Here am I, send me. And another answered and said: Here am I, send me. And the Lord said: I will send the first.

> "And the second was angry, and kept not his first estate; and, at that day, many followed after him" (Abraham 3:26-28).

The record makes it clear that this scene played out in the pre-earth life. The first estate, then, as Jude also testified, is synonymous with our pre-mortal existence. Those who kept it – or who were faithful – had the opportunity to progress to their second estate, or earth life.

Satan, however, wanted to ascend above the Father and angrily rebelled against His Plan, dragging others down with him. These did not keep their first estate and therefore were cast down and were denied the opportunity of advancing to mortality and possessing physical bodies. Instead, they now inhabit the earth, tempting and persuading mankind to sin and to rebel, as they did, against the Father and His Son.

The Lord Jesus referenced His own pre-mortal existence during His earthly ministry. In His great Intercessory Prayer, Jesus prayed to the Father and said:

> "And now, O Father, glorify thou me with thine own self with the glory which I had with thee before the world was" (John 17:5).

Jesus, though He was a Son, had glory "before the world was." Here the Lord is testifying of the pre-earth state. He could not have had glory "before the world was" if He did not exist before the world was. And is it conceivable that *only* Jesus existed before and that none of the other children of God did? The verses referenced so far put that misguided thought to rest.

Other prophets were also given glimpses of their pre-mortal existence. When the Lord called the great prophet Jeremiah, He revealed the following:

> "Before I formed thee in the belly I knew thee; and before thou camest forth out of the womb I sanctified thee, and I ordained thee a prophet unto the nations" (Jeremiah 1:5).

As noted earlier, some students of the Bible read a verse like this and look past the simple language and search for mysteries and complexities. If we read this verse in its true sense, however, we see that the Lord is simply reminding Jeremiah that he lived before his mortal birth and that the Lord knew him and had foreordained him at that time – that is, in his pre-earth life – to his earthly calling as a prophet in Israel.

The prophet Alma similarly bore record that some of the Father's children in their pre-mortal state exercised great faith and did good works and thereby were chosen as earthly prophets, high priests, and rulers. Alma stated:

> "And again, my brethren, I would cite your minds forward to the time when the Lord God gave these commandments unto his children; and I would that ye should remember that the Lord God ordained priests, after his holy order, which was after the order of his Son, to teach these things unto the people. . . .

> "And this is the manner after which they were ordained – being called and prepared from the foundation of the world according to the foreknowledge of God, on account of their exceeding faith and good works; in the first place being left to choose good and evil; therefore they having chosen good, and exercising exceedingly great faith, are called with a holy calling. . . .

> ". . . in the first place they were on the same standing with their brethren; thus this holy calling being prepared from the foundation of the world for such as would not harden their hearts, being in and through the atonement of the Only Begotten Son, who was prepared –

"And thus being called by this holy calling, and ordained unto the high priesthood of the holy order of God, to teach his commandments unto the children of men, that they also might enter into his rest" (Alma 13:1, 3, 5-6).

Alma testifies that there was a time before this earth was that our Father gathered His children and gave them His divine commandments and taught them His law and Plan. There were some intelligences who exercised their agency and became "exceedingly" faithful and did many good works. Many of these were the "noble and great ones" of Abraham's account and included men like Jeremiah whom the Lord knew and ordained before his birth. Those who hold the High Priesthood were foreordained to that calling "from the foundation of the world." They were given the special responsibility to remind the Father's children of the commandments He had given them in their pre-earth state.

Our Father's Plan is calculated to assist His children to advance step by step until they eventually become like Him and receive their exaltation in His Kingdom. This Plan was put into motion when He clothed our pre-existent intelligence with spirit element and we became His children. We then received, as spiritual toddlers, our first lessons from Him over eons and eons of time. Everything was carefully designed to help us progress, grow, and reach greater heights.

In the October 1989 General Conference, President Howard W. Hunter taught:

> "Part of our reassurance about the free, noble, and progressing spirit of man comes from the glorious realization that we all existed and had our identities, and our agency, long before we came to this world. To some that will be a new thought, but the Bible teaches clearly just such an eternal view of life, a life stretching back before this world was and stretching forward into the eternities ahead.

> "God said to Jeremiah, "Before I formed thee in the belly I knew thee; and before thou camest forth out of the womb I sanctified thee, and I ordained thee a prophet unto the nations" (Jeremiah 1:5). At another time God reminded Job that "all the sons of God

shouted for joy" (Job 38:7) before there was yet any man or woman on the earth God was creating. The Apostle Paul taught that God the Father chose us "before the foundation of the world" (Ephesians 1:4).

"Where and when did all of this happen? Well, it happened long before man's mortal birth. It happened in a great premortal existence where we developed our identities and increased our spiritual capabilities by exercising our agency and making important choices. We developed our intelligence and learned to love the truth, and we prepared to come to earth to continue our progress."[84]

Progression was the name of the game. And we each progressed through obedience to our Father's commands. The Father appointed those who had advanced further than others to positions of leadership. Yes, even in the pre-mortal world we had ample opportunity to distinguish ourselves or lapse in our studies – to be rewarded for our faithfulness and good works or to exercise our agency in a manner that hindered our personal progression. The greater intelligences, led by the Savior under the direction of the Father, went about teaching and preparing mankind to leave their Heavenly home and take their final exams here on earth.

Elder Melvin J. Ballard bore a profound testimony of the Father's Plan of Salvation when he summarized that Plan in these words:

"I proclaim it is the word of God that we all lived as separate individuals before we came into earth; that the intelligence dwelling in each of us is co-eternal with God; that it always existed and never was created or made; that in due time that intelligence was given a spirit body, which is the very child of God, our eternal Father and his beloved companion, our eternal mother. This spirit, inhabited by the eternal intelligence, took the form of its Creator and is in his image. After ages of growth and

---

[84] President Howard W. Hunter, "The Golden Thread of Choice," General Conference, October, 1989, https://www.lds.org/general-conference/1989/10/the-golden-thread-of-choice?lang=eng.

experience in that state, during which the traits, characteristics, abilities, and weaknesses we exhibit in this life, were largely developed, the various races here were established there by the exercise of our freedom and choice. Finally earth life was provided, and the spirit body, inhabited by the immortal intelligence, took up its abode in the material instrument, to be able to come into contact with the new condition and experiences afforded for the first time in our existence. After death, that which existed before and independent of the body will continue, until through the resurrection of the earth body, the union of spirit and matter will take place, providing the power and ability to touch and know all realms. We are reaping what we have heretofore sown, so shall we hereafter reap what we now sow. To guide us to success for now and hereafter the gospel of the Son of God was given. I know as well as I see you now, that I shall see you hereafter the same individuals, that as God is without the beginning of days or end, so also is the offspring of man."[85]

I suspect I have never read a more powerful and succinct summary of the entire Plan of Salvation than this given by Elder Ballard. Every word is laden with inspiration and contains precious gems of eternal truth about who we are, where we come from, and where we are going.

This apostolic witness comprehends our existence as intelligences, our birth as spirits by our Holy Father and Mother, our first lessons in the pre-earth state, our designation into various races and lineages depending upon our pre-mortal works, our spirit being clothed with a mortal body and being afforded the chance to learn and progress, our eventual resurrection with an immortal, glorified body, and our chance, if we are righteous, to continue to progress and grow and expand for eternity. Elder Ballard was an amazing apostle and his instruction is some of the purest you will find anywhere.

Another straightforward instructor is Elder D. Todd Christofferson of the current Quorum of the Twelve. In the April 2015 General Conference, he

---

[85] Bryant S. Hinckley, *Sermons and Missionary Services of Melvin Joseph Ballard* (Salt Lake City, UT: Deseret Book Company, 1949), 140.

went back to the beginning and explained our progression from intelligences to spirit children of God, and from spirit children learning in pre-existence to mortals living here on earth. He taught:

"Prophets have revealed that we first existed as intelligences and that we were given form, or spirit bodies, by God, thus becoming His spirit children—sons and daughters of heavenly parents. There came a time in this premortal existence of spirits when, in furtherance of His desire that we "could have a privilege to advance like himself," our Heavenly Father prepared an enabling plan. In the scriptures it is given various names, including "the plan of salvation," "the great plan of happiness," and "the plan of redemption." The two principal purposes of the plan were explained to Abraham in these words:

""And there stood one among them that was like unto God, and he said unto those who were with him: We will go down, for there is space there, and we will take of these materials, and we will make an earth whereon these [spirits] may dwell;

""And we will prove them herewith, to see if they will do all things whatsoever the Lord their God shall command them;

""And they who keep their first estate shall be added upon; . . . and they who keep their second estate shall have glory added upon their heads for ever and ever."

"Thanks to our Heavenly Father, we had already become spirit beings. Now He was offering us a path to complete or perfect that being. The addition of the physical element is essential to the fulness of being and glory that God Himself enjoys. If, while with God in the premortal spirit world, we would agree to participate in His plan—or in other words "keep [our] first estate"—we would "be added upon" with a physical body as we came to dwell on the earth that He created for us.

"If, then in the course of our mortal experience, we chose to "do all things whatsoever the Lord [our] God [should] command [us]," we would have kept our "second estate." This means that by our choices we would demonstrate to God (and to ourselves) our commitment and capacity to live His celestial law while outside His presence and in a physical body with all its powers, appetites, and passions. Could we bridle the flesh so that it became the instrument rather than the master of the spirit? Could we be trusted both in time and eternity with godly powers, including power to create life? Would we individually overcome evil? Those who did would "have glory added upon their heads for ever and ever"—a very significant aspect of that glory being a resurrected, immortal, and glorified physical body. No wonder we "shouted for joy" at these magnificent possibilities and promises."[86]

Who would not have shouted for joy at such glorious assurances and potential? The intelligence within us surely clamored for a greater endowment of knowledge and progression. Our spirit no doubt longed to experience life in a physical body, to enjoy the power of procreation, and to be afforded the chance to choose a mate and create an eternal family of our own. Our Father's Plan was developed to provide just such opportunities.

As we learned and came to comprehend the incredible blessings and opportunities that awaited, many of us no doubt studied diligently in the pre-earth life. While not much has been specifically revealed through official revelatory channels, it seems logical, and is attested by non-canonical sources, that pre-mortality was very much like life now. We have already discussed the wide range of personality types that existed. We noted that President McKay testified of the divine law of spiritual attraction wherein certain individuals and groups gravitated towards one another and eventually came down to earth in specific races, tribes, and lineages.

Further, we positively know from Alma and Abraham that some spirits were more obedient than others. Because of this obedience, some were ordained to the High Priesthood and given leadership posts. We know

---

[86] Elder D. Todd Christofferson, "Why Marriage, Why Family," General Conference, April, 2015 https://www.lds.org/general-conference/2015/04/why-marriage-why-family?lang=eng

that some advanced farther and possessed a greater degree of intelligence than others, such as our beloved Savior. Some became leaders while others rebelled.

We can also surmise other things about our pre-earth state. We assume that we associated with friends, taught lessons, attended classes, learned new things, enjoyed good music, conducted experiments, did charitable works, played and enjoyed leisure time, had opportunities to choose and to exercise faith, and explored the world around us. Each individual certainly developed skills, talents, aptitudes, likes, dislikes, and proclivities unique to them. Some of us learned musical instruments, others excelled in science. Some were good with words and had strong minds while others developed great spirituality and could testify with power. I think we can even say that some exhibited symptoms of laziness and carelessness while others were stalwart and true. In short, we know that a wide array of spirits existed with their unique sensibilities, capacities, and intellects.

Elder Bruce R. McConkie described this process of progression during pre-existence in these terms:

"To understand the doctrine of pre-existence two great truths must be accepted: 1. That God is a personal Being in whose image man is created, an exalted, perfected, and glorified Man of Holiness (Moses 6:57), and not a spirit essence that fills the immensity of space; and 2. That matter or element is self-existent and eternal in nature, creation being merely the organization and reorganization of that substance which "was not created or made, neither indeed can be." (D&C 93:29.) Unless God the Father was a personal Being, he could not have begotten spirits in his image, and if there had been no self-existent spirit element, there would have been no substance from which those spirit bodies could have been organized.

"From the time of their spirit birth, the Father's pre-existent offspring were endowed with agency and subjected to the provisions of the laws ordained for their government. They had power to obey or disobey and to progress in one field or another. . . .

"The pre-existent life was thus a period – undoubtedly an infinitely long one – of probation, progression, and schooling. The spirit hosts were taught and given experiences in various administrative capacities. Some so exercised their agency and so conformed to law as to become "noble and great"; these were foreordained before their mortal births to perform great missions for the Lord in this life. (Abra. 3:22-28.) Christ, the Firstborn, was the mightiest of all the spirit children of the Father. (D&C 93:21-23.) Mortal progression and testing is a continuation of what began in pre-existence."[87]

As noted, our Father designed these pre-mortal lessons for us. He was the Master Teacher, the Supreme Intelligence. We knew Him and met with him face-to-face. He sat with us, talked with us, walked with us, and taught us as an earthly dad teaches his little sons and daughters. It was a period of schooling, tutoring, learning, and progression.

President Brigham Young explained our spiritual childhood this way:

"I want to tell you, each and every one of you, that you are well acquainted with God our heavenly Father, or the great Eloheim. You are all well acquainted with Him, for there is not a soul of you but what has lived in His house and dwelt with Him year after year; and yet you are seeking to become acquainted with Him, when the fact is, you have merely forgotten what you did know. . . .

"There is not a person here today but what is a son or a daughter of that Being. In the spirit world their spirits were first begotten and brought forth, and they lived there with their parents for ages before they came here. This, perhaps, is hard for many to believe, but it is the greatest nonsense in the world not to believe it. If you

---

[87] McConkie, *Mormon Doctrine*, 589-590.

do not believe it, cease to call Him Father; and when you pray, pray to some other character.

"It would be inconsistent in you to disbelieve what I think you know, and then to go home and ask the Father to do so and so for you. The Scriptures which we believe have taught us from the beginning to call Him our Father, and we have been taught to pray to Him as our Father, in the name of our eldest brother whom we call Jesus Christ, the Savior of the world; and that Savior, while here on earth, was so explicit on this point, that he taught his disciples to call no man on earth father, for we have one which is in heaven. He is the Savior, because it is his right to redeem the remainder of the family pertaining to the flesh on this earth . . . Try to believe it, because you will never become acquainted with our Father, never enjoy the blessings of His Spirit, never be prepared to enter into His presence, until you most assuredly believe it; therefore you had better try to believe this great mystery about God.

"I do not marvel that the world is clad in mystery, to them He is an unknown God; they cannot tell where He dwells nor how He lives, nor what kind of a being He is in appearance or character. They want to become acquainted with His character and attributes, but they know nothing of them. This is in consequence of the apostasy that is now in the world. They have departed from the knowledge of God, transgressed His laws, changed His ordinances, and broken the everlasting covenant, so that the whole earth is defiled under the inhabitants thereof. Consequently it is no mystery to us that the world knoweth not God, but it would be a mystery to me, with what I now know, to say that we cannot know anything of Him. We are His children."[88]

Yes, we are His children! We lived in our Father's house for eons of time. We learned from Him directly as we grew to spiritual maturity in the realm of spirits. If we do not believe He is literally our Father, why do we

[88] President Brigham Young, *Journal of Discourses*, Vol. 4, 216, February 8, 1857, http://jod.mrm.org/4/215.

address Him as "Father"? And why did our Savior address Him as "Father" if indeed He is not the Father of us all? It is, as President Young said, inconsistent to believe He is not our Father and yet believe the scriptures which call Him our Father.

Yet, we know that we have merely forgotten our very personal relationship with God. We have only forgotten what we once knew so well. Our mind is veiled, but our memories remain intact behind that veil. Through the revelations of the Holy Spirit, the veil can be parted and we can access some of our hidden memories. By this process, it is our privilege to recall that God is our Heavenly Father and that we once lived with Him in His Heavenly Home.

President Ezra Taft Benson also testified that we are intimately acquainted with our Father in Heaven. This is one of the most powerful statements I have ever read about our close pre-mortal relationship with our Eternal Father and I commend it to you. President Benson proclaimed:

> "We once knew well our Elder Brother and His and our Father in Heaven. We rejoiced at the prospects of earth life that could make it possible for us to have a fulness of joy. We could hardly wait to demonstrate to our Father and our Brother, the Lord, how much we loved them and how we would be obedient to them in spite of the earthly opposition of the evil one.

> "Now we are here. Our memories are veiled. We are showing God and ourselves what we can do. Nothing is going to startle us more when we pass through the veil to the other side than to realize how well we know our Father and how familiar His face is to us.

> "God loves us. He is watching us. He wants us to succeed. We will know some day that He has not left one thing undone for the eternal welfare of each of us. If we only knew it, heavenly hosts are pulling for us—friends in heaven that we cannot now remember who yearn for our victory. This is our day to show what we can do—what life and sacrifice we can daily, hourly, instantly

make for God. If we give our all, we will get His all from the greatest of all."[89]

Let me repeat the line that touches my spirit so profoundly: "Nothing is going to startle us more when we pass through the veil to the other side than to realize how well we know our Father and how familiar His face is to us."

Of all the myriad of things that might startle us or cause us to stand in awe in the next life, nothing, according to this dear prophet, will affect us so deeply as remembering how familiar we are with God. We will understand that we *have* seen His face and that we *are* in His image. We will recognize Him as our *literal* Father. We will remember Him and the times we spent with Him in His house, in His presence, and under His direct tutelage. No doubt we will remember the times we walked with Him, the times we asked Him questions, and the times He hugged us tight and told us He loved us. And what of our Mother in Heaven? Yes, we will remember Her as well and will no doubt be wrapped in our Parents' loving embrace once more. What a glorious, startling, unimaginable reunion that will be!

Returning again to Brigham Young, we find that stalwart man of God teaching the following doctrine about the variety of spirits which exist, the Heavenly home from whence they came, and the Divine Kingdom they might inherit through righteous living:

"Can any man tell the variety of the spirits there are? . . . I conclude that there is as great a variety in the spiritual as there is in the temporal world, and I think that I am just in my conclusion.

"You will see people possessed of different spirits; but I will say to you what I have heretofore frequently said, and what brother Joseph Smith has said, and what the Scripture teaches, your spirits when they came to take tabernacles were pure and holy, and prepared to receive knowledge, wisdom, and instruction, and

---

[89] President Ezra Taft Benson, "Jesus Christ – Gifts and Expectations," *Ensign*, December, 1988, https://www.lds.org/ensign/1988/12/jesus-christ-gifts-and-expectations?lang=eng.

to be taught while in the flesh; so that every son and daughter of Adam, if they would apply their minds to wisdom, and magnify their callings and improve upon every grace and means given them, would have tickets for the boxes, to use brother Hyde's figure, instead of going into the pit. There is no spirit but what was pure and holy when it came here from the celestial world. There is no spirit among the human family that was begotten in hell; none that were begotten by angels, or by any inferior being. They were not produced by any being less than our Father in heaven. He is the Father of our spirits; and if we could know, understand, and do His will, every soul would be prepared to return back into His presence. And when they get there, they would see that they had formerly lived there for ages, that they had previously been acquainted with every nook and corner, with the palaces, walks, and gardens; and they would embrace their Father, and He would embrace them and say, "My son, my daughter, I have you again;" and the child would say, "O my Father, my Father, I am here again."

"These are the facts in the case, and there are none ticketed for the pit, unless they fill up that ticket themselves through their own misconduct. Are all spirits endowed alike? No, not by any means. Will all be equal in the celestial kingdom? By no means. Some spirits are more noble than others; some are capable of receiving more than others. There is the same variety in the spirit world that you behold here, yet they are of the same parentage, of one Father, one God, to say nothing of who He is. They are all of one parentage, though there is a difference in their capacities and nobility, and each one will be called to fill the station for which he is organized, and which he can fill.

"We are placed on this earth to prove whether we are worthy to go into the celestial world, the terrestrial, or the telestial, or to hell, or to any other kingdom or place, and we have enough of life given us to do this."[90]

What an incredible image! You and I once knew "every nook and corner" of Heaven. We walked the gold-paved paths of that paradise, roamed the majestic gardens, traversed the splendid palaces, and were intimately familiar with the God and Creator of all of it – our Eternal Father. As President Benson said, nothing will startle us more than to recall how familiar we are with our Father and His Heavenly abode. How wonderful it will be if we, having lived faithfully here, can return to that Kingdom and say with a clear conscious, "O my Father, my Father, I am here again"!

Yes, it was in that majestic setting that we learned the Father's Plan of Happiness. We were instructed in every detail of that Plan and knew the principles of salvation. These principles were in fact learned long before our brother Lucifer rebelled, drawing away many of our spirit siblings into darkness and captivity. We were all give ample opportunity to choose right from wrong. President Joseph Fielding Smith wrote:

> "From these scriptures we learn that our Father called a council, and the plan of salvation was presented to all. Lucifer rebelled and led away one-third of the spirits, and they were cast out with him. It is not the fault of our Eternal Father that throughout the world there are the many millions who are born without the light of the gospel. In the very beginning the commandment was given to Adam to teach his children the plan of salvation. . . .
>
> "It was necessary that all should have the plan of salvation placed before them in that spirit existence, otherwise there could have been no rebellion against the plan and if all had not had the privilege of receiving or rejecting it, there could have been no punishment for rebellion."[91]

---

[90] President Brigham Young, *Journal of Discourses*, Vol. 4, 268-269, March 8, 1857, http://jod.mrm.org/4/264.

[91] Smith, *Answers to Gospel Questions*, Vol. 3, 35-36.

Despite the fact that billions of souls rejected the universal light of God's Gospel, billions more received it. Everyone privileged to come to earth once received, whether lackadaisically or wholeheartedly, the Gospel Plan as laid down by our Father. But why did we decide this was the best Plan? Why did we willingly choose to leave a Heaven where pain, death, and suffering were not present to inhabit a fallen world where pain, death, and suffering were the mainstay? What persuaded us to leave our home to become strangers here on earth? We are told that the sons of God shouted for Joy at the opportunity to come to earth, but why?

President David O. McKay explained one simple yet compelling reason why we were so happy to move on to a new stage of life and experience. He wrote:

> "The great secret of human happiness lies in progression. Stagnation means death. With man's attitude toward service to his fellow men, with his heart compassioned and free from selfish endeavor, he will march on to the goal that is his — to become master, creator, God.
>
> "The doctrine of eternal progression is fundamental to the Church of Christ."[92]

If for no other reason, man shouted for joy at the opportunity to do and experience something new. He relished the privilege of going on yet another adventure — a new and grand adventure on a new world equipped with a new physical body to master and utilize.

Some atheists cannot come to terms with the thought held by many Christians that when man dies, he enters a glowing paradise where he will sit around singing praises to God for eternity — the proverbial angel benignly strumming his harp on a cloud forever and ever. I likewise could not believe in a "Heaven" lacking growth, diversity, and novelty. Fortunately, that dogma is untrue. The reality is much more marvelous and gratifying!

---

[92] David O. McKay, *Pathways to Happiness* (Salt Lake City, UT: Bookcraft, Inc., 1965), 240.

Stagnation means death, but life is all about progression. We have progressed over endless ages of time from intelligences to spirits, and from spirits to mortals. And when we leave mortality, our immortal spirits will continue to learn and progress and advance within the sphere best suited to their capacities and desires. Thus, man's inherent yearning for growth was a compelling factor in our decision to accept the Father's Plan of Salvation.

President Joseph Fielding Smith explained two purposes for our journey into mortality. He taught:

> "There are two purposes for life – one to gain experience that could not be obtained in any other way, and the other to obtain these tabernacles of flesh and bones. Both of these purposes are vital to the existence of man.

> "In the spirit world we saw our Father. We dwelt in his presence. He tells us in one of these revelations that we saw him, and if we are faithful, we will have the privilege of seeing him again; but we beheld a vast difference between him and us. We were spirits. He was a spirit clothed with a glorious body – an immortal body. He had become a living soul according to the definition which he himself has given, that is, a soul is a spirit and body united. We noted the difference, and naturally wanted to become like him. . . .

> "And our Father taught us that if we were faithful in the keeping of the commandments that should be given to us, that we would be like him, and would have glorious bodies shining like the sun, as his glorious body shines, and we should be called his sons and daughters, and should be clothed with the fulness of all the blessings of his kingdom."[93]

One of the chief motivating factors in our decision to leave those transcendent pre-mortal realms to become mortal on this earth and forget everything we once knew was our desperate wish to become like

---

[93] Smith, *Doctrines of Salvation*, Vol. 1, 66-68.

our Father whom we loved so dearly. Becoming like Him meant everything to us. Becoming like Him, however, required receiving a physical body and being tested in it. We knew the test would be hard. We knew that all of us would slip and fall at times. We knew that each of us would experience pain, sorrow, and loneliness. We knew some of us might even fail in the final equation. Yet, we shouted for joy at the great opportunity being afforded us – the opportunity to become like the very God of the universe!

In a BYU-I fireside address, Elder David A. Bednar noted several reasons why we understood, as we dwelt in pre-mortality, that a mortal probation was the only path that would lead to lasting happiness. He observed:

> "Our physical bodies make possible a breadth, a depth, and an intensity of experience that simply could not be obtained in our premortal estate. President Boyd K. Packer, President of the Quorum of the Twelve Apostles, has taught, "Our spirit and our body are combined in such a way that our body becomes an instrument of our mind and the foundation of our character." Thus, our relationships with other people, our capacity to recognize and act in accordance with truth, and our ability to obey the principles and ordinances of the gospel of Jesus Christ are amplified through our physical bodies. In the classroom of mortality, we experience tenderness, love, kindness, happiness, sorrow, disappointment, pain, and even the challenges of physical limitations in ways that prepare us for eternity. Simply stated, there are lessons we must learn and experiences we must have, as the scriptures describe, "according to the flesh" (1 Nephi 19:6; Alma 7:12–13). . . .

> "And in this dispensation the Lord revealed that "the spirit and the body are the soul of man" (D&C 88:15). A truth that really is and always will be is that the body and the spirit constitute our reality and identity. When body and spirit are inseparably connected, we can receive a fulness of joy; when they are separated, we cannot receive a fulness of joy (see D&C 93:33–34).

> "The Father's plan is designed to provide direction for His children, to help them become happy, and to bring them safely home to Him with resurrected, exalted bodies."[94]

In pre-mortality, we were taught that spirit and body, once joined, could experience greater joy and happiness than just a spirit by itself could. We knew that our Father, who is so cheerful and happy, had an exalted physical body and we thus wanted to imitate Him and experience the same joy.

We also learned that certain things could be learned *only* through practical experience and through the medium of a physical body. Becoming co-creators with God through the holy process of procreation is but one obvious opportunity for learning which we did not and could not enjoy in our first estate. Many experiences required us to first take upon ourselves flesh and bone and the qualities of mortality, including the ability to die.

We further ascertained that our spirit and our body, once combined, would "constitute our reality and identity." It would be an enhancement of those capabilities we already enjoyed in pre-mortality. We were therefore exhilarated to come to earth and claim our own body and commence a new stage of personal growth, complete with exciting new experiences, sensations, and opportunities. We knew this was the only way to become a truly living soul, which the Lord has defined as the combination of spirit and body (D&C 88:15), and advance to become like our Father.

Elder Richard G. Scott once taught of this glorious pre-earth state where we knew our Eternal Parents so well. He explained how excited we were at the opportunities for personal and family advancement:

> "One of the most exhilarating moments of your life—when you were filled with anticipation, excitement, and gratitude—you are not able to remember. That experience occurred in the premortal

---

[94] Elder David A. Bednar, "Things as They Really Are," *Ensign*, June, 2010, https://www.lds.org/ensign/2010/06/things-as-they-really-are?lang=eng.

life when you were informed that finally your time had come to leave the spirit world to dwell on earth with a mortal body. You knew you could learn through personal experience the lessons that would bring happiness on earth, lessons that would eventually lead you to exaltation and eternal life as a glorified, celestial being in the presence of your Holy Father and His Beloved Son. You understood that there would be challenges, for you would live in an environment of both righteous and evil influences. Yet surely you resolved no matter what the cost, no matter what the effort, suffering, and testing, you would return victorious. You had been reserved to come when the fulness of the gospel is on earth. You arrived when His Church and the priesthood authority to perform the sacred temple ordinances are in place. You anticipated being born into a home where parents would be expected to love, nurture, strengthen, and teach you truths. You knew that in time you would have the opportunity to form your own eternal family as husband or wife, father or mother. Oh, how you must have rejoiced with that prospect."[95]

As we prepared to disembark from our Heavenly port and sail to this earth for a period of testing and trial, we knew that our Father had designed a perfect Plan and that the Savior provided a means of safely returning home – even after we might stray. We knew that, no matter the challenges, we could return. We understood the blessings that awaited us for a faithful voyage and we prepared to take the leap. It is no wonder we rejoiced!

President Joseph F. Smith explained another reason we may have made the leap of faith to come to this earth. He also explained how to advance from mortality to eternal glory in the realms still distant:

"Our knowledge of persons and things before we came here, combined with the divinity awakened within our souls through obedience to the gospel, powerfully affects, in my opinion, all our likes and dislikes, and guides our preferences in the course of this

---

[95] Elder Richard G. Scott, "First Things First," General Conference, April, 2001, https://www.lds.org/general-conference/2001/04/first-things-first?lang=eng.

life, provided we give careful heed to the admonitions of the Spirit.

"All those salient truths which come home so forcibly to the head and heart seem but the awakening of the memories of the spirit. Can we know anything here that we did not know before we came? Are not the means of knowledge in the first estate equal to those of this? I think that the spirit, before and after this probation, possesses greater facilities, aye, manifold greater, for the acquisition of knowledge, than while manacled and shut up in the prison-house of mortality.

"Had we not known before we came the necessity of our coming, the importance of obtaining tabernacles, the glory to be achieved in posterity, the grand object to be attained by being tried and tested — weighted in the balance, in the exercise of the divine attributes, god-like powers and free agency with which we are endowed; whereby, after descending below all things, Christ-like, we might ascend above all things, and become like our Father, Mother and Elder Brother, Almighty and Eternal! — we would never have come; that is, if we could have stayed away.

"I believe that our Savior is the ever-living example to all flesh in all these things. He no doubt possessed a foreknowledge of all the vicissitudes through which he would have to pass in the mortal tabernacle, when the foundations of this earth were laid, "when the morning stars sang together, and all the sons of God shouted for joy." When he conversed with the brother of Jared, on the Mount, in his spiritual body, he understood his mission, and knew the work he had to do, as thoroughly as when he ascended from the Mount of Olives before the wondering gaze of the Jewish disciples, with his resurrected, glorious and immortal body.

"And yet, to accomplish the ultimatum of his previous existence, and consummate the grand and glorious object of his being, and the salvation of his infinite brotherhood, he had to come and take upon him flesh. He is our example. The works he did, we are commanded to do. We are enjoined to follow him, as he followed his Head; that where he is, we may be also; and being with him, may be like him. If Christ knew beforehand, so did we. But in coming here, we forgot all, that our agency might be free indeed, to choose good or evil, that we might merit the reward of our own choice and conduct. But by the power of the Spirit, in the redemption of Christ, through obedience, we often catch a spark from the awakened memories of the immortal soul, which lights up our whole being as with the glory of our former home."[96]

As we advanced in pre-mortality, we knew that we must take one additional step – leaving our Father's presence to be tested. We knew that we would temporarily forget everything and that we would of necessity have to walk by faith. We knew the dangers and pitfalls that awaited us. We understood that some of us, unfortunately, would make decisions that would cut us off from the full bounty of blessings offered as a reward to the righteous. We knew all of this and yet we made that leap of faith into the dark.

One of the things that gave us courage was the example of our Savior. Though He was Jehovah, the creator of worlds, He, too, would be required to go to earth where His spirit would inhabit a mortal tabernacle of flesh and bone. He, too, would have to pass through sorrow and pain. If the Savior whom we trusted so dearly understood all that was at stake, and all the challenges He would have to surmount, and was yet willing to be obedient to the Father and go to earth, it surely gave us confidence that we, with our lesser responsibilities, could also pass the test.

And so, we learned and prepared and we learned some more. The most important thing we learned in pre-mortality was how to have faith in our Father and in His Son, Jesus Christ. Elder Jeffrey R. Holland said that during those sacred moments when we take the sacrament on Sundays:

"We could remember the Savior's premortal life and all that we know him to have done as the great Jehovah, creator of heaven and earth and all things that in them are. We could remember that even in the Grand Council of Heaven he loved us and was

---

[96] Smith, *Gospel Doctrine*, 12-14.

wonderfully strong, that we triumphed even there by the power of Christ and our faith in the blood of the Lamb (see Rev. 12:10–11)."[97]

Even there, in the pre-earth state, the mercy, forgiveness, and love emanating from our Savior's Atonement was in effect. There we became humble followers of the Lord Jesus Christ. We learned to trust Him implicitly – so much so that His blood, which had not yet been shed, provided something of a preparatory redemption and salvation and helped us progress to our second estate.

In this second estate, this earth life we now find ourselves in, we must prove ourselves worthy once more. We must rekindle our faith in Christ. We must sacrifice everything once more for our Savior's cause. And if we do, the Lord, through the power of His Atonement, will heal us and aid us on our path of progression once again.

Yes, understanding this doctrine of pre-mortality places upon us heavy burdens of duty and obligation. It also lifts boulders of doubt and uncertainty from off our shoulders as we learn our true identity. As we learn that we are children of the Almighty and that we once chose to follow Jesus Christ, we understand the gravity of exercising our agency correctly in the here and now.

Before we came to earth, we understood that there would be certain terms and conditions to which we must submit. We willingly submitted to *all* of them, gave our full consent, and figuratively signed on the dotted line. This fact brings all of God's children onto a level playing field. Each of us at one time knew all the rules of the game. Each of us has agreed to be judged for our individual sins and to reap the rewards of our individual efforts. Not one of us can complain or allege unfairness because each of us read the terms and conditions and willingly signed on the dotted line.

Because we figuratively signed on the dotted line, the Lord can now ask and require certain things of us. He can require certain sacrifices, exact

---

[97] Elder Jeffrey R. Holland, "This Do in Remembrance of Men," General Conference, October, 1995, https://www.lds.org/general-conference/1995/10/this-do-in-remembrance-of-me?lang=eng.

specific punishments for misdeeds, bestow certain rewards for valiancy, give laws and commandments, and rule with complete justice and impartiality. This doctrine also explains why suffering is not unjust. In fact, the knowledge of pre-mortality is the only sound explanation I know of for the suffering we see in the world.

If man is a mere creation of God, then what inherent value does he have? If his existence began at birth, then he is no more than the Creator's play thing designed for His arbitrary amusement. And if a Creator truly created us out of nothing, and for no eternal purpose other than His own enjoyment, then the suffering we are made to endure is inherently unfair and unjust. Not only is it unfair and cruel, but if God created everything out of nothing, then He also created evil, sin, and suffering. In such a conception, there is no higher purpose involved, no personal relationship with Deity, no recourse for grievances, and certainly no justification for suffering, pain, and destruction. Rational minds patently reject such a dark, hopeless explanation for our existence.

The superlative doctrine of pre-mortality, by contrast, explains man's origin and purpose and well as the origin and purpose of sin, suffering, and death. It is a hope-filled teaching. The doctrine of our first estate teaches that man has always existed, that he has always possessed a level of intelligence, that he has always been progressing and is capable of increase, that he was given his agency in the pre-earth life, that he was fully instructed in the Gospel of Christ, that he formerly chose to follow Christ and obey the Father's commandments, and that he willingly opted to come to a fallen world of sin and ignorance to be tested and proved in the furnace of affliction and to eventually return home to be judged and rewarded according to his individual deeds.

Death, then, loses its sting when we realize man has an immortal spirit that existed in the beginning long before the creation of earth and that it is not capable of annihilation. Sin is brought into focus when we realize that man has his agency, has always had his agency, and will eternally stand or fall based on his own actions. And suffering also makes sense and loses its injustice when we know that we lived before, that we understood the trials and pains we would pass through on earth, and that we willingly and knowingly agreed to these terms and conditions for the higher purpose of progressing to the next stage of advancement, glory, and happiness. Because we knew and trusted our Father in Heaven, we knew that a perfect blend of justice and mercy would prevail either for or against us as the case required.

It also helps to know that our Heavenly Father, as all Gods have, once passed through mortal trials and is not unjustly requiring anything of us that He has not previously performed. The life of Jesus provides an even more pertinent example. Jesus, though He was the Only Begotten Son of God, suffered more than any other man. He waded through affliction, endured rejection, and was cruelly tortured and murdered in front of jeering crowds of those He called His brethren. When the Prophet Joseph Smith once protested to the Lord about his own harsh trials, the Lord responded:

> "The Son of Man hath descended below them all. Art thou greater than he?" (D&C 122:8).

The Savior also gave the Prophet words of comfort. He said:

> "And if thou shouldst be cast into the pit, or into the hands of murderers, and the sentence of death passed upon thee; if thou be cast into the deep; if the billowing surge conspire against thee; if fierce winds become thine enemy; if the heavens gather blackness, and all the elements combine to hedge up the way; and above all, if the very jaws of hell shall gape open the mouth wide after thee, know thou, my son, that all these things shall give thee experience, and shall be for thy good" (D&C 122:7).

The Savior – the One who descended below all things and suffered the combined pain of everyone who has ever lived or will yet live – testified that all our trials are for our good. They give us experience and stamp character on the soul. And, no matter how bad they are, they last only a short time. If we are faithful, the Lord will deliver us and we will be crowned in the Heavens above. With this testimony, the pre-mortal Jehovah no doubt bolstered our confidence to come into an unjust world and push through our own lesser trials that we might eventually be exalted through His grace.

Elder Neal A. Maxwell reminded us of our duties and the importance of the choices we make in the light of our understanding of pre-mortality. He observed:

> "Premortality is not a relaxing doctrine. For each of us, there are choices to be made, incessant and difficult chores to be done, ironies and adversities to be experienced, time to be well spent, talents and gifts to be well employed. Just because we were chosen "there and then," surely does not mean we can be indifferent "here and now." Whether foreordination for men, or foredesignation for women, those called and prepared must also prove "chosen, and faithful." (See Rev. 17:14; D&C 121:34–36.)

> "In fact, adequacy in the first estate may merely have ensured a stern, second estate with more duties and no immunities! Additional tutoring and suffering appears to be the pattern for the Lord's most apt pupils. (See Mosiah 3:19; 1 Pet. 4:19.) Our existence, therefore, is a continuum matched by God's stretching curriculum.

> "This doctrine brings unarguable identity but also severe accountability to our lives. It uniquely underscores the actuality of the Fatherhood of God and the brotherhood of man.

> "It also reminds us that we do not have all of the data. There are many times when we must withhold judgment and trust God, even in the midst of "all these things." Only with the help of this doctrine can we begin to understand things as they really were, are, and will become. (See Jacob 4:13; D&C 93:24.)

> "Agreeing to enter this second estate, therefore, was like agreeing in advance to anesthetic—the anesthetic of forgetfulness. Doctors do not de-anesthetize a patient, in the midst of what was previously authorized, to ask him, again, if it should be continued.

> We agreed to come here and to undergo certain experiences under certain conditions."[98]

We were no doubt impressed at the magnitude of our undertaking. As this world was created and the first of God's children were sent one-by-one to it, we must have eagerly and anxiously prepared for the cornucopia of new experiences that being mortal and having a physical body would offer. We knew that we would be under a "severe accountability" for such a privilege, yet we knew that justice would prevail and that we would have a fair chance at proving ourselves worthy.

Because of God's foresight, He knew that mortality would progress in a crescendo until the final battle between Satan and the Lord's sheep. Because of this foreknowledge, the Lord saved some of his most precious souls until these last times – individuals He knew that He could trust. These individuals had 6,000 extra years of training and preparation. They have cheerfully embraced a "severe accountability" and are now tasked with bearing off the Kingdom of God safely.

We are instructed by what Elder Maxwell once taught the youth of the Aaronic Priesthood. He said:

> "Young men, I do not believe that you are here upon the earth at this time by accident. I believe you qualified in the premortal life to come into mortality at a time when great things would be required of you. I believe you demonstrated before you came here that you were capable of being trusted under unusually difficult circumstances – that you could measure up to the most difficult challenges. . . .

> "My beloved friends, you are the vanguard of the righteous spirits to be infused into the Church in the last days. Back beyond time, it was so determined, and you were prepared – before the foundations of the world – to help save others in the latter-day world.

---

[98] Elder Neal A. Maxwell, "Premortality, a Glorious Reality," General Conference, October, 1985, https://www.lds.org/general-conference/1985/10/premortality-a-glorious-reality?lang=eng.

"You cannot keep that resplendent rendezvous if you become like the world! Make your righteous marks on the world instead of being spotted by the world.

"Be true, now, to your emotions of long ago when, as the Lord set in motion His plan of Salvation and laid the foundation of this earth, "The morning stars sang together, and all the sons (and daughters) of God shouted for joy" (Job 38:7)."[99]

We truly have a rendezvous with destiny! We are a royal generation. We learned many lessons and made many covenants and promises in the pre-earth life. It is now our time to shine. It is time for us to be true to our pre-mortal selves, and to the trust our Heavenly Father has in us, and boldly press forward in Gospel service. No one else can do the job required of us. This is why we were saved till the end when the stakes are the highest they have ever been. Remember who you are and you will find the courage and strength to do your duty to God.

In a General Conference message to the rising generation of the Church, President Ezra Taft Benson declared:

"You are not just ordinary young men and young women. You are choice spirits, many of you having been held back in reserve for almost 6,000 years to come forth in this day, at this time, when the temptations, responsibilities, and opportunities are the very greatest."[100]

Two years later while speaking at BYU, President Benson repeated and added upon his thoughts about what it means to be on earth in these momentous last days. He observed:

---

[99] Elder Neal A. Maxwell, Young Adult Fireside on Temple Square, June 23, 1985, cited in Shute, Nyman, and Bott, *Ephraim: Chosen of the Lord* Ephraim (Riverton, UT: Millennial Press, Inc., 1999), 102.

[100] President Ezra Taft Benson, "A Message to the Rising Generation," General Conference, October, 1977, https://www.lds.org/general-conference/1977/10/a-message-to-the-rising-generation?lang=eng.

"For nearly six thousand years, God has held you in reserve to make your appearance in the final days before the Second Coming of the Lord. Every previous gospel dispensation has drifted into apostasy, but ours will not. True, there will be some individuals who will fall away; but the kingdom of God will remain intact to welcome the return of its head—even Jesus Christ. While our generation will be comparable in wickedness to the days of Noah, when the Lord cleansed the earth by flood, there is a major difference this time. It is that God has saved for the final inning some of his strongest children, who will help bear off the Kingdom triumphantly. And that is where you come in, for you are the generation that must be prepared to meet your God.

"All through the ages the prophets have looked down through the corridors of time to our day. Billions of the deceased and those yet to be born have their eyes on us. Make no mistake about it—you are a marked generation. There has never been more expected of the faithful in such a short period of time as there is of us. Never before on the face of this earth have the forces of evil and the forces of good been as well organized. Now is the great day of the devil's power, with the greatest mass murderers of all time living among us. But now is also the great day of the Lord's power, with the greatest number ever of priesthood holders on the earth. And the showdown is fast approaching.

"Each day the forces of evil and the forces of good pick up new recruits. Each day we personally make many decisions that show where our support will go. The final outcome is certain—the forces of righteousness will finally win. What remains to be seen is where each of us personally, now and in the future, will stand in this fight—and how tall we will stand. Will we be true to our last-days, foreordained mission?"[101]

The eyes of eternity have been upon all generations that have come to the earth. But no generation has been more watched than ours. Prophets

---

[101] President Ezra Taft Benson, "In His Steps," BYU Devotional, March 4, 1979, https://speeches.byu.edu/talks/ezra-taft-benson_in-christs-steps/.

in all dispensations have foreseen this day and the momentous events that are occurring and will yet occur.

From the Restoration to the great gathering of Israel to the destructions and wars to the eventual return of the King of kings, this is "a marked generation." "There has never been more expected of the faithful in such a short period of time as there is of us." Are we up to the challenge? Did we prepare diligently in pre-mortality as we waited for our call to come to earth to enlist in Zion's army and fight the Lord's fight? And are we now preparing and doing all we can as we serve as the Lord's shock troops? Are we prepared, worthy, and able to fulfill the colossal shoes given to us in this final dispensation?

In 1988, Elder L. Tom Perry delivered a classic address at BYU titled "The University of Mortality." This unique and highly thought-provoking discourse started where all good discussions about man's eternal progression begin, in the pre-mortal world. Elder Perry painted this picture for his college-aged audience:

> "Imagine with me a scene from the premortal existence. The time is about two decades ago, plus or minus a few years. We see an eager spirit at the front window watching the mailbox located out by the street. The mailman arrives and a delivery is made. The spirit rushes out to the mailbox with great anticipation that a long-awaited letter has been delivered.

> "Plowing through the usual junk mail and monthly statements, we see a large white envelope. This may be it! Eagerly the letter is opened. Your name and address heads the letter. You read on: "Greetings! Your application to the 'University of Mortality' has been accepted."

> "The letter goes on to give you instructions on the date your first semester will begin and the names of your new dorm parents. There's a catalog attached detailing information and opportunities available to you in this once-in-a-lifetime experience. The long wait is over!

"With anticipation you have looked forward to this day. You remember the time of the Grand Council in Heaven when you elected to be tested as a mortal. You have watched through the centuries, and now the Lord's instructions to his prophets ring in your ears. . . .

"Now is your time to shout for joy, for now it is your turn to be on earth!"[102]

It is *our* turn now. And what are we doing with it? We prepared for eons of time before the earth was created, with at least an additional 6,000 years of preparation as we watched our brothers and sisters come and go and work out their salvation. Now what are we doing with *our* opportunity?

Perhaps, as we dwelt in pre-mortality, we were privileged to look down and watch as youthful Nephi braved the wilderness, the oceans, hunger and fatigue, Laban's guards, and the hateful violence of his own brothers to do what the Lord had commanded him. Conceivably, we rejoiced when both Alma the senior and Alma the younger turned from their wicked ways to became two of the greatest missionaries and prophets on record. Maybe we prayed for Paul as he, then known as Saul, persecuted Christ's fledgling Church; and then smiled wide as he faithfully responded to the Lord's call to the work. Perhaps our hearts ached as we watched Mormon and Moroni endure the destruction of the Nephite People at the Hill Cumorah in New York state, and as we subsequently watched Moroni wander alone for decades before depositing the sacred records in the same hill where he likely buried his friends and family.

As we no doubt witnessed these and millions of other events unfold here on this little globe, we must have been filled with emotion. I believe we would have become even more motivated to follow the Lord's laws and be faithful to Him. Both the wicked and the righteous examples would have inspired us to tread carefully and keep our feet on the covenant path. We would have resolved to hold firmly to the iron rod and not give

[102] Elder L. Tom Perry, "The University of Mortality," BYU Devotional, February 7, 1988, https://speeches.byu.edu/talks/l-tom-perry_university-mortality/.

heed to the foolish voices of the Adversary. Many of us likely studied harder, prepared more diligently, and developed even greater faith so that we could do our part when our time came to enter mortality.

Now that it *is* our time and we *are* on this earth, we must ask ourselves some pointed questions: Are we faithfully fulfilling the prophecies concerning our "marked generation"? Are we behaving like the Royal Army we are meant to be? Are we listening to the world or are we heeding the Lord's prophets? Are we walking one of many swerving paths or are we studiously walking the straight and narrow covenant path? Are we taking for granted the fact that we have been saved until this critical moment in history or are we zealously serving our Savior and standing "firm and undaunted" against Satan like modern sons of Helaman (Alma 57:19-21)?

This is a "once-in-a-lifetime experience" that determines everything. Are we giving it our all? Are we showing our Father that He was right to hold us back all these years so that we could enter the game in the closing quarter and turn the tide in favor of righteousness and truth? Are we utilizing those first lessons learned from our Eternal Father as we sat around Him, walked with Him, and grew beside Him in our pre-mortal home? Are we behaving like sons and daughters of God?

I close this chapter by answering a question that is sometimes asked in relation to the doctrine of pre-earth life. The question goes something like this: If we lived before, and if the knowledge of pre-morality is so vital to successful living, then why has this memory been taken away from us? The answer is quite simple. We are informed that one of the chief purposes of life is to be tested. The Lord said:

> "And we will prove them herewith, to see if they will do all things whatsoever the Lord their God shall command them" (Abraham 3:25).

If this earth life is a test to see if we will obey our God, it would be a very ineffective test if we retained our memories of our pre-mortal experiences with God. It would be like a teacher handing us the answer key and asking us to fill out an exam. Who would miss a single question if they had the answer key in front of them? No one. And by the same token, who could demonstrate their ability, mental ingenuity, or resourcefulness? No one.

No faith would be demonstrated, no effort exerted, and no diligence required if we had a perfect remembrance of our former state. Who would bother studying and preparing for such a pointless test? Who would have shouted for joy? Such a socialistic plan of equal rewards for no work with no incentives for righteousness and no chance for personal distinction or excellence, was in fact presented in pre-mortality by Lucifer. It was also promptly rejected by us because we knew it was a futile and inefficient plan that offered no growth, no rewards for individual righteousness, and no incentive to become godlike.

In order for a test to actually be a test, we must all start with a blank slate and have the answer key hidden from view. Then, and only then, can we each show what we learned in our studies and what we are truly capable of. Then, and only then, can you prove to your Father that you paid attention when He was teaching you in pre-mortality. Then, and only then, can I show that I am capable of conquering my individual weaknesses and standing stalwart when everything is on the line. Then, and only then, can we demonstrate that we have what it takes to hear opposite and contradictory information, sift through it, use our inborn intelligence to make independent decisions for ourselves, and choose the right.

Elder Orson Pratt described it this way:

> "What person among all the human family can comprehend what took place in his first existence? No one, it is blotted from the memory, and I think there is great wisdom manifested in withholding the knowledge of our previous existence. Why? Because we could not, if we had all our pre-existent knowledge accompanying us into this world, show to our Father in the heavens and to the heavenly host that we would be in all things obedient; in other words, we could not be tried as the Lord designs to try us here in this state of existence, to qualify us for a higher state hereafter. In order to try the children of men, there must be a degree of knowledge withheld from them, for it would

be no temptation to them if they could understand from the beginning the consequences of their acts, and the nature and results of this and that temptation. But in order that we may prove ourselves before the heavens obedient and faithful in all things, we have to begin at the very first principles of knowledge, and be tried from knowledge to knowledge, and from grace to grace, until, like our elder brother, we finally overcome and triumph over all our imperfections, and receive with him the same glory that he inherits, which glory he had before the world was."[103]

If we remain faithful in this our second estate, as we were once faithful in our first estate, we will receive a just reward. In fact, we will receive the same glory that our Master Jesus Christ received from the Father. If we overcome our mortal frailties and pass our earthly tests, we become "joint-heirs with Christ" because we too are the very children of the living God.

I start as I began by declaring that my soul loves the doctrine of pre-morality! It is the lynchpin of the Gospel of Jesus Christ. Without this understanding, life is hopeless and man would wander aimlessly like a rudderless boat at sea. But armed with the knowledge of our origin and the glimpses of our past existence and future potential that prophets have given, we can confidently place our trust in our Savior Jesus Christ and march forward to destiny. To faithfully finish our race, we must use our pre-mortal past as a lamp to light the path ahead. We must rekindle the same joyful anticipation for proving ourselves worthy in our Father's eyes that we must have felt there. If we do so, we will conquer the enemy of our soul here as we valiantly did once before in our Heavenly home.

---

[103] Elder Orson Pratt, *Journal of Discourses*, Vol. 15, 245, December 15, 1872, http://jod.mrm.org/15/241.

Chapter Fourth

Evolution

In chapter two, we quoted President Gordon B. Hinckley who declared that there is "no greater truth in all the world" than to know that we are the *literal* children of God and that we therefore have an element of His divinity within us. If this is true, and I boldly testify that it is, then we must logically conclude that the theory of organic evolution – which posits man's evolution from *lower* lifeforms to his present state as homo sapien and denies God's role in Creation – is potentially the greatest evil ever to enter the human mind.

The theory of evolution holds that the human race has gradually evolved over billions and billions of years from microscopic organisms to our present station as man. This means, to put it crudely and unscientifically, that at some point in the murky past our ancestors *had* to have been amoebas, fish, monkeys, cavemen, or some other lower species of life. Of necessity, this theory holds that there is *no* intelligent design and that all is a result of chance circumstances, billions of years of accidental development, or some fortunate "big bang."

Scientists want you to ignore the fact that they have not yet come up with a working model for *how* this supposed evolution took place or *what* precisely set this upward evolutionary track in motion. Nor do they want you to know that there is *no* official consensus and that literally *thousands* of qualified scientists refute this sectarian theory. Like the wickedest of priests, they demand blind faith in their concocted creed. They demand that you believe your existence is the result of happenstance, that you had no prior reality, that we are mere animals, that our physical bodies are not special, that you have no spirit, that this life is it, that there is no resurrection from the grave, that Jesus Christ was a fraud, that there is no sin or forgiveness for sins, that you possess no inherent intelligence or agency, and that there is no God who rules in the Heavens.

This theory belittles man. It belittles our nature and reduces us to the level of spiritless, instinct-driven animals. It severs the all-important Parent-child relationship we have with our Eternal Father. It negates the very concept of right and wrong, good and evil, Heaven and hell, God and Satan. It destroys all sense of security, stability, and confidence that individuals and societies rely on. This is because evolutionary theory rips us from the fertile Gospel soil of accountability and plants us firmly in a muck of confusion where there are no eternal laws governing moral conduct, no notions of right or wrong, no judgements and punishments for sin, and no sin at all. Under the benighted rule of evolutionary theory, jungle law *must* prevail and the only creed that is acceptable is "might makes right."

The man most responsible for popularizing this repugnant theory was Charles Darwin. While others before him postulated that man is the result of eons of evolution, it was Darwin that made this notion stick. Born in 1809, Darwin started out as a believing Christian of the Anglican faith. In later years, he recalled his desire to become an Anglican clergyman. He said: "I did not then in the least doubt the strict and literal truth of every word in the Bible."[104] This is hardly the beginning we would expect of one whose very name now implies antagonism to God and revealed religion.

Darwin's downfall began when, after dropping out of medical school and deciding not to go into the clergy, he took his fateful voyage on the *H.M.S. Beagle* to explore nature. While at sea and on the islands of the Pacific, Darwin began to doubt the account of Creation contained in the book of Genesis. His doubts intensified when he began reading books that denied or limited God's hand in Creation. The most influential of these was *Principles of Geology* by Charles Lyell which, among other things, disputed the Bible's claim that the earth is only thousands of years old and pushed the idea that Noah's Flood could not have been global. In a word, it denied the scriptural story of Creation as given by the prophets.

---

[104] John M. Brentnall and Russell M. Grigg, "Was Darwin a Christian? Did he believe in God? Did he recant evolutionism when he died?" *Christian Answers Network*, 2002, accessed August 11, 2018, https://christiananswers.net/q-aig/darwin.html.

Darwin chose to indulge his doubts, abandon his childhood faith, and trust Lyell and the scraps of finite evidence he was finding on his journey more than the revealed truths in the Bible. His evolution from believer to unbeliever quickly turned him into a bitter man who lost his love of nature, music, and art, once confessing his "curious and lamentable loss of the higher aesthetic tastes" and admitting that his mind "seems to have become a kind of machine."[105]

Because of his willful abandonment of his Christian faith, Darwin came to curse God, advocate racial eugenics, believe that morality was entirely a social construct, and support an inherently socialistic worldview where men, as mindless animals, must be forced to behave. Interestingly, all of Darwin's children were very sickly and when his favorite daughter died in 1851 he came to hate God all the more — a curious thing considering he ostensibly denied God's existence.

If Charles Darwin had not been the one to popularize this theory of evolution, someone else would have. Yet, it was Darwin and Darwin has thus earned himself a chief place of infamy in the halls of mankind's sordid history. Indeed, most of the indescribable destruction of the past century was carried out by men who found the justification for their evil deeds in his writings, as will be touched upon briefly at the close of this chapter.

Another man of science and learning who lived at approximately the same time also observed the earth and nature and came to a far different conclusion as to its origin. Thomas Jefferson, a man known for his exploration of botany, horticulture, astronomy, and the sciences, gave us this testimony of the Creator's hand in all things:

> "[W]hen we take a view of the Universe, in it's parts general or particular, it is impossible for the human mind not to perceive and feel a conviction of design, consummate skill, and indefinite power in every atom of it's composition. The movements of the heavenly bodies, so exactly held in their course by the balance of

---

[105] Charles Darwin, in Nora Barlow, ed., *The Autobiography of Charles Darwin: 1809-1882* (reprint; BooksiRead, December, 1999), 143-144.

the centrifugal and centripetal forces, the structure of our earth itself, with it's distribution of lands, waters and atmosphere, animal and vegetable bodies, examined in all their minutest particles, insects mere atoms of life, yet as perfectly organised as man or mammoth, the mineral substances, their generation and uses, it is impossible, I say, for the human mind not to believe that there is, in all this, design, cause and effect, up to an ultimate cause, a fabricator of all things from matter and motion, their preserver and regulator while permitted to exist in their present forms, and their regenerator into new and other forms. We see, too evident proofs of the necessity of a superintending power to maintain the Universe in it's course and order . . . So irresistible are these evidences of an intelligent and powerful Agent that, of the infinite numbers of men who have existed thro' all time, they have believed, in proportion of a million at least to Unit, in the hypothesis of an eternal pre-existence of a creator."[106]

Yes, the evidences of God's hand in Creation are irresistible. It is *impossible* for man to deny intelligent and divine design not only in nature, but in his own composition. "[A]ll things denote there is a God" (Alma 30:44). Jefferson was no fool. He was a man of science and learning almost without equal in his day, let alone our day of, in a great many respects, inferior wisdom. And his conclusion, merely from his own studies of nature (studies which dwarfed those conducted by Charles Darwin, in my opinion), was that there *must* be a Supreme Intelligence directing it all. Yet, one short generation after Jefferson recorded his observations and his touching testimony, Darwin published his own contrary witness born of unbelief, doubt, and cynicism.

Jefferson's logic is sound. The fact that nearly all human beings who have ever entered mortality – people in every diverse culture, on every ocean-separated continent, and in every age – have believed in a higher power, ought to suggest to the rational mind that there is something more to the notion of God than mere superstition, tradition, or social conditioning. A

---

[106] Thomas Jefferson to John Adams, April 11, 1823.

course of study for the Priesthood quorums of the Church in 1955 titled *The Divine Church Restored* included this statement:

> "The existence of God is scarcely a question for rational dispute; nor does it call for proof by the feeble demonstrations of man's logic, for the fact is admitted by the human family practically without question, and the consciousness of subjection to supreme power is an inborn attribute of mankind. . . . There is a filial passion within human nature that flames toward heaven. Every nation, every tribe, every individual yearns for some object of reverence. It is natural for man to worship; his soul is unsatisfied until he finds a deity."[107]

Yes, it is an *inborn* human trait to worship something higher. It is natural for man's soul to long for something more and to look Heavenward. Every soul has a craving for the spiritual. This feeling may be numbed, ignored, or temporarily appeased with worldly distractions or self-deception, but it cannot be erased. Each spirit, having existed before this mortal life, has a memory of the light it once enjoyed and yearns to experience it again.

Thankfully, we do not need to rely merely upon forever-changing science, man's best attempt at rational thought, or flawed mortal learning to ascertain eternal truth – we have the witness of the prophets and the Holy Ghost to show us the way. Indeed, spiritual truths *cannot* be learned by science. This type of truth can only be ascertained through the revelations of the Holy Spirit to individual human hearts.

In the October 1970 General Conference, President Ezra Taft Benson proclaimed Darwin to be a deceiver. His hammering statement, in context, reads:

> "As a watchman on the tower, I feel to warn you that one of the chief means of misleading our youth and destroying the family unit is our educational institutions. President Joseph F. Smith referred to false educational ideas as one of the three threatening

---

[107] Roy A. Welker, *The Divine Church Restored* (Salt Lake City, UT: The Church of Jesus Christ of Latter-day Saints, 1955) 175.

dangers among our Church members. There is more than one reason why the Church is advising our youth to attend colleges close to their homes where institutes of religion are available. It gives the parents the opportunity to stay close to their children; and if they have become alert and informed as President McKay admonished us last year, these parents can help expose some of the deceptions of men like Sigmund Freud, Charles Darwin, John Dewey, Karl Marx, John Keynes, and others.

"Today there are much worse things that can happen to a child than not getting a full college education. In fact, some of the worst things have happened to our children while attending colleges led by administrators who wink at subversion and amorality."[108]

According to President Benson, Darwin was a deceiver. He was one of those swindlers responsible for the subversion and amorality taught in our public institutions. And who can deny that Darwin's anti-Christ philosophy dominates our public schools, colleges, and universities? In every school and university, Darwin's creed is required reading, along with the false theories of Marx, Engels, Freud, Hegel, Jung, Dewey, Keynes, and many others who can be considered modern anti-Christs.

What have others prophets said about Darwin's theory? Do they concur with what President Benson told the Saints in 1970? I am here to tell you that they *do* agree. The purpose of this chapter is to highlight prophetic statements denouncing the false theory of organic evolution. I pray that the reader will grasp how damaging this theory is to our faith in Christ and how incompatible it is with the Gospel narrative of man's true origin.

In 1988, President Boyd K. Packer affirmed that, contrary to what we so often hear, the Church *does* have an official position regarding man's origin – a topic which naturally encompasses the idea of evolution vs creation. He spoke of the origin of the myth repeated by and circulated among many Church members which suggests the Church has taken no

---

[108] President Ezra Taft Benson, "Strengthening the Family," General Conference, October, 1970, http://scriptures.byu.edu/#:t6fc:p401.

stand on the matter. His words are powerful and straightforward and can teach us much if we open our hearts to receive them. In "The Law and the Light," President Packer asserted:

> "It is my conviction that to the degree the theory of evolution asserts that man is the product of an evolutionary process, the offspring of animals—it is false! What application the evolutionary theory has to animals gives me no concern. That is another question entirely, one to be pursued by science. But remember, the scriptures speak of the spirit in animals and other living things, and of each multiplying after its own kind (D&C 77:2; 2 Nephi 2:22; Moses 3:9; Abr 4:11–12, 24).

> "And I am sorry to say, the so-called theistic evolution, the theory that God used an evolutionary process to prepare a physical body for the spirit of man, is equally false. I say I am sorry because I know it is a view commonly held by good and thoughtful people who search for an acceptable resolution to an apparent conflict between the theory of evolution and the doctrines of the gospel. . . .

> ". . . The revelations testify of the separate creation of man in the image of God—this after the rest of creation was finished. When the revelations do not fully explain something (and there is purpose in their not doing so), there is safety in clinging to whatever they do reveal. The creation of man and his introduction into mortality by the Fall as revealed in the scriptures conform to eternal laws governing *both* body and spirit.

> "If the theory of evolution applies to man, there was no Fall and therefore no need for an atonement, nor a gospel of redemption, nor a redeemer. . . .

> "Twice the First Presidency has declared the position of the Church on organic evolution. The first, a statement published in 1909 entitled "The Origin of Man" (75–81), was signed by Presidents Joseph F. Smith, John R. Winder, and Anthon H. Lund. The other, entitled " 'Mormon' View of Evolution," signed by Presidents Heber J. Grant, Anthony W. Ivins, and Charles W.

Nibley, was published in 1929 (1090–91). It follows very closely the first statement, indeed quotes directly from it. The doctrines in both statements are consistent and have not changed. . . .

"Statements have been made by other presidents of the Church and members of the Quorum of the Twelve Apostles which corroborate these official declarations by the First Presidency.

"I should take note of one letter signed by a president of the Church addressed to a private individual. It includes a sentence which, taken out of context, reads, "On the subject of organic evolution the church has officially taken no position." For some reasons the addressee passed this letter about. For years it has appeared each time this subject is debated.

"Letters to individuals are *not* the channel for announcing the policy of the Church. For several important reasons, this letter itself is not a declaration of the position of the Church, as some have interpreted it to be. Do not anchor your position on this major issue to that one sentence! It is in conflict with the two official declarations, each signed by all members of the First Presidency. . . .

"Man is the child of God, formed in the divine image and endowed with divine attributes, and even as the infant son of an earthly father and mother is capable in due time of becoming a man, so the undeveloped offspring of celestial parentage is capable, by experience through ages and aeons, of evolving into a God. . . .

"Here we are, spirit children of God, clothed in flesh, sojourning in mortality for a season. Know that your body is the instrument of your mind, and the foundation of your character. Do not mortgage your soul for unproved theories; ask, simply ask! I have asked, but not how man was created; I have asked if the scriptures are true. And I have a witness and a testimony, and I give it unto you: That Jesus is The Christ, the Son of God; that he is our Redeemer and our Messiah; that there was the fall of man; and that he is our Mediator and our Redeemer; that he wrought the Atonement; that he is our Lord. I know him. I bear to you a witness of him, a special witness of him."[109]

Let us analyze these direct words of an apostle of God and see what they can teach us.

President Packer started his statement by declaring evolution a false doctrine. If this was all he had said, his statement would have been of great worth. However, he expounded this witness even further. Not only did he call organic evolution a false idea, but he said that "theistic evolution" – a notion which claims that evolution from lower organisms is accurate, but that it was God who initiated and oversaw the process – is equally incorrect. To President Packer, both godless and God-ordained evolution were irrevocably untrue theories that collide with Gospel teachings.

Next, President Packer appealed to the scriptures and to essential doctrines of the Gospel. Specifically, he noted that the doctrines of the Fall of Adam and the Atonement of Jesus Christ would of necessity be false if the theory of evolution is accurate. This is so because if man did not fall from a higher station, but rather ascended over time from a lower one, there is no need to redeem him and bring him *back* into God's presence. If there is no need of redemption, which the Fall makes necessary, then there is no need of Christ. And without Jesus, there is no Gospel and our faith is vain.

Most importantly, President Packer highlighted the fact that at least *two* separate First Presidencies have declared the position of the Church relative to man's origin. Their position is that evolution is a false, man-made creed and that humans are the literal children of God created in His holy image. President Packer noted that numerous apostles and prophets have confirmed this truth, including himself. Thus he testified that the notion the Church has not declared an official position on evolution is patently false.

---

[109] President Boyd K. Packer, "The Law and the Light," BYU Symposium, 1988, https://rsc.byu.edu/archived/book-mormon-jacob-through-words-mormon-learn-joy/law-and-light.

Lastly, but significantly, President Packer demonstrated that our focus should be on religion, *not* science; revealed truth, *not* mortal deductions and guesses. To be well versed in all the complexities, nuances, and conflicting theories of science, as nice is that may be, is somewhat irrelevant so long as one has a testimony of the truth imparted by the Holy Ghost. Just as so many of us can do with absolute surety, President Packer bore his special witness – gained by the Holy Spirit through prayer – that Jesus *is* the Christ and that His Gospel, no matter how bombarded by "unproved theories" it may be, is true.

Yes, because of his personal knowledge, President Packer bore his testimony that man is "the undeveloped offspring of celestial parents." He witnessed that man is now in a fallen state because of transgression, that a Redeemer is necessary to lift him up, and that the Savior carried out His beautiful Atonement for the salvation of humankind. The power of a personal witness is worth more than gold! Testimony trumps science every time.

Unless built upon eternal truth, which truth emanates from God through the workings of the Spirit and light of Christ, every false theory will inevitably fall no matter how popular they may be at present. *The Book of Mormon* teaches that "to be learned is good if they hearken unto the counsels of God" (2 Nephi 9:29). Knowledge becomes a severe stumbling block when it is not tempered by the revelations of the Almighty. No matter what some may claim, the wisdom of mortals is foolishness when it conflicts with the revealed teachings of God and the witness of the Holy Spirit. If you ever encounter a conflict between the two, cling to the Gospel in faith and you will be on the winning side 100 times out of 100.

Thankfully, we have *many* inspired witnesses to the truth and do not need to rely upon President Packer's testimony alone. Over the entire course of this dispensation, prophets and apostles have raised the warning voice against Darwin and his theories. We turn now to perhaps the best known, and most controversial, of such testimonies for further instruction.

In November 1909, under President Joseph F. Smith's administration, the First Presidency released an official doctrinal statement titled "The Origin of Man." Though, as we shall see, the statement itself says it is an official exposition of the Church's position on man's origin, many in the Church today reject it as mere opinion and go out of their way to attempt to discredit the prophets of God.

With my own ears I have heard BYU professors mock this First Presidency statement, denouncing it to their classes as "not official doctrine" or "unscientific opinion." When I protested, as I often did when I heard false doctrine being taught as truth by Latter-day Saint professors who ought to have known better, I was literally laughed at by the instructors and fellow students alike. I have also been criticized over the years, both in person and online, for defending its validity and citing it as a legitimate source of doctrine. Yet, despite the criticism and skepticism from those who ought to rally behind the prophets, the 1909 statement stands firm as a testament to the truth and to the inspiration of the apostles who wrote it.

In February 2002, this earlier statement was reprinted under President Hinckley's administration. An explanatory note accompanying this reprinting clarified:

> "In the early 1900s, questions concerning the Creation of the earth and the theories of evolution became the subject of much public discussion. In the midst of these controversies, the First Presidency issued the following in 1909, which expresses the Church's doctrinal position on these matters."[110]

To the First Presidency in 2002, the 1909 statement represented "the Church's doctrinal position" on man's origin. If the Church in 2002 believed that "The Origin of Man" was an official position, then why don't we believe it in 2018? And if it is not truly "the Church's doctrinal position" on the origin of man, then why did the Church say it was? And why is this statement still accessible and in full public view if it contains falsehoods? Were they wrong? Were they mistaken? Were they confused? Were they lying? Was President Hinckley a fallen prophet? Or

---

[110] "The Origin of Man," First Presidency, *Improvement Era*, November, 1909, 75-81. Reprinted in *Ensign*, February, 2002, https://www.lds.org/ensign/2002/02/the-origin-of-man?lang=eng.

was the Church perhaps telling the truth that many would rather not hear?

Though there is no revelation in the scriptures using the modern terms "evolution," "organic evolution," or "Darwinism," the Church *does* have an official, revealed, codified, canonized, accepted, approved, and published doctrinal position *on the origin of man*. This is demonstrably, inarguably true, factual, and unassailable. None but the dishonest or uninformed claim that the Church has no official position on the origin of man. It is semantics, then, to claim that there is no official statement on "evolution." What is the notion of evolution if not a theory about man's origin? Happily for us, the Church has an official, doctrinal, scripturally-substantiated, inspired, oft-repeated statement on man's origin.

Before the evolutionists rush to contradict me, let me preempt them by citing the only real card they have to play – one which they play over and over and over like a broken record. It is true that the Church openly says it holds "no official position on the theory of evolution." Yet, I would note the latter part of that statement which the evolutionists conveniently ignore. That same statement confirms that despite not having an official position that mentions evolution *by name*, "our teachings regarding man's origin are clear and come from revelation." What's more, this statement refers people seeking additional light and knowledge to the 1909 First Presidency declaration that is our present focus![111] Again I repeat that it is pure semantics to claim there is no official position on evolution when the Church emphatically declares an official, revealed position on man's origin – a position which is utterly incompatible with Darwin's concocted, pseudo-scientific theories that deny man's divine origins.

Regardless of what may be written by anonymous writers in Church magazines or alleged by BYU professors, and no matter how official statements may be twisted and quoted out of context by those seeking to justify their belief in the theories of men, multiple First Presidencies have reprinted the 1909 statement and refer to it as *the* "doctrinal position" on

---

[111] "What does the Church believe about evolution?" *New Era*, October, 2016, https://www.lds.org/new-era/2016/10/to-the-point/what-does-the-church-believe-about-evolution?lang=eng.

man's origin. It is the gold standard. It is what the Church refers truth-seekers to. It is, as noted, the Church's *official position* on man's origin. Thankfully we do not have to doubt its legitimacy as doctrine for we have numerous apostolic witnesses (e.g. Presidents Hinckley and Packer) who have born their testimony of this statement's validity and who have independently taught the truths it contains.

Perhaps the reason the 2002 reprint asserted that "The Origin of Man" was the Church's "doctrinal position" was the fact that the original statement *said* it was. In the original declaration, the First Presidency said that its goal was to provide "a statement of the position held by the Church upon this subject." President Joseph F. Smith and his councilors explained:

> "It is believed that a statement of the position held by the Church upon this subject will be timely and productive of good.

> "In presenting the statement that follows we are not conscious of putting forth anything essentially new; neither is it our desire so to do. Truth is what we wish to present, and truth—eternal truth—is fundamentally old. A restatement of the original attitude of the Church relative to this matter is all that will be attempted here. To tell the truth as God has revealed it, and commend it to the acceptance of those who need to conform their opinions thereto, is the sole purpose of this presentation."

To recapitulate, this 1909 First Presidency statement was not setting forth new doctrine, but was merely *reaffirming* the "original attitude of the Church" and the eternal truths of the everlasting Gospel. It was testifying of "the truth as God has revealed it." It represents then and now "the position held by the Church upon this subject." The First Presidency recommended that everyone "conform their opinions" to the doctrines they set forth.

In light of these frank statements, it appears self-evident and redundant to state that the Church *does* hold an official position on man's origin. It is also abundantly clear that the First Presidency in 1909 believed it was proclaiming the truth "as God has revealed it" and that it expected members of the Church to "conform their opinions" to those truths. Have we done so? Or are we playing the part of the rebellious and headstrong intellectual who thinks he knows better than the prophets?

The following are parts of that 1909 "statement of the position held by the Church" on the subject of man's origin and the topic of organic evolution that it unavoidably must confront:

> ""God created man in his own image, in the image of God created he him; male and female created he them." In these plain and pointed words the inspired author of the book of Genesis made known to the world the truth concerning the origin of the human family. Moses, the prophet-historian—"learned," as we are told, "in all the wisdom of the Egyptians"—when making this important announcement was not voicing a mere opinion, a theory derived from his researches into the occult lore of that ancient people. He was speaking as the mouthpiece of God, and his solemn declaration was for all time and for all people. No subsequent revelator of the truth has contradicted the great leader and lawgiver of Israel. All who have since spoken by divine authority upon this theme have confirmed his simple and sublime proclamation. Nor could it be otherwise. Truth has but one source, and all revelations from heaven are harmonious with each other. . . .

> "Adam, our first progenitor, "the first man," was, like Christ, a preexistent spirit, and like Christ he took upon him an appropriate body, the body of a man, and so became a "living soul." The doctrine of the preexistence—revealed so plainly, particularly in latter days—pours a wonderful flood of light upon the otherwise mysterious problem of man's origin. It shows that man, as a spirit, was begotten and born of heavenly parents and reared to maturity in the eternal mansions of the Father, prior to coming upon the earth in a temporal body to undergo an experience in mortality. It teaches that all men existed in the spirit before any man existed in the flesh and that all who have inhabited the earth since Adam have taken bodies and become souls in like manner.

"It is held by some that Adam was not the first man upon this earth and that the original human being was a development from lower orders of the animal creation. These, however, are the theories of men. The word of the Lord declared that Adam was "the first man of all men" (Moses 1:34), and we are therefore in duty bound to regard him as the primal parent of our race. It was shown to the brother of Jared that all men were created in the *beginning* after the image of God; whether we take this to mean the spirit or the body, or both, it commits us to the same conclusion: Man began life as a human being, in the likeness of our Heavenly Father.

"True it is that the body of man enters upon its career as a tiny germ embryo, which becomes an infant, quickened at a certain stage by the spirit whose tabernacle it is, and the child, after being born, develops into a man. There is nothing in this, however, to indicate that the original man, the first of our race, began life as anything less than a man, or less than the human germ or embryo that becomes a man. . . .

"The Church of Jesus Christ of Latter-day Saints, basing its belief on divine revelation, ancient and modern, proclaims man to be the direct and lineal offspring of Deity."[112]

I urge each person to read this statement in full and to reject and oppose those voices that would tear it down, dismiss it, or falsely claim it is merely an opinion. These were the words of the Lord's anointed and they have *never* been superseded or disavowed by subsequent presidents of the Church. Indeed, at least two First Presidencies have reprinted the statement, showing a consistency of thought among the leaders of this Church.

---

[112] "The Origin of Man," First Presidency, *Improvement Era*, November, 1909, 75-81. Reprinted in *Ensign*, February, 2002, https://www.lds.org/ensign/2002/02/the-origin-of-man?lang=eng.

Furthermore, we learn that men are "duty bound" to accept the story of Creation as expounded in the scriptures and to acknowledge the truth that "man began life as a human being." If man began life as a human being, and not as any lower form of life, then the theory of evolution is irreversibly false. It also means that not only is mainstream Darwinism, but the Christianized form of "theistic evolution," are conclusively and permanently false.

As the scripture declare, and as the First Presidency affirmed, Adam was the first man on earth. There were none before him. There were no Pre-Adamites. There was no "development from lower orders of the animal creation," as evolution teaches. There was no racial mixing with fallen angels, demigods, or extraterrestrials, as confused students of the Bible sometimes believe. We are "in the likeness of our Heavenly Father" and always have been.

Yes, President Smith and his councilors made it clear that the Church's position is that man is "the direct and lineal offspring of Deity" and that there "is nothing . . . to indicate that the original man . . . began life as anything less than a man." Our origin is divine, *not* terrestrial. We are descended from the Gods, not descended from apes. We began as spirit intelligences whose form resembled that of mortal man, as the story of Christ's pre-mortal appearance to the Brother of Jared amply attests (Ether 3:6-17).

The scripture says that "*man* was in the beginning with God" (D&C 93:29). *Man*, not animal, amoeba, or ape. From the very moment our Father coupled our intelligence with spirit, we have been in human form – in the likeness of God. The spirit, being immortal, cannot die, regenerate, reincarnate, or transmute. You began as a man or woman in the spirit, that male or female spirit now inhabits your mortal flesh, and when you pass to the next sphere of life, you retain your gender, form, and identity. It is foolishness to assume our bodies, which are designed to house our spirits, were ever anything lesser or lowlier than human in form, nature, or appearance.

If there was an intermediate lifeform between nothingness and man – a "missing link" – it must then be asked in all seriousness, what would have animated this lifeform? Adam's fleshly body had no life until God "breathed into his nostrils the breath of life; and man became a living soul" (Genesis 2:7). The First Presidency confirmed this when they said that our bodies are "quickened at a certain stage by the spirit whose tabernacle [they are]." Thus, we know that flesh has no life in and of itself but must be quickened by a spirit – a spirit resembling the form of the physical body.

We likewise know that when the spirit leaves the body, the body dies and crumbles back to the earth from which it was formed (Ecclesiastes 12:7). This is additional evidence of the preeminence of the spirit and the fact that our bodies are nothing without our spirits that were created in the beginning in the image of the Almighty. Truthfully, a body only becomes a living being when God joins it with a spirit and has no existence apart from a spirit. If man *evolved* and was once anything less than human, it then would require a corresponding less-than-human spirit to give it life and movement. But we have no evidence that such a lower species of creation exists. What we do know is that "*man* was in the beginning with God"; not Lucy or some other inferior, inhuman missing link (D&C 93:23, 29).

On a different occasion, President Joseph F. Smith took up the topic of man's origin. He again devoted time to rejecting the evolutionists' false theories. Said he:

> "We will progress and develop and grow in wisdom and understanding, but our identity can never change. We did not spring from spawn. Our spirits existed from the beginning, have existed always, and will continue forever. We did not pass through the ordeals of embodiment in the lesser animals in order to reach the perfection to which we have attained in manhood and womanhood, in the image and likeness of God. God was and is our Father, and his children were begotten in the flesh of his own image and likeness, male and female."[113]

---

[113] Joseph F. Smith, *Gospel Doctrine* (Salt Lake City, UT: Deseret Book Company, 1977), 25.

Could anything be plainer than this doctrine? We "did not spring from spawn," but existed as children of God from the beginning. We bear the image of our God and possess His attributes, sensibilities, and potential. Unless we wish to malign His character, we ought not to impugn our own by suggesting we were every anything but the children of the Father created in His divine image.

President David O. McKay added his testimony to the prophetic choir of witnesses against Darwinism. He wrote:

> "Living in deeds, living in writings, living in monuments, living in the memory of friends is not immortality; neither living in the lives of our children and our grandchildren to the latest generation. There are those who say that is the only immortality that man will have. But the author of evolution, Charles Darwin, shrank from that thought as he contemplated the greatest descent or origin in his mind of the human family, his theory, as you know. He finally came to the point that there will come a time when the human family will end. If that theory is right, all sentient beings known as man cannot live. And so he wrote: "It is an intolerable thought that man and all other sentient beings are doomed to annihilation after such a long, continued, slow progress.""[114]

It *is* an intolerable thought. It is a false notion. It is a theory debunked by the words of God and the teachings of His prophets. What a pitiful existence this would be if we evolved from some lower species to the station of intelligent man, only to go out of existence permanently upon death of the body.

Elder Bruce R. McConkie raised a particularly fierce voice against evolutionary theory. Though Elder McConkie is often wrongly accused of preaching false doctrine or making his personal opinions seem authoritative, you will note the consistency of his remarks with those expressed by the First Presidency in their binding "doctrinal position." He taught:

---

[114] McKay, *Gospel Ideals*, 50.

"Of the several theories, postulated in one age or another to explain (without the aid of revelation) the origin of man and the various forms of life, none has taken such hold or found such widespread acceptance as the relatively modern so-called theory of organic evolution. . . .

"From the day of their first announcement, these theories of organic evolution found themselves in conflict with the principles of revealed religion as such are found recorded in the scriptures and expounded by inspired teachers. . . .

"Obviously there never will be a conflict between truths revealed in the realm of religion and those discovered by scientific research. Truth is ever in harmony with itself. But if false doctrines creep into revealed religion, these will run counter to the discovered truths of science; and if false scientific *theories* are postulated, these ultimately will be overthrown by the truths revealed from Him who knows all things.

"Sometimes persons having a knowledge of the revealed truths of salvation and the evolutionistic theories of the day keep these two branches of knowledge divided between separate mental compartments. Their purpose seems to be to avoid resolving the obvious conflicts which otherwise would arise. Truth, however, is truth, and ultimately every believing person must channel his mental processes so that proper choices are made as between the truths of salvation and the theories of men. . . .

"How weak and puerile the intellectuality which, knowing that the Lord's plan takes all forms of life from a pre-existent spirit state, through mortality, and on to an ultimate resurrected state of immortality, yet finds comfort in the theoretical postulates that mortal life began in the scum of the sea, as it were, and has through eons of time evolved to its present varieties and state! Do those with spiritual insight really think that the infinite Creator of worlds without number would operate that way? . . . .

"There is no harmony between the truths of revealed religion and the theories of organic evolution."[115]

Strong words, but true nonetheless. There is absolutely *zero* harmony between the truths of the Gospel of Jesus Christ concerning man's origin and those "false doctrines" of Charles Darwin and his disciples. Nearly everything evolution teaches "conflicts" with revealed religion. The theories are "weak and puerile." They hold no water, either theologically or scientifically. Only one lacking a testimony of God's true nature can believe in the degrading Darwinist dogmas.

Tragically, there is scarcely an ideology in the world that is more prevalent and accepted as Darwinism. Its principles are found everywhere – they have even crept into most churches. Indeed, the incorrect understanding of God's nature and man's origin postulated by Darwin undergirds nearly all false religious and political systems in operation today, including all forms of socialism and communism.

In a much later address at BYU, Elder McConkie again lambasted the theory of evolution, calling it one of the seven deadly heresies – including it alongside such heresies as the Adam-God theory, the notion that resurrected man can progress from one kingdom of glory to the next, and the misguided idea that a temple marriage guarantees exaltation. Elder McConkie's denunciation of evolution was given in question format, with this great apostle expecting the hearer to fill in the black with the only logical answers. I draw out these few lines from Elder McConkie's explanation and leave the reader to study the original for himself:

> "Heresy two concerns itself with the relationship between organic evolution and revealed religion and asks the question whether they can be harmonized.

> "There are those who believe that the theory of organic evolution runs counter to the plain and explicit principles set forth in the holy scriptures as these have been interpreted and taught by Joseph Smith and his associates. There are others who think that

---

[115] McConkie, *Mormon Doctrine*, 247, 250, 256.

evolution is the system used by the Lord to form plant and animal life and to place man on earth.

"May I say that all truth is in agreement, that true religion and true science bear the same witness, and that in the true and full sense, true science is part of true religion. But may I also raise some questions of a serious nature. Is there any way to harmonize the false religions of the Dark Ages with the truths of science as they have now been discovered? Is there any way to harmonize the revealed religion that has come to us with the theoretical postulates of Darwinism and the diverse speculations descending therefrom?

"Should we accept the famous document of the First Presidency issued in the days of President Joseph F. Smith and entitled "The Origin of Man" as meaning exactly what it says? Is it the doctrine of the gospel that Adam stood next to Christ in power and might and intelligence before the foundations of the world were laid; that Adam was placed on this earth as an immortal being; that there was no death in the world for him or for any form of life until after the Fall; that the fall of Adam brought temporal and spiritual death into the world; that this temporal death passed upon all forms of life, upon man and animal and fish and fowl and plant life; that Christ came to ransom man and all forms of life from the effects of the temporal death brought into the world through the Fall, and in the case of man from a spiritual death also; and that this ransom includes a resurrection for man and for all forms of life? Can you harmonize these things with the evolutionary postulate that death has always existed and that the various forms of life have evolved from preceding forms over astronomically long periods of time?"[116]

Elder McConkie proceeded to quote scripture and bear his testimony of Adam's Fall, man's need for a Savior, and the Plan of Redemption. I testify, as he did, that Darwin's ideas and the teachings of the prophets in

---

[116] Elder Bruce R. McConkie, "The Seven Deadly Heresies," BYU Devotional, June 1, 1980, https://speeches.byu.edu/talks/bruce-r-mcconkie_seven-deadly-heresies/.

all ages do *not* harmonize. Only one can be accurate. Only one teaches the truth about man's origin, purpose, and destiny. Only one edifies, uplifts, inspires, and instructs.

In 1946, President David O. McKay lamented that: "Among the generalizations of science, evolution holds the foremost place." He added:

> "It claims: "Man is a creature of development; that he has come up through uncounted ages from an origin that is lowly. Why this vast expenditure of time and pain and blood? Why should he come so far if he is destined to go no farther. A creature which has traveled such distances and fought such battles and won such victories deserves, one is compelled to say, to conquer death and rob the grave of its victory.""[117]

Truly, the logical framework for Darwinistic evolution is feeble and falls flat when the weight of intelligent inquiry leans upon it. It is against reason, logic, and the innate whispers of the human soul. It is even against a host of scientific evidences that could be cited. The rational mind simply cannot believe it.

Fortunately, we need not rely upon science, intellectual arguments, or reason for our faith. We can rely upon the revelations of God which come to us through the Priesthood line of communication. These revelations will *always* be in harmony one with another. Whether revealed in 1909, 2002, or 2018, the truth about man's origin *cannot* change. It is a fixed reality. We must therefore make our opinions and theories conform to "the revealed truths of salvation." If we do not do so, we will eventually be overthrown with those false theories we cling to.

In one General Conference, President Boyd K. Packer bore witness against this Devilish dogma. He gave a warning not to heed the teachings of evil spirits, bringing to mind the words of our Savior who taught "that there are many spirits which are false spirits, which have gone forth in the earth, deceiving the world," including many members of the Church (D&C

---

[117] McKay, *Gospel Ideals*, 49.

50:2-4). President Packer couched his core teaching in the form of a story and then added a very simple yet scientifically sound truth. Said he:

> "[T]here is an adversary who has his own channels of spiritual communication. He confuses the careless and prompts those who serve him to devise deceptive, counterfeit doctrine, carefully contrived to appear genuine. . . .

> "Some years ago I returned home to find our little children were waiting in the driveway. They had discovered some newly hatched chicks under the manger in the barn. When they reached for them, a protective hen rebuffed them. So they came for reinforcements.

> "I soon gathered a handful of little chicks for them to see and touch.

> "As our little girl held one of them, I said in a teasing way, "That will make a nice watchdog when it grows up, won't it?" She looked at me quizzically, as if I didn't know much.

> "So I changed my approach: "It won't be a watchdog, will it?" She shook her head, "No, Daddy." Then I added, "It will be a nice riding horse."

> "She wrinkled up her nose and gave me that "Oh, Dad!" look. For even a four-year-old knows that a chick will not be a dog, nor a horse, nor even a turkey. It will be a chicken. It will follow the pattern of its parentage. She knew that without having had a course in genetics, without a lesson or a lecture.

> "No lesson is more manifest in nature than that all living things do as the Lord commanded in the Creation. They reproduce "after their own kind." (See Moses 2:12, 24.) They follow the pattern of their parentage. Everyone knows that; every four-year-old knows that! A bird will not become an animal nor a fish. A mammal will not beget reptiles, nor "do men gather . . . figs of thistles." (Matt. 7:16.) . . . .

"This is demonstrated in so many obvious ways, even an ordinary mind should understand it. Surely no one with reverence for God could believe that His children evolved from slime or from reptiles. (Although one can easily imagine that those who accept the theory of evolution don't show much enthusiasm for genealogical research!) The theory of evolution, and it is a theory, will have an entirely different dimension when the workings of God in creation are fully revealed."[118]

Without being taught, even little children understand that they are *the offspring of God*. They sense that they are special and unique. They inherently believe that they are of a royal lineage – princes and princesses in training. They realize that God is their Father and that they can speak with Him. They know without having to be told that one day they will grow to become like their Heavenly Parents. The children who grow up to discount these inborn truths are those who are taught the incorrect and false doctrines of men – doctrines designed to destroy their childlike faith.

A living creature, whether animal or man, follows "the pattern of its parentage." All life reproduces in its own image and after its own kind. No one needs a degree to witness and understand this phenomenon in nature. And it is the same with humans – when we procreate, we bring forth another human, not a dog, chicken, lizard, or snake. No human couple has to worry that when they procreate their child will be anything less or more than a human being. Such it has always been and will always be. This is because the begetting of life is governed by immutable laws upheld by God. All the theorizing and postulating in the world cannot make it otherwise.

When the truth is fully revealed, man will see as he is seen (D&C 76:94). He will know that his ancestors were not apes or pond scum. He will know that his own spirit is eternal. He will see that His Heavenly Parents rule the universe and that he once lived in Their Kingdom above. And he will then comprehend the truth that we are of "the lineage of the Gods."

---

[118] President Boyd K. Packer, "The Pattern of Our Parentage," General Conference, October, 1984, https://www.lds.org/general-conference/1984/10/the-pattern-of-our-parentage?lang=eng.

In his book *Meditation and Atonement*, President John Taylor also denounced the false concept of Darwinian evolution which was invented and popularized during his lifetime. He wrote somewhat of the laws of nature and testified of man's lineage and potential:

> "All the works of God connected with the world which we inhabit, and with all other worlds, are strictly governed by law . . . There is a perfect regularity, exactitude and order associated with all worlds; a departure from which would produce incalculable evil and irretrievable destruction and ruin. With regard to the matter of which the earth is composed, it is also governed by strict, unchangeable laws; matter possessing the same properties under the same conditions, in all parts of the world. The various grasses, herbs, plants, shrubs, flowers, minerals, metals, waters, fluids or gasses, when under the same conditions, are subject to or governed by unchangeable laws . . . The animal and vegetable creations are governed by certain laws, and are composed of certain elements peculiar to themselves. This applies to man, to the beasts, fowls, fish and creeping things, to the insects and to all animated nature; each one possessing its own distinctive features, each requiring a specific sustenance, each having an organism and faculties governed by prescribed laws to perpetuate its own kind. . . .

> "These principles do not change, as represented by evolutionists of the Darwinian school, but the primitive organisms of all living beings exist in the same form as when they first received their impress from their Maker . . . and if we take man, he is said to have been made in the image of God, for the simple reason that he is a son of God; and being His son, he is, of course, His offspring, an emanation from God, in whose likeness, we are told, he is made. He did not originate from a chaotic mass of matter, moving or inert, but came forth possessing, in an embryotic state, all the faculties and powers of a God. And when he shall be perfected, and have progressed to maturity, he will be like his Father – a God; being indeed his offspring. As the horse, the ox, the sheep, and every living creature, including man, propagates

its own species and perpetuates its own kind, so does God perpetuate His."[119]

The logic in this statement is irrefutable. The science is sound and unassailable. It is a fact of reality that each thing produces after its own kind and in its own likeness. Cows have baby calves which grow into cows. Deer produce fawns that grow into deer. Humans birth babies that grow into adult humans. And God sires children who, if they grow properly according to the laws He has established and revealed, possess all the latent ability to become like Him – gods like their Father.

Scientists have never observed one species evolve into another, and have no fossil or other evidence to prove evolutionary growth between species, for the simple fact that it is not true and completely contradicts God's eternal laws. It gives confidence to know that there is an overarching order in the universe and that all is not a result of chance or coincidence. God is a Being of order and law. He does not preside over chaos and does nothing by chance.

It is ennobling to understand that we have a higher purpose, that this earth life is a transient phase, and that we have glorious realms of possibility awaiting us. It is empowering to comprehend the Lord's design in our individual creation! Nothing is more precious than knowing you are a son or daughter of God.

President Joseph Fielding Smith was a man who took after his mortal father, the prophet Joseph F. Smith. He was not only a man of God, but a man of science and great secular learning. His teachings are some of the purest delivered in this dispensation.

While president of the Quorum of the Twelve Apostles, President Joseph Fielding Smith – at the behest of other members of that Quorum – wrote a book titled *Man: His Origin and Destiny*. From stem to stern, President Smith picked apart and deconstructed the false doctrine of organic evolution from both a spiritual *and* a scientific point of view. He explained

---

[119] President John Taylor, *The Mediation and Atonement of Jesus Christ* (reprint; Heber City, UT: Archive Publishers, 2000), 163-165.

its damaging effect on individual members of the Church and on society as a whole. He lay bare its fallacies and contradictions and set forth the revealed truth about man's origin. I encourage each of you to read and study that excellent book. I draw just a few statements from its inspired pages.

In this first passage, we see President Smith lamenting the tragedy of godless public schooling. He explained that the instruction received in public institutions too often contradicts the teachings of the Gospel as expounded by the Church and obedient parents. This influence, he said, has even invaded the Church and is leading many members astray. He observed:

> "In the home parents are commanded by revelation to teach their children these principles of the Gospel and the necessity of baptism for the remission of sins. . . .

> "In this manner they are instructed in the home. Then they go to school and find these glorious principles ridiculed and denied by the doctrines of men founded on foolish theories which deny that man is the offspring of God and that when we pray to him as our Father, our words are meaningless and that man is the offspring of some worm or *amoeba* that in some unknown way multiplied to fill the earth with all its plants and animal life. It is true that not all teachers believe and teach these foolish doctrines; but these theories do dominate the secular education of our youth. They are constantly published in our newspapers, in magazines and other periodicals, and those who believe in God and his divine revelations frequently sit supinely by without raising any voice of protest . . . Too frequently, I regret to say, unwittingly presiding officers in wards and quorums choose teachers that have scholastic training without discovering whether or not they are converted and in full faith in the doctrines of the Church. When this happens and a teacher is appointed who is filled with modernistic doctrines conflicting with what the Lord has revealed, and these theories he presents before the class, confusion is the result and we find confusion from within. Under such conditions, with enemies in our ranks, the influence of both Church and home

is further weakened and our youth more seriously impressed with these false theories."[120]

Yes, the enemies *are* in our ranks! The wolves in sheep's clothing are amongst us. They sit beside us in quorum meetings, preside in councils, visit us in our homes, instruct our children at school, and spread their confusion near and far. Their underlying error is their lack of knowledge regarding man's origin. They disbelieve the scriptures, opting instead for the "foolish doctrines" presented by the Adversary as "science."

These "foolish theories" guide and inspire the men who have "ridiculed and denied" correct Gospel principles. So prevalent are these false theories that they thoroughly "dominate the secular education of our youth." If a prophet of God told you that something your child was being taught in school was false and foolish, what would be your reaction? Would you passively allow their teachers to indoctrinate them in the ways of foolishness or would you step in to correct the errors and salvage your children's faith? Fortunately, many prophets *have* warned you of the false, man-made ideas that pass for "education" in the schools – and Darwinian evolution tops the list.

Please do not think that because you may live in a predominately Latter-day Saint community and your local school teachers are members of the Church that your children are not being indoctrinated in their school classes. They are. It is part of the mandated curriculum. It is your job as parents, however, to inculcate your children with the truth and to explain plainly that so much of what they are being taught in school is simply not in harmony with the revealed truths of the Gospel.

In order to be good stewards and care for the children Heavenly Father has entrusted you with in the manner I have described, parents must first become converted to the Restored Gospel and second become informed about what their children are being taught. Even better, I encourage Gospel-centered homeschooling whenever possible. If you research, you will find that many prophets have looked unfavorably upon public schooling and some of their most emphatic warnings concerned the false

---

[120] Smith, *Man: His Origin and Destiny*, 2-3.

ideas the youth are being taught as a matter of course in public institutions.

President Smith further elucidated what the scriptures say about man's origin and why the theory of evolution is incompatible with these teachings:

> "Modern revelation, the scriptures which have been restored in the Book of Mormon, the Book of Moses, of Abraham, the Doctrine and Covenants, all bear witness that man is the offspring of God, and that man was created in his image. Therefore there is a challenge to all these theories of men who teach the descent of man through countless ages from lower forms of life. The revelations of the Lord being true, these theories are false."[121]

> "The word of the Lord in the Pearl of Great Price, the Book of Abraham, and the Doctrine and Covenants, should carry enough weight with members of the Church to satisfy them and give them a firm foundation on which to stand. To all the members who have received the testimony through the Holy Ghost, these teachings supporting the Old Testament, will suffice. We do have in the Church, however, a great many members who do not have that abiding testimony, unfortunately. These are readily disturbed by the philosophies and theories taught in the colleges and other schools and it is difficult for them to see that the philosophical doctrines can be false. Many of the theories are proclaimed with such positive finality that those weak in the faith are confused or perhaps inclined to accept the deductions of these teachers and think that the revelations must be wrong. This is a step towards apostasy. As the Lord declared, we cannot serve two masters. We cannot accept the hypotheses of science which are in conflict with that which is here set forth in clearness, at the same time. They are diametrically opposite to each other."[122]

---

[121] Smith, *Man: His Origin and Destiny*, 269.

[122] Smith, *Man: His Origin and Destiny*, 356.

As President Smith explained, the theory of evolution presents a serious challenge to the members of the Church. This challenge comes both from without and, regrettably, from within. The "false theories" of the Adversary are tailor-made to destroy the Saints by severing them from their Eternal Father and the knowledge of their own dormant divinity. It is undeniable that the faith of many members – especially youth and new converts – has been dramatically shaken by those preaching these "foolish theories" with a tone of "positive finality." Those who preach them and those who imbibe them are making "steps towards apostasy."

Despite any air of finality with which Darwin's theories may be presented, they are "diametrically opposite" to the truths of the Restored Gospel. If the Gospel is true, then the theory of evolution is false. If the theory of evolution is true, then the Gospel is a lie. If we are really created in God's image, then the "philosophical doctrines" of the world are so much fluff. And if Darwin was a prophet of truth, then the Lord's prophets are liars and you and I are mere animals with no purpose and no connection to the stars.

If the evolutionist dogmas do not come from God and do not testify of Christ – and how can they if they deny the divinity of man and the resurrection from the grave – then they automatically come from Satan. Mormon plainly taught that "whatsoever thing persuadeth men to do evil, and believe not in Christ, and deny him, and serve not God, then ye may know with a perfect knowledge it is of the devil" (Moroni 7:17).

Those Saints who embrace the scriptures, accept the revelations of God as authoritative, and utilize the gift of the Holy Ghost, are not deceived. They know that the Darwinist theory of evolution is irreversibly opposed to the doctrine set forth in the Restored Gospel of our Lord because it denies, among other things, the Fatherhood of God, the existence of spirit, God's hand in Creation, the Fall of man, the necessity of a Redeemer, the Resurrection from the grave, and any life before or after mortal birth and death. The theory of evolution is a sandy foundation and those who build on it will fall (Matthew 7:24-27). The Gospel, by contrast, gives us a "firm foundation on which to stand."

President Smith told us what happens when men ignore these Gospel truths and turn to their own wisdom and trust in the arm of flesh:

> "As long as men of science ignore the light of truth and have no faith in the Divine Creator, they will search the hard way to find out the works of the Lord and will formulate false theories which may prove both harmful and pernicious in that they will guide their fellows who accept them away from the revealed plan leading to eternal life.

> "Unfortunately most scientists depend entirely upon their own intelligence and wisdom without a thought of divine aid. It is said repeatedly that scientists do not take God into their reckoning in the search of truth. This is an unfortunate condition, for if they were men of prayer and faith, seeking divine help they would come to the truth more readily and would avoid the many pitfalls of false hypotheses."[123]

Faith – childlike faith – dispels most errors that enter mortal minds. If the scientists and the average person alike had more faith in Christ, they would trust Him and accept His declarations that, if true, refute evolutionary theory. When faith is coupled with sincere prayer, scripture study, thoughtful and sincere pondering, and basic righteous living, no heart can be deceived for very long. By following this formula, we can "know the truth of all things" through the Holy Ghost (Moroni 10:3-5). The righteous and sincere will not be fooled by "false hypotheses," but will recognize them, by virtue of the Holy Spirit influence, as "harmful and pernicious" and destructive of faith.

I draw one final, summarizing thought from *Man: His Origin and Destiny*. President Smith wrote, warned, and witnessed that:

> "It has been truthfully said that organic evolution is Satan's chief weapon in this dispensation in his attempt to destroy the divine mission of Jesus Christ. It is a contemptible plot against faith in God and to destroy the effective belief in the divine atonement of

---

[123] Smith, *Man: His Origin and Destiny*, 22.

our Redeemer through which men may be saved from their sins and find place in the Kingdom of God. There is not and cannot be, any compromise between the Gospel of Jesus Christ and the theories of evolution. Were evolution true, there could be no remission of sins. In fact, there could be no sin. . . .

"Organic evolution tends to rob God of his mercy, his justice and his saving grace. It denies the resurrection of the dead and the gift of Jesus Christ to all men that they will live again. It denies the spiritual creation and places the earth and all of its inhabitants beyond the power of redemption. It teaches that in some unknown way and at some unknown time, life commenced in some spontaneous way in a speck of protoplasm. It cannot explain how this speck of protoplasm, or cell, happened to be. It is merely a postulate, a guess that such a thing really happened. Therefore man is beholden to no one for his existence. He is not, according to this theory, the offspring of God. He had no divine origin, no spirit in his body that is eternal. When he dies he shall return to the dust and death is the end of all. There is no other conclusion; no doctrine more hopeful than total extinction of the individual. These are the rewards offered to you and to me and to every creature through this wicked doctrine which today prevails so nearly universal, making atheists of mankind. . . .

"This is what comes naturally out of the doctrine of organic evolution. It ridicules religion. It denies the Fatherhood of God and the Sonship of Jesus Christ. It places man as the natural kin of the animal, a descendant of a rat, a worm and an amoeba. Those who like it may have this doctrine, but they have no right to attempt to drag their fellow men, who are "begotten sons and daughters unto God," down to their level. . . .

"In the spirit of fairplay we may ask WHY are these advocates privileged to teach their soul-destroying doctrines in our public schools and colleges, when the doctrines of Jesus Christ are barred? Why are so many of the textbooks adopted in these schools steeped in these theories and by these means the minds of our children poisoned and their faith destroyed? In this land of

America our fathers fought for religious and political freedom and our nation is now confronted with a far more deadly sin – the destruction of their faith in the Living God! These perpetrators of this doctrine either know that they are deceivers, or else they have been completely blinded by the arch-enemy of divine truth. Why should those who believe in the creation of man, the fall and the atonement of Jesus Christ, have to submit to these dogmatic theories being promulgated and taught in the textbooks of our schools? We should take a stand for our religious freedom from this contaminating influence which dominates so much of our education."[124]

How damning and degrading is this doctrine which is taught in every public school and school of "higher" learning in America and in the majority of schools across the globe! At its core, Darwinism assaults the basic beliefs of the Gospel, including the belief in Jesus Christ as Redeemer. The Articles of Faith are meaningless if Darwinism is correct. The Restoration of the Gospel is a total farce if Darwin was correct. In fact, everything Christians hold dear is ripped away from them by these false notions. For Latter-day Saints who believe in the everlasting nature of the soul, the reality of pre-mortality, and the promise of eternal family and marriage relationships, Darwinism is an even greater disfigurement of reality.

Annihilation of body and mind are the "rewards" guaranteed to evolutionists. Everlasting nothingness is their promised prize after a life that must necessarily be aimless and selfish. It cannot be otherwise. If there is no afterlife and no punishment or reward, there is no incentive to serve others, act kindly, give charity, or respect, defend, and love our fellow men. If Darwin was correct, there is no hope and all is bleak.

In a battle of witnesses, I side with the prophets over any group or coalition of secular scientists, no matter how popular, no matter how well accepted, no matter how deified by the intellectual community. I know our prophets are the anointed of the Lord – His servants, His chosen

---

[124] Smith, *Man: His Origin and Destiny*, 184-188.

laborers, His watchmen on the tower of Israel. I have a witness, independent of all other people, that the Savior has called prophets in our day and that these prophets deliver His word to mankind. Truly, there are "prophets in the land again" (Ether 9:28) to whom the Lord communicates His "secrets" (Amos 3:7).

One of the truths that I have felt most powerfully in my spirit, in my mind, in my bones, and in my whole frame, is that taught by the prophets regarding man's divine origin. I praise the Lord for revealing these truths anew in our day, beginning with the First Vision of Joseph Smith which shattered forever the myths surrounding God's nature and man's relationship to Him.

I know with all of my soul that President Joseph Fielding Smith was telling the truth when called evolution a "soul-destroying" dogma preached by deceivers who are inspired by the "arch-enemy of divine truth." I witness that he spoke correctly when he said that Darwinism makes atheists of mankind and drags them down. I know that this prophet of God bore accurate testimony when he lamented that our children are having their minds "poisoned" and their faith "destroyed" by the proponents of organic evolution. It is a travesty that this unscientific, hostile, anti-Christian creed is allowed to be force-fed to our youth while the sweet teachings of the Messiah are banned. Truly this is a violation of the First Amendment which guarantees to each American religious Liberty, including God-centered education in schools such as existed in public schools for most of this nation's history.

President Ezra Taft Benson once commented on President Smith's book *Man: His Origin and Destiny*. His remarks came at a time when some "educators" in the Church were publicly criticizing President Smith for his ideas, claiming he was wrong on evolution. President Benson condemned these naysayers and said that their "thesis challenges the integrity of a prophet of God." He further stated: "It is also apparent to all who have the Spirit of God in them that Joseph Fielding Smith's writings will stand the test of time." He then concluded by explaining that his purpose in mentioning this controversy was "to forewarn you about a humanistic emphasis that would tarnish our own Church and its leaders."[125]

I concur that President Smith's writings *will* stand the test of time. They have for 64 years and they will continue to bear all scrutiny. They will do so because they are based upon the scriptures which have come to earth through divine revelation.

President Benson frequently warned the Saints about the false educational ideas being taught to our youth. We have already cited his declaration that Charles Darwin – and others including the Satanist Karl Marx – was a deceiver whose philosophy has caused millions to falter. In the April 1975 General Conference, President Benson spoke of *The Book of Mormon* and why we must use it to fortify our lives, and the ways in which it does just that. In part, he said:

> "[T]he Book of Mormon exposes the enemies of Christ. It confounds false doctrines and lays down contention. (See 2 Ne. 3:12.) It fortifies the humble followers of Christ against the evil designs, strategies, and doctrines of the devil in our day. The type of apostates in the Book of Mormon are similar to the type we have today. God, with his infinite foreknowledge, so molded the Book of Mormon that we might see the error and know how to combat false educational, political, religious, and philosophical concepts of our time. . . .

> "Now, we have not been using the Book of Mormon as we should. Our homes are not as strong unless we are using it to bring our children to Christ. Our families may be corrupted by worldly trends and teachings unless we know how to use the book to expose and combat the falsehoods in socialism, organic evolution, rationalism, humanism, etc. Our missionaries are not as effective unless they are "hissing forth" with it. Social, ethical, cultural, or educational converts will not survive under the heat of the day unless their taproots go down to the fulness of the gospel which the Book of Mormon contains. Our Church classes are not as

---

[125] Benson, *This Nation Shall Endure*, 26-27.

spirit-filled unless we hold it up as a standard. And our nation will continue to degenerate unless we read and heed the words of the God of this land, Jesus Christ, and quit building up and upholding the secret combinations which the Book of Mormon tells us proved the downfall of both previous American civilizations."[126]

The Book of Mormon is the "keystone" of our religion. It "exposes the enemies of Christ" and their false philosophies. It gives us extra knowledge that we are expected to use to "combat false educational, political, religious, and philosophical concepts." These concepts include "socialism, organic evolution, rationalism, humanism, etc." These ideas are upheld by secret combinations and prove a major stumbling block to the Church. They are diminishing the effectiveness of our missionaries. They are corrupting homes and communities. "And our nation will continue to degenerate" unless we use the truths in *The Book of Mormon* to refute these Devilish doctrines.

We are also wise if we ask ourselves, "What does that great book teach about man's origin?" Like all true books of scripture, *The Book of Mormon* reveals the nature and doctrine of Christ and His Father and man's correct relationship to Them. *The Book of Mormon* affirms that we are the children of God and that without Him there could have been no Creation. Lehi taught:

> "And if ye shall say there is no law, ye shall also say there is no sin. If ye shall say there is no sin, ye shall also say there is no righteousness. And if there be no righteousness there be no happiness. And if there be no righteousness nor happiness there be no punishment nor misery. And if these things are not there is no God. And if there is no God we are not, neither the earth; for there could have been no creation of things, neither to act nor to be acted upon; wherefore, all things must have vanished away" (2 Nephi 2:13).

---

[126] President Ezra Taft Benson, "The Book of Mormon is the Word of God," General Conference, April, 1975, https://www.lds.org/general-conference/1975/04/the-book-of-mormon-is-the-word-of-god?lang=eng.

This lone verse refutes the entire foundation of evolutionary theory. And there are many such verses – veritable gems of knowledge hidden throughout the breadth of that sacred volume.

One of the best books refuting the theory of evolution is Clark A. Peterson's *Using the Book of Mormon to Combat Falsehoods in Organic Evolution*. I highly recommend each household obtain a copy of this text and use it to supplement their children's learning as the family reads through the scriptures.

In his book, Brother Peterson observed that the most successful and famous of the Nephite missionaries used the scriptural story of Creation as a powerful teaching tool. The Savior also used it as a teaching device. Brother Peterson wrote:

> "The creation account was a powerful missionary tool during Book of Mormon times. Ammon started at the beginning of creation when converting King Lamoni, (Alma 18:36) as did Aaron with Lamoni's father. (Alma 22:12) Thousands of Lamanites in seven cities were converted using this approach. (Alma 23:4-12) Christ testified that He created the heavens and the earth, and all things that in them are. (3 Nephi 9:15) Today, many records which contain accounts of creation, such as the brass plates, (1 Nephi 5:11) the sealed book, (2 Nephi 27:7) and the gold plates found by Limhi's people (Ether 1:2, 3) are being withheld from us to try our faith."[127]

Those of us who accept the scriptural witness will progress in faith and righteousness while those who do not will stagnate and retrograde. If we do not heed, use, respect, and believe in those things already revealed, we will not receive the higher light reserved for the righteous and believing Saints. Once we stop believing, we start backsliding and the Devil steals light and knowledge away from us (D&C 93:39).

Brother Peterson gave a warning that is applicable to all of us. He said:

---

[127] Clark A. Peterson, *Using the Book of Mormon to Combat Falsehoods in Organic Evolution* (San Jose, CA: Clark A. Peterson, 1992), 30.

> "[I]f we reject the scriptures, we will lose the guidance of the spirit. If we harden our hearts and do not accept creation as stated in the scriptures, but choose instead to accept the false doctrines of organic evolution or any of its associated doctrines, we will have knowledge taken away from us. This will lead to further loss of faith in the scriptures, and we will find other areas where we accept false doctrines of men. This will become a vicious circle, until we are taken captive by the devil, and we will have no chance of learning the mysteries of God throughout eternity. We will also lose our chance for exaltation."[128]

Yes, even a doctrine as seemingly inconsequential to our daily lives as the story of Creation can be the impetus for a tragic decline from faithful disciple of Christ to doubtful or half-hearted disciple to full-blown apostate. I have witnessed this process in action many times and I know it happens often. Those who deny or reject even the smallest doctrines or revealed principles eventually, unless they recant and repent, begin to question more obvious and consequential points of the Gospel until they eventually rebel against Church leaders, spend their time criticizing anyone who quotes the prophets, or commence on a crusade against the Church. We should all cross ourselves and exercise that childlike faith that our Savior so frequently implored us to develop (3 Nephi 11:37-38).

Other scriptural passages could be cited in refutation of Darwin's theories. I list only two more: 1) Moses' inspired account of the Creation which, if its chronology and testimony are to be taken at face value, suggests that Adam was created *before* the animals and was designated as "the first flesh upon the earth, the first man also," thus negating any and all possibility of an upward evolution from lower species (Moses 3:5-9, 19-20); and 2) Abraham's account of the seven creative periods and the Lord's reckoning of the time span in which these things were done (Abraham 3:4; Abraham 5:13; 2 Peter 3:8).

It is high time that we turned to the scriptures and studied them diligently, for they speak the truth. The Lord has not left us in the dark. He

---

[128] Peterson, *Using the Book of Mormon to Combat Falsehoods in Organic Evolution*, 22.

has flooded the earth with light and truth, but we must open our spiritual eyes in order to perceive the pure intelligence that is being communicated. When we do this, we will understand the scriptures and we will know that our prophets speak the truth – even when they say unpopular or hard things. We would do well to remember Nephi's rebuke:

> "Wherefore, the guilty taketh the truth to be hard, for it cutteth them to the very center.
>
> "And now my brethren, if ye were righteous and were willing to hearken to the truth, and give heed unto it, that ye might walk uprightly before God, then ye would not murmur because of the truth, and say: Thou speakest hard things against us" (1 Nephi 16:2-3).

The Lord is standing at the door and knocking. Will we let Him in?

Elder Melvin J. Ballard of the Quorum of the Twelve Apostles once referred to the greater intelligences of Heaven helping us, the lower intelligences, and handed a firm rebuke to the flawed and pseudo-intellectual reasoning of atheists who demand tangible proof of God's existence before believing in Him and man's divine origin. He taught:

> "Communications from higher intelligences have been brought to this world, revealing who we are, why we are here, and where we are going.
>
> "Greater than all other intelligences is the one called God. It has been proclaimed by these revelations that man is the child of God. Why look for the origin of man on this world, one of the latest and smallest of the universe? It is just as reasonable to look for the first evidence in this city. We know that there are older cities from which men come; so there are older worlds from which men come. We should wait until we have searched them, if we do not believe the divine revelations of man's origin, before definite conclusions are made. Those who do not believe their God because they have not seen him, or having eyes they do not see the evidences of his existence in this world, should wait until they have seen outside of their own state or country and have

traversed this small globe, and if he or the evidences of his existence are not found, then wait until a few of the millions of worlds, more glorious and splendid than ours, have been visited before saying that he is not; perchance he may be found there. This is eternal life to know the only true God and Jesus Christ, who he has sent. I know that my Redeemer lives as well as I know that I live. . . .

"The tangible evidences are so great that I know that God lives as well as I know that I see you and that you have an existence. I know that he is the Father of the spirits of all flesh. I know that his son Jesus Christ, our Savior, the Mighty Master of the elements, who has promised to bring us forth from the grave and give us immortal life, lives as well as I know that I live and exist. . . .

"If the Great Creator shall care for the sparrow, give to the withered flower the sweet assurance of another springtime, renew the life of the pulseless grain, reclothing it through a thousand resurrections, shall he leave neglected the soul of men, the height of his creation, sons and daughters in his own image?

"The soul may stand calm in the presence of death; it is the child of an eternal God and will never know annihilation."[129]

It must be admitted even by the hardened skeptic that Elder Ballard's reasoning and logic are sound. Yet, those who deny God's existence deny not only spiritual truth, but the scientific method. They cut corners, ignore evidence, and dismiss eyewitness testimonies – yet they pay religious devotion to the theory of evolution which no one has ever witnessed, no scientist has ever tested or replicated, and for which no credible evidence exists.

Though they have not explored even one trillionth of the endless depths of space, many scientists are prepared to pass judgement on what may or may not exist there. Because they do not see our Celestial God here on this telestial earth, they assume – without any proof except their own

---

[129] Hinckley, *Sermons and Missionary Services of Melvin Joseph Ballard*, 137-139.

prejudice – that He does not exist and, moreover, that He *cannot* exist elsewhere. This is very dishonest reasoning and flies in the face of the established scientific method. Such a flimsy methodology would be laughed out of any honorable court of law where facts and evidence hold sway. It is also the same defective reasoning used by the anti-Christs and apostates of *The Book of Mormon* record and the Saints should be wary of indulging it even for one moment (Jacob 7:9; Alma 30:23-28, 40-48; Helaman 16:18-20).

The truth is, as Elder Ballard recounted, that "man is the child of God." Tangible evidence exists of this relationship between the higher intelligences of Heaven and the lower intelligences who are slowly moving along the path of eternal increase. And millions of individuals, myself included, have received the very real and literal assurances from the Spirit that a higher realm exists. I have had too many direct communications from the other side to doubt for one second their veracity. I bear witness of the reality of the spirit world and of a God who hears and answers prayers.

This short life is barely a blip on the radar of Heaven. We are strangers here. This is only a temporary residence – a place of testing, trial, and growth. We existed before as the children of God in the spirit and in the future will we be resurrected and enjoy continued existence. I testify of these things. Yet, all of these are verities denied by evolutionists. If we follow their creed, we will be hopeless, rudderless, and miserable.

Truth is what we must cling to – the truth, the whole truth, and nothing but the truth. Many years ago, Elder Albert E. Bowen of the Quorum of the Twelve said:

> "Man's destiny and the means of achieving it – the gospel – must be taught even though it collides with political programs."[130]

It is not popular to teach about God and it is even less popular to teach the scriptural account of Creation. Instead, evolutionary theory dominates

---

[130] Elder Albert E. Bowen, in Newquist, ed., *Prophets, Principles and National Survival*, 45.

the scene. Our youth are bombarded throughout 15 years of compulsory schooling, and for an additional span of four or more years in universities, with godless Darwinism. Do we think they can survive this onslaught of lies without also being taught the Gospel in *at least* equal measure?

C.F. Potter, one of the co-signers of the first *Humanist Manifesto*, laughed at the idea that parents can curb the tide of humanism by merely sending their children to Church on Sunday. He gloated:

> "Education is thus a most powerful ally of humanism, and every American public school is a school of humanism. What can the theistic Sunday schools, meeting for an hour once a week, teaching only a fraction of the children, do to stem the tide of a five-day program of humanistic teaching?"[131]

Indeed, what *can* the Church do if parents allow their children to be smothered in an avalanche of anti-Christ propaganda denigrating his or her royal lineage? How can children grow properly in a spiritual sense if their parents deprive them of religious instruction in the home while allowing public school teachers and the media to indoctrinate them? How can we honestly believe that a short scripture reading, a nightly prayer, and perhaps a Family Home Evening now and then can protect our children from the Adversary with his honed system of deceit and indoctrination? Parents, we must do better. Our homes must become beacons of light for our families – centers of education surpassing anything our children might receive in the public schools.

Please do not be naïve – the humanist push *is* a deliberate plot to destroy people by first destroying Christianity and making public schools into secular centers of indoctrination. In 1983, John Dunphy – another avowed humanist revolutionary – wrote:

> "I am convinced that the battle for humankind's future must be waged and won in the public school classroom by teachers who correctly perceive their role as the proselytizers of a new faith:

---

[131] Ted Flynn, *Hope of the Wicked: The Master Plan to Rule the World* (Herndon, Virginia: MaxKol Communications, Inc., 2000), 6.

a religion of humanity that recognizes and respects the spark of what theologians call divinity in every human being. These teachers must embody the same selfless dedication as the most rabid fundamentalist preachers, for they will be ministers of another sort, utilizing a classroom instead of a pulpit to convey humanist values in whatever subject they teach, regardless of the educational level—preschool day care or large state university. The classroom must and will become an arena of conflict between the old and the new—the rotting corpse of Christianity, together with all its adjacent evils and misery, and the new faith of humanism."[132]

The humanists – and these are closely allied with the hardcore communists in back of all this – are openly erecting a new religion. This Devilish humanist creed, depending on which version you look at, either: 1) rejects God outright as in the case of atheism and Darwinism; or 2) rejects God's supremacy in favor of other gods or cosmic forces, as in the case of occultism, paganism, Wicca, and the New Age movement.

Both strains of this anti-Christ dogma are allied in their endeavor to destroy Christianity and fundamentally transform our society. Both atheism and occult worship lead men to reject their Creator, deny Jesus Christ, and adopt perverse views, habits, and attitudes. This nearly universal indoctrination is preparing mankind to accept Lucifer's religion – an occultic, theocratic, worldwide despotism – when it is eventually unveiled.

And though some like Dunphy claim to respect the spark of divinity within each person, theirs is a radically different conception of what this "divinity" entails. It is one born of pride and egotism, *not* an understanding that we are the children of God. We will discuss this counterfeit doctrine more in chapter five. In short, public schools that teach "the theories of Huxley, of Darwin, or of Miall" rather than the truth

---

[132] "Government school classrooms: temples of humanism?" Creation Ministries International, accessed August 17, 2018, https://creation.com/government-school-classrooms-temples-of-humanism.

about God and His Restored Gospel, are "where young infidels are made,"[133] to quote the prophet Brigham Young.

The Lord has placed a heavy burden upon parents in relation to the education of their young. It is *their duty* to see that their children are taught the truth and are not led astray by false teachings. I repeat: It is *their duty* and its discharge, for good or evil, will be answered upon their own heads. The revelations warn:

> "I have commanded you to bring up your children in light and truth" (D&C 93:40).

> "And again, inasmuch as parents have children in Zion, or in any of her stakes which are organized, that teach them not to understand the doctrine of repentance, faith in Christ the Son of the living God, and of baptism and the gift of the Holy Ghost by the laying on of the hands, when eight years old, the sin be upon the heads of the parents. . . .

> "And they shall also teach their children to pray, and to walk uprightly before the Lord" (D&C 68:25, 28).

> "And these words, which I command thee this day, shall be in thine heart:

> "And thou shalt teach them diligently unto thy children, and shalt talk of them when thou sittest in thine house, and when thou walkest by the way, and when thou liest down, and when thou risest up. . . .

> "And thou shalt write them upon the posts of thy house, and on thy gates. . . .

> "Then beware lest thou forget the Lord" (Deuteronomy 6:6-7, 9, 12).

---

[133] Brigham Young to Willard Young, October 19, 1876, in President Spencer W. Kimball, "The Second Century of Brigham Young University," BYU Devotional, October 10, 1975, https://rsc.byu.edu/archived/called-teach-legacy-karl-g-maeser/beginnings-brigham-young-academy-1876-84#_edn15.

When the theory of evolution is taught in schools to the exclusion of the doctrine of man's true origin, then men are being prepared for hell. If to know God is to know oneself, and if to know God is eternal life, then to reject one's own nature as well as God's by embracing false theories, is to embrace spiritual death. I believe parents who allow their children to imbibe humanism, Darwinism, Marxism, and very other destructive ism, without countering these lies with Gospel truth and spiritual light will stand accountable before their Maker.

To entrust one's children to the Church is not enough. While Gospel principles and doctrines never change, those principles are transmitted by flawed human beings – and even sometimes by wolves in sheep's clothing. President J. Reuben Clark, Jr. once warned the Saints:

> "The ravening wolves are amongst us, from our own membership, and they, more than any others, are clothed in sheep's clothing, because they wear the habiliments of the priesthood; they are they to whom Brother Widtsoe referred, as distorting the truth. We should be careful of them."[134]

Yes, we should be careful of anyone – even members of the Church – who is entrusted to teach. We must ensure that what is being taught conforms to the positions the Church has taken and the plain doctrines expounded in scripture.

At a General Conference of the Church, President Benson warned of the "subversion" of the Church Educational System, Church culture, and Church worship by members who had forsaken the revealed truths of God and replaced them in their hearts with the theories of men. He covered many points from the wickedness of birth control to the myth of world overpopulation to the perversion known as sex education, but it is the following comment that is most relevant to our discussion:

> "The world worships the learning of man. They trust in the arm of flesh. To them, men's reasoning is greater than God's revelations.

---

[134] President J. Reuben Clark, Jr., "Beware of False Prophets," General Conference, April, 1949, http://scriptures.byu.edu/#:t191:p527.

The precepts of man have gone so far in subverting our educational system that in many cases a higher degree today, in the so-called social sciences, can be tantamount to a major investment in error. Very few men build firmly enough on the rock of revelation to go through this kind of an indoctrination and come out untainted. Unfortunately, of those who succumb, some use their higher degree to get teaching positions even in our Church educational system, where they spread the falsehoods they have been taught. President Joseph F. Smith was right when he said that false educational ideas would be one of the three threats to the Church within (*Gospel Doctrine*, pp. 312-13)."[135]

Are we guilty of worshiping the "learning of man"? Do we trust more in the findings and guesses of scientists than the revealed knowledge of God? Do we, because of our earthly accolades, university degrees, and so-called advancement, discount the beliefs held by the ancients about the Creation, Flood, young earth, and other such scriptural accounts? According to President Benson, very few people are so firmly rooted in the Gospel as to be able to safely pass through university education without becoming contaminated with falsehoods. What a sobering thought! Let us examine ourselves closely to ensure that we are not, even inadvertently, spreading falsehoods and lies under the name of education, science, and learning.

One individual who has considered the ideas of evolutionary theory and rejected them was President Gordon B. Hinckley. President Hinckley once recounted:

"I remember when I was a college student there were great discussions on the question of organic evolution. I took classes in geology and biology and heard the whole story of Darwinism as it was then taught. I wondered about it. I thought much about it. But I did not let it throw me, for I read what the scriptures said about our origins and our relationship to God. Since then I have become acquainted with what to me is a far more important and

---

[135] President Ezra Taft Benson, "To the Humble Followers of Christ," General Conference, April, 1969, http://scriptures.byu.edu/#:t685:p401.

wonderful kind of evolution. It is the evolution of men and women as the sons and daughters of God, and of our marvelous potential for growth as children of our Creator."[136]

President Hinckley was tightly tethered to the Gospel. He knew what was in the scriptures and believed what he read. As a result, he did not sink under the tempestuous waves of intellectualism that crashed down upon him in university. Instead, he held fast to the truth and eventually came to understand and relish man's true potential as a child of God.

President Joseph Fielding Smith once answered a critical query regarding his stance on organic evolution thus. Note his dismay at the wide acceptance of these theories as "fact" by some who consider themselves learned:

"I will state frankly and positively that I am opposed to the present biological theories and the doctrine that man has been on the earth for millions of years. I am opposed to the present teachings in relation to the age of the earth which declare that the earth is millions of years old. Some modern scientists even claim that it is billions of years old. Naturally, since I believe in modern revelation, I cannot accept these so-called scientific teachings, for I believe them to be in conflict with the simple and direct word of the Lord that has come to us by divine revelation.

"If you have the idea that all capable and intelligent professors and scientists hold to these evolutionary doctrines, let me tell you that there are many who do not do so, and they are just as renowned and capable in their fields . . . not all the great thinkers and men of science are evolutionists and not all of them believe in these fantastic ages of the mortal earth.

"I regret that modern education in this country and largely in other countries, is dominated today by men holding these views."[137]

---

[136] President Gordon B. Hinckley, "God Hath Not Given Us a Spirit of Fear," *Ensign*, October, 1984, https://www.lds.org/ensign/1984/10/god-hath-not-given-us-the-spirit-of-fear?lang=eng.

President Smith was a man who said what he meant and meant what he said. Was he telling the truth when he said that the pseudo-scientific "teachings" of modern evolutionists and the geological scientists "cannot" be reconciled with the Gospel? I believe he was, but you may judge for yourself. One thing is certain – he believed that he was telling the truth. When a prophet bears his testimony of a principle of the Gospel, we ought to sit up and take notice.

Another man whose sincerity I do not doubt for an instant is our current prophet, President Russell M. Nelson. In an *Ensign* article titled "The Magnificence of Man," this learned, inspired servant of the Lord proclaimed:

> "Through the ages, some without scriptural understanding have tried to explain our existence by pretentious words such as *ex nihilo* (out of nothing). Others have deduced that, because of certain similarities between different forms of life, there has been a natural selection of the species, or organic evolution from one form to another. Many of these people have concluded that the universe began as a "big bang" that eventually resulted in the creation of our planet and life upon it.

> "To me, such theories are unbelievable! Could an explosion in a printing shop produce a dictionary? It is unthinkable! Even if it could be argued to be within a remote realm of possibility, such a dictionary could certainly not heal its own torn pages or renew its own worn corners or reproduce its own subsequent editions!

> "We are children of God, created by him and formed in his image. Recently I studied the scriptures to find how many times they testify of the divine creation of man. Looking up references that referred to *create, form* (or their derivatives), with either *man, men, male,* or *female* in the same verse, I found that there are at least fifty-five verses of scripture that attest to our divine creation. . . .

---

[137] Smith, *Answers to Gospel Questions*, Vol. 5, 112-113.

> "It is incumbent upon each informed and spiritually attuned person to help overcome such foolishness of men who would deny divine creation or think that man simply evolved. By the Spirit, we perceive the truer and more believable wisdom of God."[138]

What an incredible statement from an incredible man! As one spiritually attuned, President Nelson took the opportunity to declare his witness of our divine origin and sound the warning voice against the "foolishness of men who would deny divine creation or think that man simply evolved." He even named organic evolution as one of the false theories that the spiritually blind cling to.

I think it is impossible for one who believes the scriptures to simultaneously believe the doctrine of organic evolution. Surely, such a person cannot claim to have truly read the scriptures. And if he has, then I apply Moroni's comment:

> "Behold I say unto you, he that denieth these things knoweth not the gospel of Christ; yea, he has not read the scriptures; if so, he does not understand them" (Mormon 9:8).

One who *does* understand the scriptures is President Russell M. Nelson, the prophet, seer, and revelator for our day. It was he who said the theories of the Darwinists are "unbelievable." These ideas, said he, cannot even be argued "within a remote realm of possibility." One of the things that makes them so unbelievable, besides the sheer illogic of these unscientific, evidence-lacking theories, is the multitude of scriptural testimonies of divine Creation – at least fifty-five of them.

Brothers and sisters, isn't it time we got with the program? Shouldn't we finally accept the teachings of the Savior's prophets, both ancient and modern? Isn't it about time we humbled ourselves and bowed our meager intellects before the wisdom the holy scriptures and the burning witness of the Holy Ghost?

---

[138] President Russell M. Nelson, "The Magnificence of Man," *Ensign*, January, 1988, https://www.lds.org/ensign/1988/01/the-magnificence-of-man?lang=eng.

Dozens upon dozens of additional quotations from presidents of the Church, apostles, and other General Authorities confirming the truth of man's origin could be cited. I trust, however, that these are sufficient to convince any honest soul of the reality. Only those past feeling or unwilling to sincerely ask God for a confirmation of these things will still subscribe to the everlastingly false dogma of Darwinian evolution after reading these unapologetic statements from inspired men of God – prophets of the Almighty. I bear my personal witness that the theory of man's evolution from a lesser species to our current form is entirely, eternally false. I firmly believe that one will eventually lose his faith if he embraces this Satanic notion in whole or part.

It is only fair, after having discussed why evolution is a false dogma, to discuss the truth about our physical creation on earth. There are many things we do not know and which will be revealed at a future time, however we know the basics. President Brigham discoursed on this subject of physical creation perhaps more than any other prophet of this dispensation. On one occasion, President Young taught:

> "The life that is within us is a part of an eternity of life, and is organized spirit, which is clothed upon by tabernacles, thereby constituting our present being, which is designed for the attainment of further intelligence. The matter composing our bodies and spirits has been organized from the eternity of matter that fills immensity. . . .

> "Jesus Christ says, "And this is life eternal, that they might know thee the only true God, and Jesus Christ, whom thou has sent." We are not now in a capacity to know him in his fulness of glory. We know a few things that he has revealed concerning himself, but there are a great many which we do not know. When people have secured to themselves eternal life, they are where they can understand the true character of their Father and God, and the object of the creation, fall, and redemption of man after the creation of this world. These points have ever been subjects for speculation with all classes of believers, and are subjects of much interest to those who entertain a deep anxiety to know how to secure to themselves eternal life. Our bodies are organized from

the eternity of matter, from such matter as we breathe, and from such matter as is found in the vegetable and mineral kingdoms. This matter is organized into a world, with all its appendages, by whom? By the Almighty; and we see it peopled by men and women who are made in the image of God.

"All this vast creation was produced from element in its unorganized state; the mountains, rivers, seas, valleys, plains, and the animal, vegetable, and mineral kingdoms beneath and around us, all speaking forth the wonderful works of the Great God. Shall I say that the seeds of vegetables were planted here by the Characters that framed and built this world—that the seeds of every plant composing the vegetable kingdom were brought from another world? This would be news to many of you. Who brought them here? It matters little to us whether it was John, James, William, Adam, or Bartholomew who brought them; but it was some Being who had power to frame this earth with its seas, valleys, mountains, and rivers, and cause it to teem with vegetable and animal life.

"Here let me state to all philosophers of every class upon the earth, When you tell me that father Adam was made as we make adobies from the earth, you tell me what I deem an idle tale. When you tell me that the beasts of the field were produced in that manner, you are speaking idle words devoid of meaning. There is no such thing in all the eternities where the Gods dwell. Mankind are here because they are the offspring of parents who were first brought here from another planet, and power was given them to propagate their species, and they were commanded to multiply and replenish the earth. The offspring of Adam and Eve are commanded to take the rude elements, and, by the knowledge God has given, to convert them into everything required for their life, health, adornment, wealth, comfort, and consolation. Have we the knowledge to do this? We have. Who gave us this knowledge? Our Father who made us; for he is the only wise God, and to him we owe allegiance; to him we owe our lives. He has brought us forth and taught us all we know. We are not indebted to any other power or God for all our great blessings."[139]

Man was not made in the same way a brickmaker makes bricks, or "adobies." That is, he was not taken and formed by hand or through some evolutionary process. He was not pieced together from lifeless elements. He was not formed through some spontaneous blowing of the wind or wave the magical wand which brought the raw elements together. This is an "idle tale." Neither were the animals made in this manner.

To be sure, all living beings on this earth were made of the materials constituting this earth, the raw element of the universe, but it was *not* an evolutionary or arbitrary process of any sort. Adam's body was created through procreation. Adam was commanded to create bodies for others in the same manner in which his own tabernacle had been created – by taking "the rude elements" and, through the natural processes of his body, begetting bodies after his image through procreation.

To further clarify this revolutionary point, we quote from three others of President Young's sermons and then supplement these with additional witnesses:

> "God has made His children like Himself to stand erect, and has endowed them with intelligence and power and dominion over all His works, and given them the same attributes which He Himself possesses. He created man, as we create our children; for there is no other process of creation in heaven, on the earth, in the earth, or under the earth, or in all the eternities, that is, that were, or that ever will be. As the Apostle Paul has expressed it, "For in him we live, and move, and have our being." "Forasmuch then as we are the offspring of God, we ought not to think that the Godhead is like unto gold, or silver, or stone, graven by art or man's device." There exist fixed laws and regulations by which the elements are fashioned to fulfill their destiny in all the varied

---

[139] President Brigham Young, *Journal of Discourses*, Vol. 7, 285-286, October 9, 1859, http://jod.mrm.org/7/282.

kingdoms and orders of creation, and this process of creation is from everlasting to everlasting."[140]

"Though we have it in history that our father Adam was made of the dust of this earth, and that he knew nothing about his God previous to being made here, yet it is not so; and when we learn the truth we shall see and understand that he helped to make this world, and was the chief manager in that operation.

"He was the person who brought the animals and the seeds from other planets to this world, and brought a wife with him and stayed here. You may read and believe what you please as to what is found written in the Bible. Adam was made from the dust of an earth, but not from the dust of this earth. He was made as you and I are made, and no person was ever made upon any other principle."[141]

"Things were first created spiritually; the Father actually begat the spirits, and they were brought forth and lived with Him. Then He commenced the work of creating earthly tabernacles, precisely as He had been created in this flesh himself, by partaking of the coarse material that was organized and composed this earth, until His system was charged with it, consequently the tabernacles of His children were organized from the coarse materials of this earth."[142]

We do not discuss these powerful principles often in our Sunday School meetings, or in any meetings, frankly, yet the prophets have taught them more than once in this dispensation. President Brigham Young was emphatic on the point. Other apostles, before and after him, have also taught it plainly enough.

---

[140] President Brigham Young, *Journal of Discourses*, Vol. 11, 122, June 18, 1865, http://jod.mrm.org/11/119.

[141] President Brigham Young, *Journal of Discourses*, Vol. 3, 319, April 20, 1856, http://jod.mrm.org/3/316.

[142] President Brigham Young, *Journal of Discourses*, Vol. 4, 218, February 8, 1857, http://jod.mrm.org/4/215.

Now, I add a quick caution. Do not allow yourself, in your private studies, to be hoodwinked by those who twist President Brigham Young's words and preach the "Adam-God theory" – that is, the theory which holds that Adam is our Heavenly Father. This false idea comes from a sermon given by President Young which was incorrectly transcribed. The notion spread from there and now has a cult following despite being repeatedly denounced by numerous presidents of the Church and by the holy scriptures. My favorite refutation of this false theory is found in Elder Mark E. Petersen's book *Adam: Who is He?* I leave you to study Elder Petersen's words prayerfully as we proceed with our present topic.

President George Q. Cannon bore witness that what President Brigham Young taught on the subject of man's earthly origin was the truth. On October 12, 1861, he wrote the following in *The Latter-day Saints' Millennial Star* about President Young's teachings of man's origin:

> "He unmistakably declares man's origins to be altogether of a celestial character – that not only is his spirit of heavenly descent, but his bodily organization too, – that the latter is *not* taken from the lower animals, but from the originally *celestial* body of the great Father of humanity.

> "Taking the doctrine of man's origin as seen from this higher point of view, and comparing it with the low assumptive theories of uninspired men . . . how great the contrast appears! "Look on this picture" – Man, the offspring of an *ape!* "And on this" – Man, the image of *God*, his *Father!* How wide the contrast and how different the feelings produced in the breast! In the one case, we instinctively shrink with dread at the bare insinuation; while in the other, the heart beats with higher and warmer and stronger emotions of love, of adoration, and praise; the soul is cheered and invigorated in its daily struggles to emancipate itself from the thraldom of surrounding evils and darkness pertaining to this lower sphere of existence, and is animated with a purer and

nobler zeal in its onward and upward journey to that Divine Presence whence it originally came."[143]

Indeed, what a noble, inspiring, uplifting feeling this knowledge gives! Who can truly be satisfied and happy if they believe their ancestors were apes or any other lower form of beast or creature? We are not from below, but from above. *We are of the lineage of the Gods!*

President Joseph F. Smith taught this principle as well. In 1912, the First Presidency under President Smith, clearly taking their cue from President Brigham Young, wrote that:

> "Our father Adam – that is our earthly father – the progenitor of the human race of man, stands at the head being 'Michael the Archangel, the Ancient of Days,' and was not fashioned from earth like an adobe, but "begotten by his Father in Heaven." Adam is called in the Bible "the son of God"" (Luke 3:38).[144]

I will point out that Luke 3:38 has been amended by the Prophet Joseph Smith to read ". . . Adam, who was formed of God, and the first man upon the earth," as opposed to "Adam, which was the son of God." Yet, Adam was also a son of God apparently formed by the Father the way that all people are formed here upon the earth.

Another time, President Smith stated:

> "God originated and designed all things, and all are his children. We are born into the world as his offspring; endowed with the same attributes. The children of men have sprung from the Almighty, whether the world is willing to acknowledge it or not.

---

[143] President George Q. Cannon, *The Latter-day Saints' Millennial Star*, Vol. 23, October 12, 1861, 654, https://contentdm.lib.byu.edu/digital/collection/MStar/id/22135.

[144] First Presidency letter to Samuel O. Bennion, February 26, 1912, see James F. Stoddard III, "A Response to the Erroneously Attributed "1910 First Presidency Message,"" LDS Answers, September 20, 2016, accessed August 29, 2018, http://ldsanswers.org/a-response-to-the-erroneously-attributed-1910-first-presidency-message/; and "Adam and Eve Were Physically Begotten by God," ScottWoodward.org, accessed August 29, 2018, http://scottwoodward.org/creation_adambegottenbygod.html.

He is the Father of our spirits. He is the originator of our earthly tabernacles. We live and move and have our being in God our heavenly Father."[145]

The Father is the originator, or progenitor, of our physical tabernacles as He is the primal ancestor of our spirits. In order to make these glorious bodies mortal, Adam had to choose to transgress a lower law to bring about death and mortality. Eventually, we will again inhabit immortal bodies such as Adam had in the Garden of Eden, yet of a more permanent and glorified character.

President Heber C. Kimball also taught this doctrine. He stated quite clearly:

> "Now, brethren, you have got a spirit in you, and that spirit was created and organized—was born and begotten by our Father and our God before we ever took these bodies; and these bodies were formed by him, and through him, and of him, just as much as the spirit was; for I will tell you, he commenced and brought forth spirits; and then, when he completed that work, he commenced and brought forth tabernacles for those spirits to dwell in. I came through him, both spirit and body. God made the elements that they are made of, just as much as he made anything."[146]

To President Heber C. Kimball, we came through God "both spirit and body." Our bodies "were formed by him, and through him, and of him, just as much as the spirit was." He is truly the Father in every sense of the term. This earth was organized upon natural principles. And mankind came to earth through the most natural and divine of all processes – procreation. We are in the likeness of our Heavenly Parents more than we sometimes allow ourselves to believe.

I bear witness that we came not from a lower species but from a higher state, that God is our beloved Heavenly Father, that we are literally His

---

[145] Smith, *Gospel Doctrine*, 62.

[146] President Heber C. Kimball, *Journal of Discourses*, Vol. 6, 31, November 8, 1857, http://jod.mrm.org/6/28.

children, and that we descended from the Gods! If we could only grasp how remarkable our lineage is, it would change us in the very depths of our being. I pray that we will reject the notion of Devilish Darwinism and instead embrace the truth of our sacred lineage as the offspring of God Almighty.

There is one additional reason that I raise my voice so emphatically against Darwinism. I refer to Darwinism's track record of unparalleled destruction and misery. The horrors of the 20th Century came about largely because of the Darwinist philosophy, or because of those philosophies justified and undergirded by the theory of evolution. Let me briefly explain.

My first two books are respectfully titled *A Century of Red* and *Red Gadiantons: What the Prophets Have Taught about the Communist Secret Combination that Threatens Mankind.* As the titles suggest, these books cover communism and secret combinations. I am something of an expert on the communist conspiracy and the occult workings of Luciferianism. I sincerely desire more people would read my books in order to comprehend the enemy we are up against. It is a *commandment* to awake to a sense of our awful situation caused by secret conspiracies (Ether 8:24) and I commend my books to you as tools to aid in that awakening process.

In my second book, *Red Gadiantons*, I provide dozens of statements from the Church and General Authorities regarding communism. For instance, the following is the *official* position of the Church on communism, issued by the First Presidency under President David O. McKay during General Conference in April 1966:

> "The position of this Church on the subject of Communism has never changed. We consider it the greatest satanical threat to peace, prosperity, and the spread of God's work among men that exists on the face of the earth. . . .

> "The entire concept and philosophy of Communism is diametrically opposed to everything for which the Church stands – belief in Deity, belief in the dignity and eternal nature of man, and the application of the gospel to efforts for peace in the world.

Communism is militantly atheistic and is committed to the destruction of faith wherever it may be found. . . .

"Communism debases the individual and makes him the enslaved tool of the state, to which he must look for sustenance and religion. Communism destroys man's God-given free agency.

"No member of this Church can be true to his faith, nor can any American be loyal to his trust, while lending aid, encouragement, or sympathy to any of these false philosophies; for if he does, they will prove snares to his feet."[147]

Yes, communism is the *"greatest satanical threat"* to the Church and to mankind as a whole. This is significant because communism presupposes a belief in Darwinist evolution and a total rejection of God. Behind the scenes, communism is Satanic and its chief leaders were avowed Satanists who formed the world's largest and most destructive secret combination. I provide ample evidence for this in my books. But for our purposes here, we note that communism is outwardly atheistic and views man as an evolved creature to be molded and used by the state.

Embracing Darwin's false ideas is often the first step in a person's journey from normal to communist, from moral to amoral, and from Christian to atheist – or worse. One example will suffice. Joseph Stalin, the world's second greatest mass murderer behind fellow communist Mao Tse-tung, started his life as a Christian. He attended a Christian school, sang in the choir, and planned – like Darwin originally had – to become a priest. However, Stalin's life dramatically altered course when he secretly read a banned book titled *On the Origin of Species* by one Charles Darwin.[148] From the moment Stalin read that blasphemous book, he devolved into a veritable monster who delighted in thievery, rapine, death, and wanton destruction, who led a debauched and hedonistic private life, and who headed the most sadistic and brutal regime in world history.

---

[147] President David O. McKay, "Only One Standard of Morality," April 9, 1966, Conference Report, 109-110, http://scriptures.byu.edu/#:t5c7:p51c.

[148] Simon Sebag Montefiore, *Young Stalin* (New York: Alfred A. Knopf, 2007), 49.

Every genocidal dictator of the last century, as far as I can ascertain in my studies, was a Darwinist – and many were simultaneously Darwinists and Satanists. This seeming paradox is not surprising at all when we recall that Satan appeared to the anti-Christ Korihor as an angel of light and told him to preach the doctrine of atheism (Alma 30:52-53). Among Korihor's teachings included principles that appear lifted straight out of Darwin's own work, such as a repudiation of a Creator, a rejection of sin, judgement day, and the need for a Savior, a denial of an afterlife, and a belief in the survival of the fittest (Alma 30:12-18). In like manner, the Devil has inspired the modern anti-Christ communists who have become the biggest proponents of the theory of evolution on planet earth.

The communists – and their socialist, humanist, secularist, progressive, libertine, liberal, and democratic dupes and allies – have institutionalized Darwin's teachings, elevating him to the level of a prophet. Karl Marx, a false prophet in his own right, was enamored with Darwin. The two were contemporaries and they received their inspiration from the same evil source. Marx once wrote to a fellow conspirator:

> "Darwin's book is very important and serves me as a basis in natural science for the class struggle in history."[149]

Darwinism thus became the basis, or justification, for Marx's philosophy of class warfare and violent global revolution. This evolutionary basis was reiterated time and time again by Lenin, Stalin, Mao, and other communist kingpins. Latter-day Saint historian W. Cleon Skousen identified this humanistic dogma as underpinning the communist version of "morality." He wrote:

> "Marx and Engels accepted the fact that the remaking of the world will have to be a cruel and ruthless task and that it will involve the destruction of all who stand in the way. This is necessary, they said, in order to permit the Communist leadership to wipe out the social and economic sins of human imperfection in one clean sweep and then gradually introduce a society of

---

[149] Harun Yahya, *Communism in Ambush: How the Scourge of the 20th Century is Preparing for Fresh Savagery* (Istanbul: Global Publishing, 2003), 15.

perfect harmony which will allow all humanity to live scientifically, securely and happily during all future ages.

"However, before striking out on such a bold course, the founders of Communism realized they would have to develop a whole new approach to morals and ethics for their followers. Lenin summarized it as follows: "We say that our morality is wholly subordinated to the interest of the class struggle of the proletariat" . . . This concept is simply intended to say that "the end justifies the means." It is not wrong to cheat, lie, violate oaths or even destroy human life if it is for a good cause. This code of *no* morals accounts for the amoral behavior on the part of Communists which is frequently incomprehensible to non-Communists."[150]

The Marxist version of "morality" is the same that the Devil revealed to Korihor – "whatsoever a man did was no crime" (Alma 30:17). Indeed, the only amoral act for a communist is to *not* serve the conspiracy's interests. Again, we note the parallel to Nephite secret conspirators who were oath-bound to support their fellow schemers and the Gadianton cause at all costs – even if it required murder, theft, or violation of the laws of the land (Helaman 6:21-30). Beyond that, they were free to debauch themselves or behave in any manner they chose.

The only reason these conspirators would not fear divine retribution for their crimes is if they believed some form of Darwinism/atheism or if they had assurances from Satan that he would win his war against God and that his followers would be rewarded for their devotion. Inasmuch as the majority of communists and their allies are not part of the sworn Brotherhood of darkness, it is reasonable to assume that the former is true; namely, that they believe man is a mere animal, a creature of happenstance and evolution.

It would almost appear as if the Apostle Paul was talking about the communists and their evolutionist allies when he said:

---

[150] W. Cleon Skousen, *The Naked Communist* (Salt Lake City, UT: The Reviewer, 1985), 38.

"[W]hen they knew God, they glorified him not as God, neither were thankful; but became vain in their imaginations, and their foolish heart was darkened.

"Professing themselves to be wise, they became fools. . . .

"Who changed the truth of God into a lie, and worshipped and served the creature more than the Creator" (Romans 1:21-22, 25).

The brilliant Turkish historian Harun Yahya has written much about the communist-Darwinist connection. In his phenomenal book *Communism in Ambush*, he explained:

"When examined closely, the theories of Marx-Engels and Darwin appear to be in total harmony, as if they have arisen from a single source. Darwin applied materialist philosophy to nature, while Marx-Engels applied it to history. . . .

"Savagery is the evident, natural result of the Communist idea that a human being is just another "species." As Marx never tired of pointing out, Communism is based on Darwin's theory of evolution, which describes human beings as advanced animals and which suggests that conflict and struggle among peoples, oppression, cruelty, use of force are natural and legitimate. If someone who accepts this philosophy has enough power and resources, he will find it easy to commit all kids of cruelty. . . .

"Communism is definitely rooted in Darwinism — not a "deviant version of Darwinism," but authentic Darwinism. The source of the ideas that human beings are a species of animal, that history progresses through a natural and inevitable conflict, that no one is responsible for his actions is Charles Darwin. Darwin simply proposed the theory; the Communists implemented it. The bloody account of 20th-century Communism, which presents all the nonsense of dialectical materialism in the guise of "science," is in reality applied Darwinism."[151]

---

[151] Yahya, *Communism in Ambush*, 14, 81, 85.

Communism is completely and thoroughly "rooted in Darwinism." It is the purest expression of Darwinism in action. The theory of organic evolution provided the foundation for the philosophy that the Church has called the "greatest satanical threat" to mankind – an ideology responsible for the greatest mass murders and genocides in world history. More than 100 million human beings were slaughtered in Soviet Russia and Red China alone, to say nothing of the billions of humans enslaved by socialistic regimes and the tens of millions of souls who lost their lives in world wars initiated by these enemies of God and humanity.

It appears reasonable to say that one cannot be a communist without first being an evolutionist. Communism does not make sense unless seen as a product of evolution – an attempt to use the "natural" forces of struggle and class warfare to create the "new Soviet man" and forcibly turn the world into a "utopia." What is certain to me is that anyone who believes man evolved from lower lifeforms or that he is just a brute beast is right at home in the communist camp.

It is true that people are not born communists or socialists. Rather, they are led there by a gradual loss of faith in God and humanity engendered by the "false educational ideas" President Benson warned about so emphatically, chief among which is the theory of organic evolution. The origin of the communist species, then, is Darwinism.

The aim of this false evolutionary religion is to destroy his man's faith in his Creator and to retrograde his mental faculties. And this is the inevitable effect upon those who indulge these pseudo-scientific concepts. They reject the light and love darkness, thus condemning themselves by rejecting their own eternal nature and the nature of man and God (D&C 93:31-32).

Yet, notwithstanding the almost universal popularity of Darwin's false theories, the truth is that man is the *literal* offspring of God. His is descended from the lineage of the Gods! Man cannot erase his spiritual DNA. He cannot, as much as he might try, obliterate the fact that he is a child of the Eternal Father. Man's very soul rebels at this unnatural thought and a person who embraces it becomes miserable like Charles Darwin became after rejecting God in favor of mammon (Matthew 6:24).

The Church's position relative to man's origin is clear – *we are His literal offspring*. We lived with Him for an infinitely long period of time in the pre-earth state. We are His sons and daughters and, as such, have inherited His attributes, potentials, and powers. We are gods in embryo. If we keep the commandments, we can be brought back into God's presence through the Redemption of Jesus Christ and the cleansing effects of His blood. Any theory that denies these truths cannot edify, only leads to darkness, and comes directly from Satan (D&C 50:23).

The Devil, who is "an enemy to all righteousness" (Alma 34:23), wants us to deny our royal heritage. He assaults our spiritual pedigree by numbing our minds and deadening our spirits with incoherent theories that belittle and degrade our very nature and make a mock of the holy scriptures. Let us be exceedingly careful whose side we choose to stand on. Only the truth can "make [us] free" (John 8:32) while error causes us to "walk in darkness" (D&C 95:12) and "fall into the ditch," where no doubt Marx and Darwin – the "blind leaders of the blind" – now reside with their dark master (Matthew 15:14).

Chapter Fifth

Godmen – Satan's Counterfeit

For every truth God reveals, Satan presents a cheap counterfeit. Satan is unintelligent and can only *react* to God's actions. When God acts, the Adversary reacts in an inferior, crude, and impish manner. His impotence is on full display each and every time he attempts to mirror what the incomparable Lord has done.

Satan presents forgeries, counterfeits, and imitations while the Lord gives us the genuine article. Often, Satan's forgeries are so dazzling that they blind us to the lies and we only glimpse the slivers of truth strategically impeded throughout the counterfeit in order to more effectively deceive. The Devil's increased effort to deceive is a sign that the Lord's Kingdom is growing stronger.

President James E. Faust observed:

> "I think we will witness increasing evidence of Satan's power as the kingdom of God grows stronger. I believe Satan's ever-expanding efforts are some proof of the truthfulness of this work. In the future the opposition will be both more subtle and more open. It will be masked in greater sophistication and cunning, but it will also be more blatant. We will need greater spirituality to perceive all of the forms of evil and greater strength to resist it. But the disappointments and setbacks to the work of God will be temporary, for the work will go forward (see D&C 65:2)."[152]

---

[152] President James E. Faust, "The Great Imitator," General Conference, October, 1987, https://www.lds.org/general-conference/1987/10/the-great-imitator?lang=eng.

While Satan has enjoyed stunning success in blinding minds and hearts and enslaving billions of God's children, he knows his days are numbered (Revelation 12:12). Therefore, his propaganda will increase and his counterfeits will multiple – both in number and ferocity. They will be delicately sophisticated yet ever "more blatant" to those who have the spirit of discernment.

Elder Bruce R. McConkie explained the Devil's power to deceive by imitation in this way:

> "Lucifer is the Great Imitator. He patterns his kingdom after that of God the Lord. The Lord proclaims a plan of salvation; Satan sponsors a plan of damnation. Signs follow those who believe and obey the law of the gospel, and false signs, false wonders, false miracles attend the ministry of the Master of Sin. Knowledge is power, and because he knows more about many things than mortal men, the Great Imitator is able to blind the eyes and deceive the hearts of men and to put his own seal of verity, that of false miracles, on his damning philosophies. Thus those who place themselves wholly at his disposal have power to imitate the deeds of the prophets, as the magicians of Egypt imitated the miracles of Moses and as Simon the sorcerer sought to duplicate the works of Peter."[153]

The Devil always imitates the works of the Lord, but for his own evil purposes. He does not edify or save, he demeans and damns. While the Lord has His Priesthood that blesses lives, serves, and performs saving ordinances, Lucifer has his own priesthood that teaches the art of self-aggrandizement, deceives, and ultimately drags people "carefully down to hell" (2 Nephi 28:21). When God calls and inspires prophets, Satan sends his false ministers to preach the gospel of damnation. When the Lord raises up a Joseph Smith or Brigham Young, the Devil raises up a Charles Darwin or Karl Marx. Always and forever, Satan operates by counterfeits.

---

[153] Bruce R. McConkie, *Doctrinal New Testament Commentary*, Vol. 3 (Salt Lake City, UT: Bookcraft, Inc., 1990), 524-525.

President M. Russell Ballard has warned the Saints about false prophets and deceivers – even among the membership of the Church. He said:

> "When we think of false prophets and false teachers, we tend to think of those who espouse an obviously false doctrine or presume to have authority to teach the true gospel of Christ according to their own interpretation. We often assume that such individuals are associated with small radical groups on the fringes of society. However, I reiterate: there are false prophets and false teachers who have or at least claim to have membership in the Church. There are those who, without authority, claim Church endorsement to their products and practices. Beware of such. . . .

> "Therefore, let us beware of false prophets and false teachers, both men and women, who are self-appointed declarers of the doctrines of the Church and who seek to spread their false gospel and attract followers by sponsoring symposia, books, and journals whose contents challenge fundamental doctrines of the Church. Beware of those who speak and publish in opposition to God's true prophets and who actively proselyte others with reckless disregard for the eternal well-being of those whom they seduce. Like Nehor and Korihor in the Book of Mormon, they rely on sophistry to deceive and entice others to their views. They "set themselves up for a light unto the world, that they may get gain and praise of the world; but they seek not the welfare of Zion" (2 Ne. 26:29). . . .

> "Regardless of which particular false doctrines they teach, false prophets and false teachers are an inevitable part of the last days. "False prophets," according to the Prophet Joseph Smith, "always arise to oppose the true prophets". . . .

> "However, in the Lord's Church there is no such thing as a "loyal opposition." One is either for the kingdom of God and stands in

defense of God's prophets and apostles, or one stands opposed."[154]

In every Gospel dispensation, there have been false teachers and false prophets who have labored to lead the people of God astray. These are most easily identified by their opposition to the positions taken by the *true* prophets who are called of God and ordained through His Priesthood. Some members have been deceived into thinking they can keep one foot in the Church and one in Babylon, or that they may pick and choose which doctrines to believe and which to reject, but the reality is that they must take a stand for or against the Church.

There is no middle ground in spiritual and moral matters. We either declare our allegiance for Christ and His Gospel Plan or we, by default, link arms with the opposition. Joseph Fielding McConkie once said:

> "We cannot march with both the Israelites and the Philistines. Light and darkness will never meet. Christ and Satan will never shake hands. As to Christ and His gospel, there can be no middle ground, no neutrality. You stand with the prophets or against them."[155]

If we stand against the prophets, we will be dragged down to an everlasting destruction like apostates and scoffers in former days. Nephi testified of the terrible fate awaiting those who lift up their heads in pride and fight against the Lord's servants. He said:

> "[T]he great and spacious building was the pride of the world; and it fell, and the fall thereof was exceedingly great. And the angel of the Lord spake unto me again, saying: Thus shall be the destruction of all nations, kindreds, tongues, and people, that

---

[154] President M. Russell Ballard, "Beware of False Prophets and False Teachers," General Conference, October, 1999, https://www.lds.org/general-conference/1999/10/beware-of-false-prophets-and-false-teachers?lang=eng.

[155] Joseph Fielding McConkie, "The First Vision and Religious Tolerance," in *A Witness for the Restoration: Essays in Honor of Robert J. Matthews*, ed. Kent P. Jackson and Andrew C. Skinner (Provo, UT: Religious Studies Center, Brigham Young University, 2007), 177–99.

shall fight against the twelve apostles of the Lamb" (1 Nephi 11:36).

The biggest difficulty, however, arises not when members openly leave the Church and renounce their membership, but when they remain within the Church, corrupting other members from within either through their misunderstanding of true doctrine or through deliberate deception. On this note, the Prophet Joseph Smith taught:

> "A man must have the discerning of spirits before he can drag into daylight this hellish influence and unfold it unto the world in all its soul-destroying, diabolical, and horrid colors; for nothing is a greater injury to the children of men than to be under the influence of a false spirit when they think they have the Spirit of God. Thousands have felt the influence of its terrible power and baneful effects. Long pilgrimages have been undertaken, penances endured, and pain, misery and ruin have followed in their train; nations have been convulsed, kingdoms overthrown, provinces laid waste, and blood, carnage and desolation are habiliments in which it has been clothed.
>
> "The Turks, the Hindoos, the Jews, the Christians, the Indian; in fact all nations have been deceived, imposed upon and injured through the mischievous effects of false spirits."[156]

Even the most well-meaning individuals can easily be led astray by "false spirits" who reveal lies and half-truths to those who do not assiduously guard themselves against deception. The most precarious spiritual state to be in is when we are living in error or hold wrong ideas and principles, but still believe we are doing God's work. We see this condition exhibited every day. Many believe they are righteous, yet cling to the false theories of men, such as Darwinism and socialism. When they embrace falsehoods, yet believe they are righteous and worthy and learned, then the Devil has cheated their souls and has taken them captive.

---

[156] Joseph Smith, *Documentary History of the Church*, Vol. 4, 573, April 1, 1842, https://byustudies.byu.edu/content/volume-4-chapter-33.

Helaman chapter 16, verses 15 and 22, describe how the Devil cheated the souls of a generation of Nephites. We read:

> "[T]he people began to harden their hearts, all save it were the most believing part of them . . . and began to depend upon their own strength and upon their own wisdom. . . .

> "And many more things did the people imagine up in their hearts, which were foolish and vain; and they were much disturbed, for Satan did stir them up to do iniquity continually; yea, he did go about spreading rumors and contentions upon all the face of the land, that he might harden the hearts of the people against that which was good and against that which should come."

The Nephites began to disbelieve the prophets and instead turned to their own strength and so-called wisdom. Instead of believing the revealed word, they believed their own theories and intellectual learning and trusted in the arm of flesh (2 Nephi 4:34). Because the Devil whispered rumors in their ears, the Nephites imagined up "foolish and vain" things, adopted unsound ideas, and became a wicked People. Their hearts were hardened against that which was true and good and worthy and they clung to their errors while boasting about how sophisticated and strong they were. The only ones who survived this mass delusion were the "more believing part" of the People – those who exercised childlike faith in the revelations of God as delivered through the prophets.

President Dallin H. Oaks expressed his desire that the Saints develop discernment so that they might detect the falsehoods of Satan's modern deceptions and false religious practices. He stated:

> "This power of discernment is essential if we are to distinguish between genuine spiritual gifts and the counterfeits Satan seeks to use to deceive men and women and thwart the work of God. . . .

> "Satan-inspired and man-made counterfeits of spiritual gifts have been present throughout our religious history. This is evident from the enchantments wrought by Pharoah's sorcerers and magicians (see Ex. 7:11, 22; Ex. 8:7), and from Isaiah's warnings

against "wizards that peep, and that mutter" and "them that have familiar spirits" (Isa. 8:19). The Savior warned against false Christs and false prophets who "shall show great signs and wonders, insomuch, that, if possible, they shall deceive the very elect . . . according to the covenant." (JS—H 1:22.) The Apostle John said, "Try the spirits whether they are of God: because many false prophets are gone out into the world." (1 Jn. 4:1.)"[157]

Like in ancient times, the Master Deceiver is going throughout the land spreading lies and urging people to adopt false traditions like those of ancient days. We must develop spiritual maturity and fortify ourselves with the armor of God so that we will not be "tossed to and fro, and carried about with every wind of doctrine, by the sleight of men, and cunning craftiness, whereby they lie in wait to deceive" (Ephesians 4:14).

President Brigham Young also taught and warned of Satan's counterfeits. He warned that the Devil was giving false revelations and visions to mankind and convincing them, through his deceptive power, that *these* were the true communications from Heaven. Said he:

> "If true principles are revealed from heaven to men, and if there are angels, and there is a possibility of their communicating to the human family, always look for an opposite power, an evil power, to give manifestations also: look out for the counterfeit.

> "There is evil in the world, and there is also good. Was there ever a counterfeit without a true coin? No. Is there communication from God? Yes. From holy angels? Yes; and we have been proclaiming these facts during nearly thirty years. Are there any communications from evil spirits? Yes; and the Devil is making the people believe very strongly in revelations from the spirit world. This is called spiritualism."[158]

---

[157] President Dallin H. Oaks, "Spiritual Gifts," *Ensign*, September, 1986, https://www.lds.org/ensign/1986/09/spiritual-gifts?lang=eng.

[158] President Brigham Young, *Journal of Discourses*, Vol. 7, 240, September 1, 1859, http://jod.mrm.org/7/237.

Satan is a revelator. He reveals his doctrines and philosophies to men and women across the globe. Often, he inspires men to mingle these ideas with scripture so as to better deceive those well-meaning people who do not have true testimonies or who lack discernment. The entire Spiritualist movement, kicked off by the Fox Sisters in 1848, is a part of this deception concocted by Lucifer. The key takeaway from President Young, however, is that we must *always* be on guard against counterfeits, because there truly are evil spirits communicating with man.

One final quote on counterfeits ought to suffice before we move on to the meat of our discussion. Latter-day Saint author Leon R. Hartshorn once wrote:

> "Truth applied falsely can be most damaging. One has to look closely to tell a counterfeit. If a counterfeit is known to an intended victim, then it is worthless, so the counterfeiter tries in every way to keep the real truth hidden so that the deception may be successful and the unsuspecting made a victim.

> "Satan is an excellent counterfeiter, but he also has an additional deception that is confusing and harmful. Let me illustrate. If a salesman sold glasses to a person with perfect vision, it would be wrong and harmful. If one persuaded a healthy person that he needed a wheelchair or that he needed an operation, that would be wrong and harmful . . . All of the services or products mentioned, in the right setting, are not only necessary, but beneficial, and all but indispensable. . . .

> "Evil individuals, or perhaps just thoughtless individuals, have a way of perverting obviously good things and making it sound as if one must possess them or incorporate them into her life immediately."[159]

The logic of these statements is manifest. Often, deceivers (and sometimes merely "thoughtless individuals") convince people to misapply

---

[159] Leon R. Hartshorn, *A Mother's Love* (Bountiul, Utah: Horizon Publishers, 1980), 21-22.

and misuse that which is inherently good and right. If something good is used inappropriately, it frequently becomes detrimental. As Brother Hartshorn noted, a perfectly healthy person has no need of an invasive surgery. A surgery performed on a healthy individual can offer no benefits and may in fact prove either harmful or, in some cases, fatal. So it is with truth and righteous acts.

What is true under one set of circumstances might be absolutely false if misinterpreted or misapplied under other circumstances. For instance, to teach that man must be baptized is not only correct doctrine, but a commandment and a prerequisite for eternal life. However, if that baptism is performed by someone not holding proper Priesthood authority, it is null and void. If it is performed on those who have not repented and who have no faith, it is ineffectual. If it is performed by sprinkling as opposed to the true method of immersion, it is annulled. If innocent children who are not capable of sin because they have not reached the age of accountability are baptized, it is a great evil notwithstanding the fact that those above the age of accountability are commanded to be baptized.

By another comparison, the sacred powers of procreation are not only good and holy, but absolutely essential to fulfilling the Father's Plan of Salvation. Sex between man and woman is to be celebrated when performed within the marriage covenant. When properly used, this power is a godly, holy, ennobling power. Yet, when this power is used by those not legally and lawfully wedded, it becomes a great abomination – a "whoredom" – and will drag one down to damnation if he or she does not repent. It is the same with intellectual counterfeits.

It is obvious from the above quotations that the prophets have been greatly concerned about deception and the false ideas that have attempted to gain a foothold among members of the Church. In chapter four, we discussed the damnable theory of evolution and how it has made major inroads in the Church and throughout the world. In this chapter, we will highlight some of the other Devilish counterfeit doctrines popular in our day. We will focus on Satan's counterfeit of the Gospel's declaration that men may become gods. We will discuss how this seminal truth has been misapplied and misshapen so horribly over the generations that to believe the counterfeit is to deny Jesus Christ and His Atonement.

One of the oldest lies the Devil has used to entice mankind is the one he told Eve in the Garden of Eden. He said that if Eve disobeyed God and partook of the forbidden fruit, she would "be as gods" (Genesis 3:5). As we have thoroughly documented in the first three chapters of this work, one of the most glorious Gospel truths is that we are *literally* children of God and, thus, have the germ of divinity within us. We have a potential to become like our Eternal Father because we inherited His abilities when He begot us as His spirit children. We are the very children of God and, thus, "heirs of God" and "joint-heirs with Christ," as the Apostle Paul taught (Romans 8:17). Or, as the Psalmist revealed, God said: "Ye are Gods" (Psalms 82:6) – a truth which Jesus confirmed during His ministry (John 10:30-36).

Yes, we are of the lineage of the Gods! We are gods in embryo with unlimited potential. It is not surprising, then, that Satan chose this powerful promise to counterfeit. And it is also not surprising that uninspired opponents of The Church of Jesus Christ of Latter-day Saints wrongly equate our doctrine on man's potential for godhood with the Devil's lie in the Garden of Eden. That we do not erroneously conflate these two diametrically opposed ideas, let us analyze the fundamental differences.

The notion that we may become gods is true. It is scriptural, Biblical, and has been taught by prophets both ancient and modern. Anyone who has taken the time to read chapters one through three of this work has seen dozens of references from the scriptures and writings of modern prophets expounding this principle, and I have cited three such Bible verses above in this chapter. Though it is rejected by modern Christendom, it is beyond dispute that the scriptures – yes, even the Holy Bible – teach this doctrine. It is also beyond dispute that Satan plays off of this truth and spins his own web of lies to blind and deceive.

Satan's distorts this Heavenly principle in many ways. We will speak of two of them: 1) The lie that man can self-deify without any aid from the

Savior Jesus Christ and without compliance to Gospel laws; and 2) the myth that man *is* God – that is, God with a capital G.

Perhaps Satan's most common lie regarding man's potential for godhood is his teaching that *through our own efforts* we may become gods – or "Godmen" as they are sometimes called.[160] Through our own learning, study, and experience, he claims, we may attain the status of a god or even God. We do not need the Gospel of Jesus Christ. We do not need a Savior. We do not need to comply with the Ten Commandments or the other laws of the Restored Gospel. We need no ordinances, revealed religion, or organized theology. We only need the proper focus and desire and we may, through meditation, study, and sheer will power, come into harmony with the divine essence of the cosmos and become gods.

We are, says the Devil, wholly divine; we just haven't realized it yet. Thus, he has come to give us the forbidden knowledge of good and evil so that our eyes may be opened that we may see who we really are – gods trapped in mortal flesh. By achieving self-realization and enlightenment and coming into communion with the higher powers of the universe – often through psychic or occult practices – we understand that we are a part of God, we learn to transcend mortal bounds, and we access our God-potential. This is the substance of Lucifer's first great lie.

Satan's second great lie about man's potential to become gods is that we may become *God*; that is, God with a capital G. This fib is normally coupled with the mystical idea that God is a genderless essence or cosmic force and that we are merely emanations of that force. Therefore, if we are created of the same identical substance as this galactic essence called God, or if we are merely emanations or projections of that essence, then logically that means *we* are God – we just haven't realized it yet. This is perverse reasoning and denies the personhood and identity of God our Father, yet it is a philosophy held by potentially billions of people across the earth.

---

[160] I have taken the term "Godmen" from researcher Caryl Matrisciana who has applied it to the Eastern gurus who are sometimes seen by their disciples as gods in human flesh. See Matrisciana's incredible 1991 documentary film "The Pagan Invasion, Volume 2: Invasion of the Godmen" for more information.

Additionally, to suppose that *we* are God is to suppose we have the power of God or at least that we may obtain it through our own efforts; that is, we can create our own gods and reality. The scriptures, however, put this myth to rest. While speaking of seership, Ammon said that:

> "a gift which is greater can no man have, except he should possess the power of God, which no man can; yet a man may have great power given him from God. . . .

> "Thus God has provided a means that man, through faith, might work mighty miracles; therefore he becometh a great benefit to his fellow beings" (Mosiah 8:16).

And while speaking of the related gift of prophecy, Peter taught:

> "For the prophecy came not in old time by the will of man: but holy men of God spake as they were moved by the Holy Ghost" (2 Peter 1:21).

As these verses suggest, man *can* be endowed with power from God for specific purposes. These spiritual gifts are meant to be used for the "benefit [our] fellow beings" and are never given for self-aggrandizement. Prophecy, seership, spiritual rebirth – these come through God and *not* because of our own will power, wisdom, or skill.

We do not and cannot perform miracles of ourselves. We cannot heal the sick through our own energy vibrations or attunement to the universe, as the energy healers claim. We cannot be born again without God's grace. We cannot save ourselves. We cannot deify ourselves. To think we can do any of these things of our own will and choice is inherently self-centered and prideful, does not seek the benefit and exaltation of others, and dismisses the notion of a Savior and a personal God. The takeaway, then, is that it is God and only God who grants these powers and performs these miracles, and He does so only in accordance with His will. Man has no opportunity to force His hand.

These two great lies are what Latter-day Saints are often accused, by "orthodox" Christians, of believing. Anyone who possesses intellectual honesty and who has read this book with an open mind knows now that this accusation is *utterly false* and without foundation. We agree that man can become like God, as the Old and New Testaments both teach, but the similarities between our revealed doctrine and the suppositions and theories of others ends there. Yet, notwithstanding the wide gulf between our doctrine and what the world teachers, Latter-day Saints are almost always lumped in with mystics, Eastern thinkers, occult gurus, and New Agers by people who call themselves mainstream Christians.

Because The Church of Jesus Christ of Latter-day Saints is so often criticized, misjudged, and slandered regarding this point, I want to offer a defense. For the remainder of this chapter, I will examine various teachings of cults, Eastern religions, and New Age proponents and compare and contrast these with the truths of the Restored Gospel of Jesus Christ as proclaimed by the Church that bears His holy name. If you take away nothing else from this chapter, please take away the fact that our doctrine regarding man's opportunity to become like his Heavenly Father is radically different from, and even incompatible with, the New Age and occult notions of deification and self-deification.

Let us begin our contrasting by discussing a couple of doctrines relative to man's physical body, the Resurrection, and the afterlife. An almost universal belief held by apostate Christians, Buddhists, Hindus, Jews, pagans, and others, posits that man will *not* have a physical body in the afterlife. They view our mortal tabernacles as temporary prisons. They see them as limiting and unnatural. Most Christians, basing their theories upon mistranslations in the Bible and the man-made creeds of the Dark Ages, believe the lie that God is *only* a spirit, similar to what Eastern religions teach. Yes, God has a spirit and one might even say that He *is* a spirit Being. But He *also* possesses a tangible, exalted body that can only be in one place at one time and which is the glorified temple of His Spirit.

We must never forget the universal promise of the Savior's Atonement that *all* mankind will regain their physical bodies in the Resurrection and will stand before the judgement bar of God. The Apostle Paul confronted those who disbelieved in a literal resurrection when he wrote:

> "Now if Christ be preached that he rose from the dead, how say some among you that there is no resurrection of the dead?

"But if there be no resurrection of the dead, then is Christ not risen;

"And if Christ be not risen, then is our preaching vain, and your faith is also vain" (1 Corinthians 15:12-14).

Paul then testified of the Resurrection and the abolition of death:

"But now is Christ risen from the dead, and become the firstfruits of them that slept.

"For since by man came death, by man came also the resurrection of the dead.

"For as in Adam all die, even so in Christ shall all be made alive. . . .

"The last enemy that shall be destroyed is death" (1 Corinthians 15:20-22, 26).

Death was an enemy that entered the word only *after* Adam's and Eve's transgression. Long before they partook of the forbidden fruit, Adam and Eve were granted bodies to house their spirits. Before their Fall, physical death did not exist (2 Nephi 2:22; Moses 4:25). Their bodies, then, were immortal. The Atonement of Jesus Christ restores this former condition of immortality through the power of the Resurrection.

The prophet Ezekiel alluded to a literal resurrection from the grave when he painted this somewhat macabre, yet hopeful, picture:

"Again he said unto me, Prophesy upon these bones, and say unto them, O ye dry bones, hear the word of the Lord.

"Thus saith the Lord God unto these bones; Behold, I will cause breath to enter into you, and ye shall live:

"And I will law sinews upon you, and will bring up flesh upon you, and over you with skin, and put breath in you, and ye shall live; and ye shall know that I am the Lord. . . .

". . . I will open your graves, and cause you do come up out of your graves. . . .

"And shall put my spirit in you, and ye shall live" (Ezekiel 37:4-6, 12, 14).

And, finally, Job testified of a literal resurrection for mankind when he declared:

> "And though after my skin worms destroy this body, yet in my flesh shall I see God:
>
> "Whom I shall see for myself, and mine eyes shall behold, and not another; though my reins be consumed within me" (Job 19:26-27).

In his flesh he will see God. In other words, in the next life, Job will have a physical body of flesh and bone when he stands before God — a body purified from deformities, injuries, and pain. With his physical eyes he will see His Father. This is the testimony of Job and all Bible-believing Christians must accept it.

Yes, the Bible teaches the doctrine of a physical Resurrection sufficiently for anyone to understand. Yet, the Restored Gospel sounds an even greater witness. I draw this line from *The Book of Mormon*:

> "The soul shall be restored to the body, and the body to the soul; yea, and every limb and joint shall be restored to its body; yea, even a hair of the head shall not be lost; but all things shall be restored to their proper and perfect frame" (Alma 40:23).

Not one hair of our head will be lost and each of our bodies will be perfected! This is what awaits mankind at some future date after we pass through the veil because of the great sacrifice of the Son of God, our Master Jesus Christ.

The Gospel truth about physical bodies is truly glorious and hope-filled. We know that we will be like our Savior. When Jesus was resurrected, He took upon Himself a physical body of flesh and bone that was capable of being felt and of eating food (Luke 24:36-43). Modern revelation confirms that the Father and Son both have perfected and exalted bodies "of flesh and bones as tangible as man's" (D&C 130:22). We also know that the righteous dead "looked upon the long absence of their spirits from their bodies as a bondage" (D&C 138:50). We understand from *The Book of Mormon* that in the Resurrection "the spirit and the body shall be reunited again in its perfect form; both limb and joint shall be restored to its proper frame, even as we now are at this time" (Alma 11:43). And, finally, as we detailed in chapter three, gaining a physical body was one of the two basic reasons we left our pre-mortal abode to come to earth. We could not progress to become like our embodied Eternal Father without it.

Almost all of these truths have been taken away from humanity through generations of apostasy. And this is the tie-in to our present subject. Because of mankind's apostasy, the truth has been covered and we have accepted false doctrines which lead us to gratify our pride and follow our own spiritual paths rather than the one brightly marked by God. The "creeds of the fathers, who have inherited lies" have been "strongly riveted" upon the hearts of men in the earth and they know almost nothing of God or their own potential and destiny (D&C 123:7).

Elder Bruce R. McConkie wrote of some of the ways mankind, in its apostate condition, have sought to commune with God:

> "[U]ntold millions have worshiped before the thrones of false Christs. Some deluded fanatics have bowed before persons professing to be saviors or to have the power to confer salvation. Other hosts of misguided souls have trekked to desert monasteries, to mountain hermitages, to Jesuit retreats, and to the meeting places of secret cults – all acting under the specious assumption that in the place of their choice they would find Christ . . . And virtually all the millions of apostate Christendom have abased themselves before the mythical throne of a mythical Christ whom they vainly suppose to be a spirit essence who is incorporeal, uncreated, immaterial, and three-in-one with the Father and Holy Spirit."[161]

Whether through the worship of personal "saints" and icons, embracing the errors of monastic living, the following of false gurus and religious teachers, or the practice of false rituals and rites, mankind have been

---

[161] McConkie, *Mormon Doctrine*, 269.

"feeling their way" forward and "wandering in strange roads" (1 Nephi 8:31-32).

Among the most misguided of religionists are those who believe Satan's lies about the body being a hindrance to progression and who, consequently, conceive of God as an essence, a force, or a mystical spirit rather than an individual Man whose Spirt and body are inseparably connected and everlastingly exalted. And this belief ultimately lends itself to the belief that *we* are God because God is everywhere and in everything.

The conviction that God is an omnipresent essence rather than an exalted Man is part and parcel of Hinduism, the primary belief system of the vast subcontinent of India. In his book *The Essentials of Hinduism*, the Hindu author Swami Bhaskarananda thoroughly catalogued the tenets of Hinduism. Among other things, he mentioned the "supersensuous truths" of Hinduism, the limiting nature of the physical body, the theory of reincarnation, and God-realization. I draw several quotations from his text:

> "[When the] mind is purified or transformed throughout spiritual discipline into an extraordinary mind, it can transcend the barriers of the sense world and reach the outermost frontier of the world of time and space. It can then glimpse what lies beyond the domain of the senses. It gains extraordinary capabilities. It becomes all-knowing; it can know all the events of the past, present and the future. . . .

> "Hinduism has the unique distinction of having no known founder . . . The eternal and supersensuous truths discovered by ancient Indian sages are the foundation of Hinduism. . . .

> ". . . Various saints and Divine Incarnations at different times have appeared on the stage, played their individual roles, and enriched Hinduism with their teachings. . . .

> "Any ancient religion can be compared to the attic of an old home. Unless the attic is regularly cleaned, it gathers dust and cobwebs and eventually becomes unusable. Similarly, if a religion

cannot be updated or cleaned from time to time, it loses its usefulness and cannot relate anymore to changed times and people. . . .

". . . Hinduism believes in God's omnipresence and speaks of the presence of Divinity in every human being. At any given point of time Divinity is equally present in all, but not equally manifest. . . .

". . . All without any exception will eventually attain moksha [or "liberation achieved through God-realization"]. Some highly evolved souls may accomplish this in this life, or after their death. Others who are not as evolved may need several more incarnations. Conscious effort or sincere spiritual practice, however, can help one to achieve this goal faster. . . .

". . . Eventually [man] realizes that searching for Infinite Bliss through such finite external means will lead him nowhere.

"This awareness inspires him to turn around and consciously search for that fountain of Infinite Bliss within himself. When he arrives at this perennial source of Infinite Bliss, all his wants and cravings disappear. He then experiences God – the all-pervading Divinity – both within himself and without. He experiences God as the essence of everything and every being . . . He transcends all suffering, fear and sorrow . . . He sees himself as part of a Divine play where God is playing all the roles, including his own. He can no longer identify with his body-mind-complex, which is subject to birth, change, decay and death. He gains the unshakable conviction that he is the eternal Divine Spirit – deathless and birthless."[162]

An entire volume would be necessary to pick apart all the theological errors and untruths in these few statements. The chief errors, however, are these: 1) Hinduism sees God as an "essence" that pervades all things and is omnipresent; 2) Hinduism sees man as part of as this God-essence

---

[162] Swami Bhaskarananda, *The Essentials of Hinduism: A Comprehensive Overview of the World's Oldest Religion* (Seattle, WA: Viveka Press, 2009), 3-5, 8-9.

and, indeed, as God himself; 3) Hinduism believes in reincarnation and the transmutation of the soul and the eternal evolution of man; 4) Hinduism rejects the need for normal human senses and instead grasps at a mystical notion of cosmic consciousness; 5) Hinduism claims it has no founder, yet acknowledges the hand of otherworldly entities in shaping its corrupt beliefs; and 6) Hinduism does not believe in eternal truth or the concept of an "everlasting" Gospel, but maintains that religion must change with the circumstances and adapt to fit the sensibilities of men.

On the issue of omnipresence, which at first glance sounds much like the doctrine taught in *The Doctrine and Covenants* that God "is above all things, and in all things, and is through all things, and is round about all things" (D&C 88:41), Elder Bruce R. McConkie has written:

> "It is by reference to this true doctrine of *omnipresence* that the sectarian world attempts to justify its false creeds which describe Deity as a vague, ethereal, immaterial essence which fills the immensity of space and is everywhere and nowhere in particular present. God himself, of course, is a personal Being in whose image man is created. (Gen. 1:26; 5:1; Moses 2:26; 6:9), but he is also an immanent Being, meaning that the light of Christ shines forth from him to fill all space. This "light proceedeth forth from the presence of God to fill the immensity of space – The Light which is in all things, which giveth life to all things, which is the law by which all things are governed, even the power of *God who sitteth upon his throne*, who is in the bosom of eternity, who is in the midst of all things." (D&C 88:12-13.)

> "God is the *Creator*; the power, light, influence, and spirit that goes forth from his person to fill all immensity is a *creature* of his creating. Thus it was that Paul, speaking of apostate peoples, said they had "*changed the truth of God into a lie, and worshipped and served the creature more than the Creator*, who is blessed for ever." (Rom. 1:25.)"[163]

---

[163] McConkie, *Mormon Doctrine*, 544-545.

Thus, God Himself is not everywhere present – His *influence* is. The light of Christ is in all things and through all things, not the physical Christ Himself. God can only be in one place at one time. The Son, Jesus Christ, can only be in one place at one time. The powerful influence of Holy Ghost, who is not embodied, can be everywhere present, though even He has a spirit body that cannot be divided or occupy two places at once. The light that shines forth from the throne of God and from the glorious Personages comprising the Godhead is that presence that fills space. We must never confuse the creature with the Creator; the light of Christ with Christ Himself; or God's presence with His actual person. Yet, this is precisely what Hinduism and other apostate creeds teach.

As is obvious, Hinduism lacks the light of Gospel truth in the fundamental aspects relating to God's nature, man's origin, and man's relationship with God. Hinduism is not alone, however, in believing that man has no true individuality apart from this cosmic force that pervades all nature, life, and substance in the universe. M. Scott Peck, a man who touts himself as a Christian, gave this theory about man being God:

> "To put it plainly, our unconscious is God. God within us. . . . Since the unconscious is God . . . we may further define the goal of spiritual growth to be the attainment of Godhood by the conscious self . . . to become totally, wholly God . . . a new life form of God. . . .

> "God wants us to become Himself (or Herself or itself). We are growing toward godhood. God is . . . the source of the evolutionary force and . . . the destination."[164]

In harmony with Hindu theology, this man's version of Christianity holds that *we* are God, that God is an asexual essence or force, and that by individualized "spiritual growth" and God-realization we attain godhood. There is no room in this conception for Jesus Christ and His Atonement since godhood can supposedly be attained independently.

---

[164] Dave Hunt, *Occult Invasion: The Subtle Seduction of the World and Church* (Eugene, Oregon: Harvest House Publishers, 1998), 342.

Along similar lines, the Dalai Lama has spoken of cosmic consciousness and our necessity of aligning with it:

> "From the Buddhist point of view, our consciousness has the potential to know every object. Because of obstructions we are, at present, unable to know everything. However, by removing these obstructions gradually, it is ultimately possible to know everything."[165]

We can plainly see the weaving of lies and truths into this Buddhist philosophy. Of a truth, one day in the future – after we have been purified by the blood of Christ and changed in the inner man by the Spirit – we will comprehend all things, even God (D&C 88:49-50). Yet, we cannot do this by ourselves. We cannot raise our "consciousness" to the level of God by meditation, mantras, fasting, or any of the other methods often proposed by Eastern gurus. Our bodies are not "obstructions" to knowledge – our body and spirit combined constitutes the soul of man. And knowledge comes not from some vague "consciousness" – and certainly not "universal consciousness" or "God consciousness" as it is sometimes referred to – but through the Holy Ghost according to God's will (2 Peter 1:21; D&C 88:68; Jacob 4:8).

In the Jewish mystical tradition, as embodied in the Kabbalah, we see this same pagan ideology repeated. In Kabbalistic thought, God is an essence – a series of divine emanations of energy and presence. God is incomplete without man, according to the Kabbalah. This God-force combines both male and female aspects and is constantly evolving – a thought incredibly similar to the Hindu conception. Author and Kabbalist Daniel C. Matt has written:

> "The rabbinic concept of *Shekhinah*, divine immanence, blossoms into the feminine half of God, balancing the patriarchal conception that dominates the Bible and the Talmud . . . According to the Kabbalah, every human action here on earth affects the divine realm, either promoting or hindering the union of Shekhinah and her partner – the Holy One, blessed be he. God

---

[165] Hunt, *Occult Invasion*, 338.

is not static being, but dynamic becoming. Without human participation, God remains incomplete, unrealized. It is up to us to actualize the divine potential in the world. God needs us. . . .

". . . In this primal state, God is undifferentiated being, neither this nor that, no-thingness."[166]

The falsehoods are plain to behold. To say that "God needs us," that He is "incomplete, unrealized" without man, and that He is ever-evolving and "becoming," borders on blasphemy. It is certainly a rejection of the Gospel teaching that our "Father which is in heaven is perfect" (Matthew 5:48), that "he is the same yesterday, today, and forever" (1 Nephi 10:18), that in Him "is no variableness, neither shadow of turning" (James 1:17), and that "from eternity to eternity he is the same, and his years never fail" (D&C 76:4). God is perfect, God is definable, God is our literal Father and we bear His image. He is not, as the Kabbalists think, "no-thingness."

Furthermore, the Kabbalah teaches that man has no unique spirit identity and will one day merge with the cosmic essence and lose all individuality and free will. It teaches that once man joins with the God-force, there is no necessity for a Messiah; man having become his own savior. Daniel Matt explained, complete with the usual nonsensical jargon of Kabbalistic thought, that:

"Beyond Hokhmah is the Nothingness of Keter, the annihilation of thought. In this ultimate sefirah human consciousness expands, dissolving into Infinity. . . .

". . . [Isaac] Luria taught that the first divine act was not emanation, but withdrawal. Ein Sof withdrew its presence "from itself to itself," withdrawing in all directions away from one point at the center of its infinity, as it were, thereby creating a vacuum. This vacuum served as the site of creation. . . .

"Into the vacuum Ein Sof emanated a ray of light, channeled through vessels. At first, everything went smoothly; but as the

---

[166] Daniel C. Matt, *The Essential Kabbalah: The Heart of Jewish Mysticism* (San Francisco, CA: HarperSanFransisco, 1996), 1-2, 8.

emanation proceeded, some of the vessels could not withstand the power of the light, and they shattered. Most of the light returned to its infinite source, but the rest fell as sparks, along with the shards of the vessels. Eventually, these sparks became trapped in material existence. The human task is to liberate, or raise, these sparks, to restore them to divinity. This process of *tiqqun* (repair or mending) is accomplished through living a life of holiness. All human actions either promote or impede *tiqqun*, thus hastening or delaying the arrival of the Messiah . . . Luria's teaching resonates with one of Franz Kafka's paradoxical sayings: "The Messiah will come only when he is no longer necessary; he will come only on the day after his arrival."'"[167]

This ludicrous, anti-Christ philosophy dates to ancient times, though some place the "official" founding date in the much more recent past. Is it any wonder that Nephi, speaking of the ancient Jews from whom his family had been separated by God, said: "[T]heir works were works of darkness, and their doings were doings of abominations" (2 Nephi 25:2)? And the Savior's own rebuke to the Kabbalistic and Talmudic leaders of His day was as the crack of a fiery whip:

"Ye neither know me, nor my Father. . . .

". . . ye seek to kill me, a man that hath told you the truth. . . .

"Ye are of your father the devil, and the lusts of your father ye will do. He was a murderer from the beginning, and abode not in the truth, because there is no truth in him" (John 8:19, 40, 44).

Curiously, the Kabbalah's chief text, the Zohar, "may have been composed through automatic writing, a technique in which the mystic would meditate on a divine name, enter a trance, and begin "to write whatever came to his hand."'"[168] Automatic writing is essentially necromancy or consulting with "familiar spirits," which practice is expressly forbidden in numerous locations in the Bible (Deuteronomy 18:10-12). As we will

---

[167] Matt, *The Essential Kabbalah*, 11, 15.

[168] Matt, *The Essential Kabbalah*, 6.

discuss presently, however, the Devil has been actively divulging false doctrines to man through ancient occult practices like automatic writing, overshadowing, channeling, necromancy, divining, and direct manifestations and visitations by evil spirits posing as angels of light (2 Corinthians 11:14).

In a 1974 *Ensign* article, we read the following:

> "In recent years there has been increased interest throughout the Western world in the occult and mystical-type religions. This is not a revival of the spirituality characteristic of the ancient patriarchs and prophets of Israel, but is a type of magic and spiritualistic wizardry that the true prophets vigorously opposed. . . .

> "The scriptures show that the enchantments and the spells of the wizard, the medium, and the necromancer are characteristic of the false religions and superstitions of the world, and that those who practice such are actually in competition with the true prophets and apostles. All who are acquainted with the spirit and faith of Jesus Christ will want nothing to do with any form of divination and spiritual wizardry."[169]

All forms of magic, mediumship, and necromancy are from Satan. There are no exceptions. They are counterfeits. Their practitioners, as well-intentioned as they may be, are ensnared by the Evil One.

The *New Era* once ran an intriguing article discussing astrology and the deceptive nature of occultism and Eastern religious philosophies. In the article, Bjarne Christensen explained:

> "And many young people go into the occult sincerely determined to make a success of it by learning all the proper techniques of magic. *Time* magazine, September 27, 1968, said of them:

---

[169] Robert J. Matthews, "What the Scriptures Say about Astrology, Divination, Spirit Mediums, Magic, Wizardry, and Necromancy," *Ensign*, March, 1974, https://www.lds.org/ensign/1974/03/searching-the-scriptures?lang=eng/.

""Hippies, with their drug-sensitized yen for magic, are perhaps the prime movers behind this phenomenon. Not only do they sport beads and amulets that have supposed magical powers, they also believe firmly and frighteningly in witchcraft."

"In major cities, shops devoted to selling amulets, potions, candles, herbs, magical tools, incense, and ceremonial garments have opened up.

"Such concern for the arcane on the part of some people is an attempt to find enrichment for perplexed and arid lives. Disillusioned with life as they now find it, they hope to find answers by using the power of magic to create a meaningful existence. This suggests that the occult may be a form of religion. Psychologists compare the fascination for the occult to the fast-rising pseudo interest in Oriental religions such as Zen Buddhism. A belief in reincarnation, for example, is considered part and parcel of astrology. "Never before in history has a single society taken up such a wide range of religious and near-religious systems at once," states an article in *Life* magazine.

"Of course, many people just go into the supernatural wanting something new and sensational to play with, something to dip into from time to time. Indeed, many Church members, both young and old, have, as millions of others, searched for artificial guidance in one of the 1200 daily newspapers in the United States that now carry horoscope columns. But whatever the motivation for this new interest in astrology, it is evident that the movement is already the victim of exploiters who have moved in for the financial kill."[170]

The resurrected Lord told the Nephites that, when He returned in the end times, He would destroy "the sorcerers" (3 Nephi 24:5). Many prophets also foretold of sorcery in the last days – our days. Members of The

---

[170] Bjarne Christensen, "The Precarious Age of Aquarius," *New Era*, November, 1972, https://www.lds.org/new-era/1972/11/the-precarious-age-of-aquarius?lang=eng.

Church of Jesus Christ of Latter-day Saints should have absolutely nothing to do with the mélange of occultic practices gaining ascendency in our society.

Today, exponentially more than in 1974, we are witnessing the rise of the New Age movement and a host of psychic and paranormal phenomena. We first touch upon psychic phenomena before discussing the threatening New Age movement. In a book called *Master Guide to Psychism*, Harriet Boswell wrote extensively of psychic abilities and attributed them to a benevolent source. Among the psychic/occult practices she championed we find: Mediumship; astral projection; Ouija boards; table tilting; supernatural healings; prophecy; telekinesis; automatic speaking/writing/painting; teleporting; spirit photography; clairvoyance; and so forth.

As we have just noted above, the Devil pours out psychic powers upon those who open themselves to his seductive influence. Through this necromancy, so plainly denounced in the Bible, people believe they are accessing the spirits of the dead or the legitimate powers of the netherworld when in reality they are communicating with Satan's henchmen. These demonic impostors possess a great deal of information about those who have lived and who are alive – even "secret" information the individual thinks only he or she knows – and are thus able to weave their lies together so carefully with true information about the individuals or events in question that they deceive hosts of people. Messages received through these counterfeit sources, however, ought to be discarded as spurious and harmful.

Many people are susceptible to such spiritual sophistry because they have embraced elements of the Eastern school of thought that portrays God as a mystic force and man as an emanation of that force. If they are part of this God-force, then *they* are divine and do not need outside help. Why do you need a bishop, priest, or organized religion if you only need to raise your consciousness in order to commune with God? In this conception, salvation is merely a matter of self-realization and connecting with "God."

Unfortunately, many Christians have fallen into the trap of rejecting organized religion in favor of self-study and alternative methods to find

"God." No matter whether it is a Christian or a person of another creed who embraces this philosophy, the attitude is the same. The individual comes to believe, in essence, that it doesn't matter if you access your higher self – this mystical God-force – through a medium, Ouija board, spirit guide, or meditation. The important thing is you do access it. If psychic abilities like astral projection or occult methods like séances and mediumship help, so be it. So long as you access the "God" within, all is acceptable and right.

In this vein, Harriet Boswell wrote:

> "We are instruments expressing the Creative Mind of God – in a sense we are creators ourselves. Why not sensitize ourselves so that we can receive and express the higher creative impressions which emanate from the source of all things? . . . .
>
> "It is true in a sense that we are not really individuals; we are component parts of a great whole. Nonetheless, we are individuals in this respect: a clock is made up of many parts, each part with its own particular function which contributes to the usefulness and efficiency of the clock's operation . . . We must each discover for ourselves, from the Great Clockmaker, what component part we are. Psychic awareness is the practical answer. . . .
>
> "Until man consciously accepts his own relationship to the original Creative Intelligence, by whatever name he might call it . . . he is only half-alive. To be wholly alive he must have psychic awareness.
>
> "Even to say that there is no other God than man, is an expression of man's recognition of a Supreme Being of some sort, since we cannot conceive of or deny anything that does not have some possibility of existence . . . It is the spark of the supreme Creator innate in each of us that makes us individual in talents, personalities, etc. We each create ourselves in expression according to our own sense of value, initiative and, in a way, adventuresomeness. . . .

"By seeking within, developing the psychic consciousness found there, you can become aware of the part of you which is non-physical. When you are not aware of that part of your inner self which is capable of demonstrating at least one of the nine gifts of spirit which God gave man, you are violating the best part of yourself – the divine part of your nature. . . .

". . . One must become subjective in order to know. Truth is such an individual thing – we can believe only that which we accept as valid by our own personal standards. Our truths are determined through experiences, either spiritual, emotional or physical. Occasionally we accept as truth an objective observation, but generally the subjective is more definite and satisfying."[171]

This attitude of seeking the "God" within – even through psychic practices – is readily apparent here. To Boswell, man creates his own gods. Instead of being created in God's image, man creates his personal gods in his own image the same as all idol-worshiper of the past. Truth, as Boswell claims, is subjective. To each his own – there is no constant. The way to manipulate the "Creative Intelligence" that defines reality is through psychic practices like mediumship and meditation.

Unfortunately, this outlook is increasingly prevalent. Truth is discarded as subjective and man has adopted "situational ethics" in place of constant verities. God has been replaced with whatever personal idol the individual wishes to create. The very notion of God as an intelligent Being has been replaced with the Eastern idea of an indefinable galactic force whose power we can best access through psychic/occult practices, shamans, mediums, séances, etc. These self-indulgent lies are, as the anti-Christ Korihor admitted, and as Harriet Boswell echoed, "pleasing unto the carnal mind" (Alma 30:53) and much more "satisfying" than old-fashioned, limiting, stuffy "truth."

Brothers and sisters, avoid the entire gamut of psychic practices and ideas. They administer nothing but spiritual death.

---

[171] Harriet A. Boswell, *Master Guide to Psychism* (West Nyack, NY: Parker Publishing Company, Inc., 1969), 18-22.

Now we address the New Age movement. The term "New Age" is an umbrella term covering a host of mystical, occultic, and apostate traditions that have blended together Eastern and Western metaphysics to produce a hodgepodge philosophy that is destroying faith in Jesus Christ on a massive scale. Latter-day Saint author David Balmforth wrote what to me is the best introduction to the New Age movement. In his book *New Age Menace: The Secret War Against the Followers of Christ*, Balmforth described the New Age program thus:

> "Many Americans have never heard of the New Age movement yet they already accept and believe in many of its practices and teachings. "New Age" ideas are becoming increasingly popular throughout the world. They embrace trance channeling, crystal healing, reincarnation, spirit guides, spirit mediums or channelers, ESP, crystals, Karma, out of body travel, the ancient practices and beliefs of occultism, mind sciences, Eastern mysticism, metaphysics and many others. The New Age movement emphasizes the paranormal, the harnessing of specific mental powers and procedures to draw energy from crystals, as well as "channeled" messages and instructions from the dead. . . .

> ". . . It should come as no surprise that these teachings, which blend Eastern and Western religious sources, are in direct opposition to those of Jesus Christ.

> "The New Age Movement has a master plan to overthrow Christianity and all other religions that refuse to worship Lucifer. . . .

> "New Age leaders, along with their enlightened spirit guides, teach the doctrine of selfism. They teach that man is the only god; there is no other. They accept Jesus as a great teacher but reject all claims of his divinity as the son of God. In their view, Jesus Christ is no more God than anyone else is. The New Age believes that Jesus became "the Christ" only after he purified himself of "bad karma" by going through numerous incarnations. In their view he is only one of many "masters" who assist humanity from a superior (though not always the highest) plane of existence.

"There is an increasing appeal in New Age circles toward the pagan belief in an "earth mother" deity, as opposed to a heavenly Father. They deny the sacrifice and atonement of Jesus on the cross. . . .

"New Age ideology is based upon astrologically defined beliefs rather than those that are biblically defined. Thus the New Age is thoroughly occultic and completely unchristian."[172]

The New Age movement is rapidly expanding into every segment of our society. It has made its greatest inroads under the names "science," "medicine," and "health." Yoga, energy healing, holistic medicine, hypnosis, crystal work, emotion coding, visualization, reflexology, acupuncture, transcendental meditation, psychedelic drugs, altered states of consciousness, trance induction, astrology, and other occult practices have exploded in popularity in what can only be described as a major sign of the times.

Most Christians think nothing of practicing Yoga, for example, despite the fact that Yoga is a *religious* tradition borrowed from Hinduism and that Hindus believe it is impossible to separate the physical stretching from the religious aspect of awakening one's inner "serpent power," or Kundalini, and thereby "yoking" with the Hindu god Brahman.[173]

Among Church members, it is sad to relate that not only is Yoga popular, but that many thousands have become ensnared with an even more dangerous practice: Energy healing. Energy healing is alternatively called therapeutic touch, Christ-centered energy healing, faith-based energy healing, hand-motion treatment, etc., and has been officially denounced

---

[172] David N. Balmforth, *New Age Menace: The Secret War Against the Followers of Christ* (Bountiful, Utah: Horizon Publishers and Distributors, Inc., 1996), 23-24, 26-27.

[173] See Dave Hunt's book *Yoga and the Body of Christ: What Position Should Christians Hold?* for a great analysis of the very real dangers of Yoga.

by the Brethren.[174] If one needs a healing, they should seek a blessing at the hands of properly authorized Priesthood holders. Sadly, many such delusions are overcoming the Saints and fellow Christians of other denominations.

Elder Orson Pratt warned us against accepting Satanic deceptions which come to us under the name of science. He also referred to, and warned of, the Spiritualist movement sparked by the Fox Sisters that Brigham Young mentioned in a quotation cited earlier. He noted that this movement is headed by apostates – those who have rejected the truth of the Gospel and turned to fables (2 Timothy 4:4). And he highlighted the damning effects these false manifestations were having upon society. Said Elder Pratt:

> "But instead of calling upon men and beginning something great and good, in a godlike manner, he called upon certain females, residing not far from where the plates of the Book of Mormon were found, where the people had been warned, perhaps, longer than in any other portion of the United States. These ladies, Misses Fox by name, began bringing forth supernatural manifestations. Others did the same in a short time, and they have continued until the present day and have spread over the whole United States and many other parts of the world. If you go forth and make inquiries in regard to these manifestations, you will find that there are several millions of people in this country that believe in them. What a change between now and forty years ago! Then you could scarcely find one in the whole Christian world that would admit the probability of new revelation or supernatural manifestations; now there are millions in the United States alone!

---

[174] In his October 2017 General Conference talk "The Trek Continues!" President M. Russell Ballard repeated the Church's statement on energy healing which warns: "We urge Church members to be cautious about participating in any group that promises—in exchange for money—miraculous healings or that claims to have special methods for accessing healing power outside of properly ordained priesthood holders."

"Do these manifestations affect, for good, those who believe in them? Do they cause them to repent of their sins? No; they who blaspheme the name of God almost with every breath, and that will cheat and take every advantage possible of their brethren; they who will lie and steal and do every species of wickedness and abominations are the very ones that the devil works through; still the whole Christian world, apparently, are now willing to admit new revelation. Oh, yes! They have forgotten how they persecuted the Latter-day Saints because they believed in new revelation, and they can now believe in revelation by wholesale! They will not believe in records given through the medium of the prophets; but they are ready enough to believe if a wicked man who will blaspheme the name of Jesus is the medium and is made a participant in this great power. Such characters do not need any organization from God, they do not need any baptism, ordinances or Priesthood.

"The devil has invented various names for his manifestations in order to get the people to swallow them down; the same as the doctors. When they wish to administer some nauseous kind of medicine, they sweeten it up a little. So the devil has sweetened up these things in such a way that he has got almost all these manifestations under the name of science. If you want to see a species of devilism made manifest, it comes out under a scientific phraseology, under the specious name of electrobiology, animal magnetism, or some such popular name—names that have been given to real sciences, which have their laws, founded in nature, are now given to these supernatural manifestations. Why does Satan use these artifices? Because the people at the present day have become naturally scientific, or a great many of them have; and the devil thinks if he can only invent a real, nice, beautiful name, with some resemblance to a scientific name, a great many of these persons will swallow it down, and think it all right. . . .

"Some of the worst kind of apostates—apostates who had turned away from everything good, from every principle of righteousness, had become great mediums. Some of them were writing mediums; some of them would work with a table; some would have manifestations in one way and some in another. . . .

"When we heard these things we saw, truly, that as the devil did manifest his power in ancient times among the Egyptians, because they had persecuted the people of God, put to death their young infants, and shed innocent blood, even so, directly in the midst of our nation, his evil power was again manifested in strong delusion. Having persecuted the Saints of God, and having shed the blood of His prophets and Saints and driven them from place to place, and banished them beyond the Rocky Mountains, thinking that they had certainly got rid of them, and that they would perish there. Having become so exceedingly wicked, we saw that the devil was showing forth his power on the right hand and on the left, for their delusion and destruction.

"Now let us again speak of the apostates. Apostates seem to be the greatest mediums in Spiritualism, where they have neither order, church, nor Priesthood. These apostates, generally, had fallen into the idea that Jesus, and the apostles and prophets of ancient times, were living in barbarous ages, far behind the civilization of our day, but that they were called upon to open up a wonderful dispensation, and to reveal light far superior to that which had ever been revealed by any prophet who ever lived on the earth. This seems to have been the general idea of those apostates called mediums."[175]

The Adversary quickly concocted the Spiritualist movement as a counterfeit to the Lord's Gospel which had recently been restored. The early Brethren spoke frequently of this evil. As Elder Pratt noted, millions of Americans were hoodwinked by this demonstration of the Devil's power. Satan spoke to man through mediums, divulged secrets through visions, relayed instructions via automatic writing, and generally captivated entire generations with his sorceries. Today, the occult in all its forms has become wildly popular. The occult has in fact become so

---

[175] Elder Orson Pratt, *Journal of Discourses*, Vol. 13, 69-71, December 19, 1869, http://jod.mrm.org/13/62.

popular that Wicca – that is, Witchcraft – is now *the fastest-growing religion in America* and Britain![176]

Wicca is a hodgepodge of divergent "spiritual paths." Everyone has their own traditions and the traditions of one coven or practitioner might differ from that of another. Many Wiccans, however, believe in Eastern-style monism. Monism essentially refers to the belief in the oneness of all things – that all things are God or are an emanation from God. Or, in the Hindu concept, all is an illusion (i.e. maya). In their book *Generation Hex*, Dillon Burroughs and Marla Alupoaicei explained this Wiccan belief thus:

> "Wiccans worship the Great Mother Goddess, and her partner, the Horned God (also called Gaius or Pan), but these and a host of other pagan deities are said to represent various aspects of an impersonal creative force called "The One" or "The All" – reflecting the current influence of Eastern monism popularized in New Age thought. Wiccans regard all aspects of nature – plants, rocks, planets – as having spirit."[177]

As we have already noted in relation to Hinduism, there is a kernel of truth in this counterfeit. Nonetheless, it is a counterfeit which blatantly violates the first, and often second, of the Ten Commandments.

---

[176] Josh Kimball, "Wicca Experts Encourage Christians to Engage America's 'Fastest-Growing' Religion," *The Christian Post*, September 21, 2008, accessed August 14, 2018, https://www.christianpost.com/news/wicca-experts-encourage-christians-to-engage-america-s-fastest-growing-religion-34408/; Neela Banerjee, "Wiccans Keep the Faith With a Religion Under Wraps," *The New York Times*, May 16, 2007, accessed August 14, 2018, https://www.nytimes.com/2007/05/16/us/16wiccan.html; and "Wicca: What's the Fascination?" *The Christian Broadcasting Network, Inc.*, accessed August 14, 2018, http://www1.cbn.com/books/wicca%3A-what%27s-the-fascination%3F; and Michael Snyder, "The Fastest Growing Religion In America Is Witchcraft," *TheTruthWins*, October 30, 2013, accessed August 14, 2018, http://thetruthwins.com/archives/the-fastest-growing-religion-in-america-is-witchcraft.

[177] Dillon Burroughs and Marla Alupoaicei, *Generation Hex: Understanding the Subtle Dangers of Wicca* (Eugene, Oregon: Harvest House Publishers, 2008), 46.

Like many New Age and occult religious traditions, Wicca is also pantheistic. Pantheism is incredibly similar, if not identical in most respects, to monism and can be described in this way:

> "Another common philosophy, *pantheism*, teaches that God is Everything, and Everything is God. According to this worldview, everything in creation is a part of God. This includes the sun, the moon, trees, turtles, and rocks; everything has a divine nature. Julia Phillips and Matthew Sandow state, "To a Wiccan, all of creation is divine, and by realizing how we are connected to the turning of the seasons and to the natural world, we come to a deeper understanding to the ways in which we are connected to the God and Goddess."

> "Pantheism takes the loving, personal God of the Bible and converts Him into an impersonal force. It suggests that if we are part of God, then we can't be sinful, and therefore, we have no need for a Savior. Principles like these can lead people to worship creation rather than the Creator. . . .

> "Ecology is one of Wicca's most revered tenets because Wiccans envision the earth as a living goddess who blesses her people with her abundance."[178]

We can readily see the counterfeit nature of this doctrine. Yes, God has organized all matter into planets and other creations. He has formed the bodies of animals and of humans from the dust of the earth. Every living thing, including the earth itself, *does* in fact have a spirit and a degree of intelligence. However, these are *not* emanations from God, but His creations. They are not literally part of Him. He is a distinct Being, a Holy Man of flesh and bones. He is an individual Being, just as each of us are and ever will be unique individuals.

The Devil has taken the idea that intelligence and spirit animate all things and has exaggerated it. By exaggerating this truth, he lessens the importance of God and effectively shunts Him to the side. If *all* is God,

---

[178] Burroughs and Alupoaicei, *Generation Hex*, 93-94.

then there is no need to worship the Creator as a personal, individual Being – and certainly not as our Father. In fact, we would be our own God and figurative Father in this pantheistic conception. "All is One" is a popular saying throughout the world. In fact, all is not one. Each of us has an individuality – an intelligence – separate and apart from every other creature in the cosmos. We are not merely part of a cosmic essence, a galactic force, or some collective God-consciousness.

As individuals with agency, we are liable to sin. In fact, each of us sins regularly. As such, we need a Savior to atone for our sins and to set up a program to bring us back into the presence of God. To believe that God is everywhere and in everything, and that we are all connected because we are all a part of God or His direct emanations, is to reject our own individuality, the Fall of man, and the need for a personal Savior to redeem us and bring us back to God. We see this doctrine preached almost universally throughout the world today. It has its most appealing encapsulation in the West through the mishmash of spirituality known as the New Age movement.

The foundation for this New Age menace can be found in the teachings of the Russian Helena Blavatsky and her followers. Blavatsky was an occultist and medium who claimed that Ascended Masters of Wisdom – that is, more highly-evolved beings of wisdom and light – had appeared to her and instructed her in what to teach. For Latter-day Saints, this should immediately ring alarm bells. Korihor, you will recall, was visited by the Devil masquerading as an angel of light. The Devil – posing as a benevolent being, perhaps even a big brother – told him what to teach and spun a yarn about reclaiming the people who had "gone astray after an unknown God" (Alma 30:53). This is precisely what happened with Blavatsky.

In her most famous work, *The Secret Doctrine*, Blavatsky laid out her ideology. *The Secret Doctrine* is one of the most obtuse and convoluted books I have ever attempted to read. In it, Blavatsky mangled the Gospel, conflated Eastern and Western conceptions of God into a jumbled mess, criticized Christianity, condemned Jehovah as a cruel Being, and defended the liberating force of the universe which she said the Christians have wrongly labeled Satan. Most importantly, she also praised Lucifer as the liberator of mankind. These are the things Blavatsky was taught by her so-called Masters of Wisdom.

It is striking how often I have come across accounts of these Ascended Masters of Wisdom in my research. Numerous people around the globe have been visited by these imposters. Entire books have been both dictated by these otherworldly beings or conveyed through automatic writing and then published as a new gospel to mankind.

These Masters of Wisdom are led by a figure name Lord Maitreya. Sometimes he is referred to as "the Christ." He is expected to come to the earth and consolidate mankind in a global theocratic socialist government. At that time, his followers say that the Jews will recognize him as "the Messiah," Christians will call him "the Christ," Hindus will hail him as "the Avatar" or "Krishna," Muslims will call him the "Imam Mahdi," Buddhists will recognize him as "the Fifth Buddha," and so on. Together with his fellow Ascended Masters, Maitreya will govern this earth and usher in a *new age*, or golden age, for humanity.

Some Wiccans also believe in these Ascended Masters, though the call them by a different name. We are informed:

> "Most Wiccans do not believe in the biblical view of angels, but rather in beings called "the Watchers." Raven Grimassi describes them as "an ancient race who have evolved beyond the need for physical form.""[179]

It is my firm opinion that these Masters of Wisdom – these "Watchers" – are nothing but Satan and his fallen hosts, who rebelled during the pre-earth life and were cast down to the earth, posing as angels, saints, deceased figures of the past, etc. The predictions of this coming Maitreya and his legions are stunningly similar to the story of the Anti-Christ foretold by John in the book of Revelation. It appears to me that this New Age narrative has been carefully designed to parallel elements of the true prophesies concerning Christ's Second Coming so as to confuse and

---

[179] Burroughs and Alupoaicei, *Generation Hex*, 47.

deceive humanity into worshiping this false "Christ," or Maitreya, when he appears.

As noted, a host of individuals have come forward claiming revelations and teachings from these "higher" beings. Heads of state, U.S. presidents, ambassadors, royalty, religious leaders, and others are counted among Lord Maitreya's disciples. They are quietly moving the world towards the occult both in belief and behavior. Society is being led like lambs to the slaughter.

While the Ascended Masters have apparently stalked the earth for millennia, they began openly unveiling themselves during the Nineteenth Century – the time, not coincidentally, coinciding with the restoration of the Gospel. The timing of these demonic manifestations is another evidence of the truthfulness of the Restored Gospel. While the Heavens were closed, Satan was restricted in the scope of manifestations he could give. However, when the Lord broke the silence and poured down light upon the Prophet Joseph Smith and others, the Devil's hands were untied and he was again able to flood the earth with his own revelations in at least equal proportion.

Blavatsky was not alone in her enterprise of spiritual deception. She was joined by other very influential figures and occultists such as Alice Bailey, Annie Besant, C.W. Leadbeater, and Colonel Olcott – all of whom also claimed to be in contact with higher beings from other realms of existence and most of whom wrote numerous books detailing the teachings received from these so-called Masters. Blavatsky and her group founded a philosophy and an organization. The organization is called the Theosophical Society and the ideology is Theosophy.

Theosophy has become internationally influential and wields tremendous power in the communist-controlled United Nations. Theosophy, similar to the Restored Gospel, takes what it calls "truth" from all religions and synthesizes them into one whole. In fact, Theosophy's catchphrase is that "there is no religion higher than truth." In the case of Theosophy, however, the adherents incorporate many false concepts into their creed, such as Hindu reincarnation.

As should be expected, Theosophists do not worship Jesus Christ as the Savior or Son of God, but believe Him to be only one of many advanced individuals who came to the earth to bring new light and usher in a new golden age. This higher source of light, to the Theosophists, is Lucifer, whose pre-earth title meant "lightbearer." As noted, Blavatsky made her love for Lucifer clear in her arduous tome *The Secret Doctrine*.

Author Ted Flynn, in his excellent book *Hope of the Wicked*, wrote of the New Age movement that:

> "The New Age has what it calls "the Christ," but this "Christ" is not the Christ of the Gospels. In the New Age views, Jesus is separate from Christ; Jesus is a great man, like Buddha or Confucius, but not God – He is simply a way to "the Christ." It is this view of Christ that New Agers want Christians to adopt. They want to change Christian theology and philosophy. Again, they separate Jesus from Christ. St. John the Evangelist had already faced this blasphemy back in the first century. He wrote, "Who is a liar, but he who denieth that Jesus is the Christ? This is Antichrist, who denieth the Father, and the Son." (1 John 2:22)."[180]

Theosophy, like Wicca and nearly all New Age religious organizations, is essentially a buffet-style spirituality. They pick and choose what they want to believe in. They feel no need of God's "strict" commandments and laws – they can walk their own "path" to God. They completely reject the eternal principle of obedience to law. Obedience to divine law and truth is the essence of Freedom – especially in the Gospel sense. And this truth and Freedom are granted to mankind only through Jesus Christ. Outside of Him there is no salvation, progression, or exaltation.

Truly, the New Age movement and the Theosophical ideology behind it are anti-Christ. They deny the Lord, dismiss the need for an Atonement, confuse the origin of man, teach false principles like reincarnation, reject the direction of prophets and organized religion with its beautiful ordinances, and preach that man may become as the Ascended Masters of Wisdom through advanced and independent study and effort.

---

[180] Flynn, *Hope of the Wicked*, 153.

At least one prophet has spoken directly against Theosophy. President Joseph F. Smith taught:

> "This idea of theosophy, which is gaining ground even among so-called Christians, in these latter days, is a fallacy of the deepest kind. It is absolutely repugnant to the very soul of man to think that a civilized, intelligent being might become a dog, a cow, a cat; that he might be transformed into another shape, another kind of being. It is absolutely repulsive and so opposed to the great truth of God, that has been revealed from the beginning, that he is from the beginning always the same, that he cannot change, and that his children cannot change. They may change from worse to better; they may change from evil to good, from unrighteousness to righteousness, from humanity to immortality, from death to life everlasting. They may progress in the manner in which God has progressed; they may grow and advance, but their identity can never be changed, worlds without end – remember that; God has revealed these principles, and I know they are true. They assert their truth upon the intelligent mind and soul of man."[181]

Theosophy, with its jumble of metaphysical dogmas and Eastern religious teachings, is "absolutely repugnant" to the true Gospel of Jesus Christ. It simply is not a philosophy that an "intelligent mind" can accept. It is a Luciferian counterfeit concocted to pull men away from God by handing them fake revelations when they reach out in their natural longing for the divine.

Theosophist C.W. Leadbeater spoke of the evolutionary nature of this counterfeit program and of the direct guidance being given by these Devilish Masters of Wisdom. Notice that his conception of God as a force is the same as that held in Hinduism. And also note how this godhood can allegedly be attained. He wrote:

> "The existence of Perfected Men is one of the most important of the many new facts which Theosophy puts before us. It follows logically from the other great Theosophical teachings of karma

---

[181] Smith, *Gospel Doctrine*, 27.

and evolution by reincarnation. As we look round us we see men obviously at all stages of their evolution — many far below ourselves in development, and others who in one way or another are distinctly in advance of us . . . Some of us in the process of that development have already succeeded in unfolding some of those higher senses which are latent in every man, and will be the heritage of all in the future; and by means of those senses we are enabled to see the ladder of evolution extending far above us as well as far below us; and we can also see that there are men standing upon ever rung of that ladder.

"There is a considerable amount of direct testimony as to the existence of these Perfected Men whom we call Masters. . . .

"This galaxy of human genius that enriches and beautifies the pages of history is at the same time the glory and the hope of all mankind, for we know that these Greater Ones are the forerunners of the rest, and that They flash out as beacons, as veritable lightbearers to show us the path that we must tread if we wish to reach the glory which shall presently be revealed. We have long accepted the doctrine of the evolution of the forms in which dwells the Divine Life; here is the complementary and far greater idea of the evolution of that Life itself, showing that the very reason for that wondrous development of higher and higher forms is that the ever-swelling Life needs them in order to express itself. Forms are born and die, forms grow, decay and break; but the spirit grows on eternally, ensouling those forms, and developing by means of experience gained in and through them; and as each form has served its turn and is outgrown, it is cast aside that another and better form may take its place.

"Behind the unfolding form burgeons out ever the Life Eternal, the Life Divine. That Life of God permeates the whole of nature, which is but the many-colored cloak which He has donned; it is He Who lives in the beauty of the flower, in the strength of the tree, in the swiftness and grace of the animal as well as in the heart and soul of man. It is because His Will is evolution that all life everywhere is pressing onward and upward; and it is therefore that the existence of Perfected Men at the end of this long line of ever-unfolding power and wisdom and love is the most natural thing in the world. . . .

"The records of every great religion show the presence of such Supermen so full of the Divine Life that again and again They have been taken as the very representatives of God Himself. . . .

"Human progress is slow, but it is constant; therefore the number of the Perfected Men is increasing, and the possibility of attaining to Their level is within the reach of all who are willing to make the stupendous effort required. In normal times we should need many births before we could gain Adeptship, but just now it is possible for us to hasten our progress on that Path, to compress into a few lives the evolution which otherwise would take many thousands of years. That is the effort which is being made by many members of the Theosophical Society; for there is in that Society an Inner School which teaches men how to prepare themselves more rapidly for this higher work."[182]

According to Leadbeater, the number of Perfected Men – the Masters of Wisdom – are increasing in the earth. They are spreading their message that man can study and, by his own "evolution" over the course of several reincarnated lifetimes, can move upward on the evolutionary ladder toward godhood. While on earth, they may even become veritable "Supermen" among mere mortals. They may achieve this through intense study. That is what the Theosophical Society is all about – giving people the opportunity, through teaching the "secret doctrine" of Lucifer, to become adepts to Maitreya and his Masters. Please recall that a prophet of God has called Theosophy "absolutely repugnant."

In his book *Masters and the Path*, from which I took the above quotations, Leadbeater describes Maitreya's planned appearance to mankind. He said that at the time he shows himself, many of his followers, or "Adepts," will inhabit the bodies of specially-prepared members of the Theosophical

---

[182] C.W. Leadbeater, *Masters and the Path* (1925; Kessinger Publishing, 1996), 1-2, 3-4, 50.

Society in order to better carry out their work. Without saying the words, Leadbeater described a mass demon possession. These nonchalant writings of occultists like Leadbeater should shock us into action when we realize how literally they are fulfilling John's prophecies in the book of Revelation.

Freemasonry is another corrupted philosophy that agrees with the New Age thesis that men may become supermen by their own study and diligence. The Prophet Joseph Smith described Masonry as an apostate version of the ancient temple rites – hence the similarity to those same rites and symbols revealed in our dispensation through the Prophet. High-level English Freemason Walter Leslie Wilmshurst, in his revealing book *The Meaning of Masonry*, wrote of a Mason's ascent from a "natural man" to what amounts to godhood. He explained:

> "[F]rom grade to grade the candidate is being led from an old to an entirely new quality of life. He beings his Masonic career as the natural man; he ends it by becoming through its discipline, a regenerated perfected man. To attain this transmutation, this metamorphosis of himself, he is taught to first purify and subdue his sensual nature; then to purify and develop his mental nature; and finally, by utter surrender of his old life and losing his soul to save it, he rises from the dead a Master, a just man made perfect, with larger consciousness and faculties, an efficient instrument for use by the Great Architect in His plan of rebuilding the Temple of fallen humanity, and capable of initiating and advancing other men to a participation in the same great work.

> "This – the evolution of man into superman – was always the purpose of the ancient Mysteries, and the real purpose of modern Masonry is, not the social and charitable purposes to which so much attention is paid, but the expediting of the spiritual evolution of those who aspire to perfect their own nature and transform it into a more god-like quality. And this is a definite science, a royal art, which it is possible for each of us to put into practice; whilst to join the Craft for any other purpose than to study and pursue this science is to misunderstand its meaning . . .

"The genuine secrets of a Master Mason," the true knowledge of ourselves, the conscious realization of our divine potentialities.

"The very essence of the Masonic doctrine is that all men in this world are in search of something in their own nature which they have lost, but that with proper instruction and by their own patience and industry they may hope to find. Its philosophy implies that this temporal world is the antipodes of another and more real world from which we originally came and to which we may accelerate our return by such a course of self-knowledge and self-discipline as our teaching inculcates."[183]

Members of The Church of Jesus Christ of Latter-day Saints will see many similarities in our own revealed doctrine. This, I remind you, is because Masonry was once an authentic version of true temple rituals – or at least incorporated true elements into it. However, the Masonic creed – though it possesses some truths – has become corrupted. It is now a thoroughly apostate dogma that has incorporated many occult, pagan, Kabbalistic, Spiritualist elements into its philosophy. As Wilmshurst noted, Masonry is the successor of the ancient pagan Mystery Religions.

Please also note that Masonry, as described by Wilmshurst, purports that man can "accelerate" his own perfection through a course of study. In other words, man can perfect and deify himself. They make no mention of the Lord's Atonement. His blood means absolutely nothing to Masons. It is inconsequential. No faith in Jesus Christ is needed for a Mason to perfect himself. In fact, the Fall of man is seen merely as an allegory and the only way to remedy the situation is by obtaining secret knowledge and so-called God-consciousness.

According to many Masons – and this belief harmonizes with the Theosophists, New Agers, Kabbalists, and others – Jesus was just one of many enlightened teachers sent from God and by no means *the* Master Teacher, *the* Lord, or *the* Redeemer of mankind. Instead, by esoteric "self-knowledge," diligent study, and consciousness-raising, the Mason believes

---

[183] W.L. Wilmshurst, *The Meaning of Masonry* (New York: Gramercy Books, 1980), 46-48.

he can become "perfected" and "god-like" – a "superman" among men. Masonry is thus a complete rejection of Jesus Christ, His redemptive Atonement, and His Gospel ordinances and the Priesthood by which they are performed.

These Satanic delusions are by no means of recent origin. From the very beginning of the world – from the time Cain entered into a secret combination with Lucifer and slew his brother Abel (Moses 5:18, 26-31) – lies have gone forth into the four quarters of the earth. Many Masons and occultists date the start of occultism, or the search for hidden secrets and mysteries, back to Egypt. Mason Albert Churchward, for instance, spent a large part of his book *The Arcana of Freemasonry* tracing Freemasonry and all pagan religions back to ancient Egypt. He shared these fascinating observations which give us insight into how Satan operates through secret societies:

> "From the downfall of the old Egyptian Empire, five thousand years ago, or more, up to the last few hundred years, we have passed through a dark and degenerate age. Then our altars were thrown down, our Brotherhood scattered over the face of the earth, and some of our secrets were lost to many. But there were remnants of the Brotherhood who went forth from Egypt into various parts of the world, carrying the true doctrines and secrets with them, some one part, some another."[184]

> "These Sacred Mysteries were the same amongst the priests of the Mayas, and in Central and South America, the Druids, and the priests of Egypt, and the same as we practise. The similarity of the rites practised in the initiation and other ceremonies, the identity of the sings, symbols, and tokens, proves that all these had been communicated from one to another, from one centre of origin. Only in Old Egypt can we find that origin; it is all there.

> ". . . The so-called Christian cult which is the supposed latest in evolution is, in fact, the oldest. What I mean by this is that the

---

[184] Albert Churchward, *The Arcana of Freemasonry: A History of Masonic Signs and Symbols* (San Francisco, CA: Weiser Books, 2005), 111-112.

> whole of the Christian doctrines were the same as the original Stellar [cult] if you give it the esoteric rendering. The same tale of the Son of God coming on earth, being crucified, and rising again is at least a million years old, and all the different cults are one and the same rendered esoterically."[185]

> "The old faith has never died, and we Freemasons have it in the purest form."[186]

According to many Freemasons, like Churchward, their dogma is the oldest in the world, dating all the way back to Egypt. In this, there is a kernel of truth, as I will briefly detail.

Predating all other religions was the revelation of the Gospel of Jesus Christ to Adam (Moses 5:56-59). The Priesthood authority was also given to Adam so that he could perform saving ordinances for his posterity (Moses 6:7). Adam and Eve "made all things known unto their sons and their daughters" (Moses 5:12). Many of their children rebelled, however, and "loved Satan more than God. And men began from that time forth to be carnal, sensual, and devilish" (Moses 5:13). They formed vicious secret combinations that spread great wickedness throughout the earth (Moses 5:51; Moses 6:15). After the Flood destroyed these perversions, they came back with a vengeance when Satan revealed his secret plans and pagan mysteries to the peoples in Egypt and Babylon.

Shortly after Noah's Flood, Egypt was discovered and founded (Abraham 1:23-24). Because the Egyptians were of the cursed lineage of Cain – through Egyptus, the wife of Noah's son Ham – they were denied the Priesthood (Abraham 1:27). They were, however, blessed with at least a portion of Gospel knowledge and "wisdom" (Abraham 1:26). Tragically, as time progressed, the Egyptian pharaohs pretended to have the true Priesthood authority and quickly turned the Gospel truths they possessed into a sophisticated form of idolatry and paganism that even included human sacrifice (Abraham 1:8-11, 17, 27). Yet, though they warped,

---

[185] Churchward, *The Arcana of Freemasonry*, 123-124.

[186] Churchward, *The Arcana of Freemasonry*, 205.

distorted, and added upon the original teachings learned from Noah, the Egyptians maintained a number of truths found in the original Gospel.

From Egypt, this apostate version of the Gospel was spread into various parts of the world through a secretive Brotherhood, the so-called Mystery Religions, the Jewish Kabbalah, and other mediums. Because of the ancient date of these apostate creeds, many esotericists, New Agers, Masons, Wiccans, etc., believe it is the true faith and that Christianity is only a later manifestation. Some even say that Christianity stole their traditions when, in truth, the opposite happened. The pagan cults took some of the Gospel's teachings, such as the true doctrine that man may become like his Heavenly Father, and misapplied them under different names.

History has been so twisted that it is now mainstream to refer to the pagan and heathen religions as "pre-Christian." Hinduism, Judaism, Egyptian Hermeticism, Asatru, Wicca, and various occult traditions all claim to predate Christianity. Many of them, especially in Europe, demand their traditions, rituals, doctrines, and holidays back from the Christians. The verses from *The Pearl of Great Price* just cited, however, thoroughly refute the notion that any occult or pagan religion predated Christianity. Christianity did not evolve nor was it revealed only by Jesus in the flesh – it was a revelation to Adam and has been handed down and confirmed by angels and prophets ever since.

To recap, the Gospel of Jesus Christ was delivered in its purity to Adam and, as people later rebelled and followed Satan, they changed the doctrines. These doctrines retained an echo of the truth, however. This largely accounts for the similarities between certain doctrines of the Restored Gospel and those found in Eastern, pagan, and New Age religious traditions. In the future, then, when you are confronted with pagan claims of validity based on the grounds of great antiquity, remember that "all things were confirmed unto Adam, by an holy ordinance, and the Gospel preached, and a decree sent forth, that it should be in the world, until the end thereof; and thus it was" (Moses 5:59).

In the book *The Gospel Through the Ages*, commissioned as a course of study for Melchizedek Priesthood quorums for 1946 and written by Elder Milton R. Hunter, we have extensive descriptions of pagan doctrines and rites. Among other things, this book is designed to demonstrate that these various religions retain many of the truths revealed in the beginning to Adam and the patriarchs, albeit in a corrupted form. Some even have much truth but simply do not understand what they possess.

Adam was taught that the Son of God would come to redeem mankind and that through Him men could also become the sons of God. Moses' account tells that God cursed the apostate peoples of the earth: "For they would not hearken unto his voice, nor believe on his Only Begotten Son, even him whom he declared should come in the meridian of time, who was prepared from before the foundation of the world" (Moses 5:57). Thus, the knowledge of a God coming to earth to die for mankind became engrained in nearly every culture on earth.

Elder Milton Hunter explained that most ancient cultures had the idea of savior-gods who would come to redeem their nations. The similarities with the true story of Jesus Christ coming to redeem mankind, being born of a virgin, being crucified for the sins of the world, rising from the dead, and promising salvation and resurrection to His followers, are truly stunning. Elder Hunter wrote of this tradition as established in Egypt:

> "The Egyptian "Osiris was claimed to be the savior of the world, both in his life and death." His devotees believed that he had wrought many noble benefits for mankind while in life, and that through his death he had overcome the powers of darkness. Following his death he became the "Lord of the Underworld and Ruler of the Dead." As a result of his resurrection and the observance of the cult rituals, the worshipers were promised a glorious resurrection and that, if they so chose, they could become gods. . . .

> "The Egyptian mother-goddess, Isis, the "eternal savior of the race of men," promised her worshipers:

> ""Thou shalt live in blessedness; thou shalt live glorious under my protection. And when thou hast finished thy life-course and goest

down to the underworld, even there in that lower world thou shalt see me shedding light in the gloom of Acheron and reigning in the inmost regions of Styx: thou thyself shalt inhabit the Elysian fields and shalt continually offer worship to me, ever gracious."

"It so happened in this pagan cult that Isis acted in conjunction with Osiris as savior-gods, while in the true Gospel the Savior of the world and the Judge of the dead was a male God. This is further evidence of the alterations made in paganism."[187]

The Egyptian traditions are fascinating and they are making a comeback among many in the world today. They are, however, "alterations" of the original Gospel of the Savior.

Furthermore, of the Babylonian tradition of the savior-god Tammuz, Elder Hunter wrote:

"The Babylonian goddess Ishtar, the deified personification of motherhood, was known to Bible writers as Ashtoreth. With her was associated a young and active deity called Tammuz. He was crucified, it was claimed, and afterwards resurrected and deified; and thereupon, becoming a savior, he promised similar blessings to cult members. . . .

"Julius Firmicus speaks of Tammuz as "rising from the dead for the salvation of the world.""[188]

Of a similar Greek tradition, Elder Hunter recorded:

"It was believed that the Greek "Bacchus or Dionysus, born of the virgin Semele to be the liberator of mankind, was torn to pieces," died, resurrected, immortalized, and deified. . . .

"It was claimed that Bacchus, Dionysus-Zagreus and Persephone – three savior-deities – were begotten by Zeus, the chief of the Greek gods, and born to mortal virgins. Obviously this belief was

---

[187] Hunter, *The Gospel Through the Ages*, 155.

[188] Hunter, *The Gospel Through the Ages*, 158.

an adulterated version of Jesus Christ being the Only Begotten Son of God, a fact known and proclaimed by all the holy prophets beginning with Adam. . . .

"Citizens of the Greek world were familiar with Aphrodite and Adonis, "the goddess of love and her impetuous young husband." Adonis, an ardent young hunter, was killed by a wild boar. The grief of his goddess lover brought about his resurrection; and thereafter cult members were promised that they also would rise from death. Obviously this was another drastically altered form of the true Savior doctrine."[189]

The last example I will cite of this religious appropriation is Mithraism. The pagan religion of Mithraism, which possibly originated in Persia and came to dominate Rome and much of the Mediterranean at the time of the early Church, shared a comparable account to that found in the Gospel. According to Elder Hunter:

"Mithraism, the Mystery cult which promised during the early Christian centuries to make itself the universal religion, claimed Mithra to be a mediator between God and man and also a savior, just as Jesus of Nazareth was both Mediator and Savior. He was regarded by his devotees as a divine being, a humanized savior-god. After performing a number of unusual feats, according to tradition he ascended to heaven and became "the god of light, the upholder of truth and the enemy of error," and the judge of the dead. . . .

"Nowhere in ancient paganism was there a god who in his functions resembled more closely the true Savior of mankind than did Mithra. By the time Mithraism reached the Mediterranean world, its beliefs and practices were greatly adulterated; yet the evidence is extensive enough to show beyond question that this ancient religion was a modified form of the true Gospel and that

---

[189] Hunter, *The Gospel Through the Ages*, 156, 158.

is roots extended back into the divine revelations from heaven."[190]

The similarities to Christ's true story are indeed striking. Mithra, like Tammuz, Osiris, and other pagan deities, all attempted to usurp the station of Savior occupied by Jesus Christ, the Only Begotten Son of the Eternal Father.

These historical accounts are mentioned for two reasons: 1) To impress upon your mind that Satan is and always has been highly active in spreading his counterfeit ideas; and 2) to demonstrate a common pattern for how he deceives.

When Satan lies, he often does it by telling the truth. This truth, however, is misapplied and taught out of context. Truth misapplied becomes a lie. His best lies are those mingled with truth. I repeat, Satan lies best when he tells the truth.

Satan's counterfeits are everywhere. All throughout time he has created forgeries to confuse and distract mankind. As we have witnessed, the Adversary has gone so far as to repeat and spread the idea of the coming of a Savior to redeem mankind. Of course, when this truth is ripped out of its context and the label of Savior is given to another besides Jesus Christ, it becomes a gross lie and a solemn mockery of the Son of God.

By spreading the idea of savior-gods *before* the actual appearance and Atonement of Jesus Christ, Satan sought to discredit and confuse the world. If every nation had the notion of a Savior, what would be so special about a new Savior arising in the backwaters of Palestine? And if there is a Savior in Israel, why can't there be one in the more sophisticated Babylon, Greece, or Egypt?

Furthermore, Satan spread the lie of ecumenicism and promoted the equality of divergent "spiritual paths" so that when the new Israeli Savior taught the exclusivity of His Gospel, it would offend others who had their own savior-god and believed their worship of him brought salvation and eternal blessings. Thus, the Father of Lies spread the idea of savior-gods

---

[190] Hunter, *The Gospel Through the Ages*, 156-157.

to confuse mankind and muddy the waters at the time the true Messiah appeared in Jerusalem. And in the 21st Century, Lucifer is resurrecting these false deities to again mislead people and create antipathy towards the Restored Gospel of Jesus Christ.

Understanding, then, that Satan lies most effectively by telling the truth out of context, we consider again the idea of man becoming like God. We quote further from Elder Hunter. In *The Gospel Through the Ages*, he expounded the popular pagan belief – taken from the true Gospel which predated them all – that men may become gods:

> "The Mystery Religions, pagan rivals of Christianity, taught emphatically the doctrine that "men may become Gods." Hermeticism, which had its rise in Egypt in the second or third centuries B.C., was a prominent religion in the Mediterranean world during the period of the rise of Christianity. Its literature, *Corpus Hermeticum*, professes to be revelations from Hermes from his divine father and teacher. Hermes declared: "We must not shrink from saying that a man on earth is a mortal god, and that God in heaven is an immortal man." This thought very closely resembles the teachings of the Prophet Joseph Smith and of President Lorenzo Snow.

> "This religion taught that it was perfectly possible for man, even while living in mortality, to become a god. It also maintained, as does the true Gospel doctrine, that the spirit of the man who had become deified was immortal. To quote from Hermetic literature: "The natural body can be dissolved, the spiritual body cannot be." The worshiper was taught that after he left this mortal life he would "be brought into the troops of the gods and the souls that have attained bliss."

> "Such teachings as the following appear in the theology of Orphism – another prominent pagan rival of Christianity: "'Happy and Blessed One, you shall be God instead of mortal.' . . . Thus the initiated, having lived a life of Orphic purity, finally became 'God from man'." . . . .

"The Great Mother Mystery Religion furnishes another example which deified its cult members. All holders of the priesthood, the *Galli*, were eunuch-priests and were regarded as gods. Each one was also called Attis, the name of the male god of this religion. "Just as Attis was believed to have attained the state of deity by the passion of emasculation, so by the way of self-mutilation, the *Gallus* became a god instead of mortal."

"In the same religion, as well as in the Mithraic Mysteries, a baptism in blood, known as *taurobolium*, was practiced. As the neophyte emerged from the trench, drenched and dripping in blood, he presented himself to the expectant throng or worshipers. "They did obeisance to him as to a god, as to one who had been born again to a divine life."

"Much evidence has been presented which shows that throughout history human beings had the belief that "men may become Gods." During certain periods the prophets have thoroughly understood this sublime truth; and at other times the doctrine has practically vanished from the earth. For example, during the early centuries A.D., both Christians and pagans accepted this doctrine wholeheartedly. Then there came a period, which lasted for hundreds of years, in which the "divine-man doctrine" was lost, except as it applied to kings. During this period, often spoken of as the "Dark Ages," a drastic phase of the Great Apostasy was the loss of the true interpretation of this Gospel truth and its warped and adulterated application to the families of earthly royalty.

"Therefore, during the early part of the nineteenth century, it required divine revelations from God to the Prophet Joseph Smith and other Mormon leaders to restore to mankind in all of its purity and majesty the eternal truth that the goal of human life is that *"men may become Gods.""*[191]

---

[191] Hunter, *The Gospel Through the Ages*, 110-112.

We can see from these examples that the concept of man becoming a god has been widely accepted by the human race at various times. Unfortunately, this truth has long been broken off from the Gospel of Jesus Christ and, thus, is almost universally misapplied, as in the cases of Hinduism and the New Age movement cited earlier. The idea has been mangled and there are now as many definitions of what godhood means as there are alleged ways of achieving it.

One sect may teach that man can meditate his way to enlightenment while another believes self-mutilation opens the pearly gates. A religion may teach that one must find and follow a guru, or master teacher, and yield complete devotion to him in order to advance spiritually. Still another may teach that death, and the "freeing" of one's spirit from the lowly body, or even the complete dissolution of one's self, brings instant deification or union with the cosmic force in the universe. This last concept is depicted in Star Wars, a tale deliberately based on Eastern mystical concepts of God. To the world, there are a million ways to return to God and to become like Him.

None of these alternative paths lead one to exaltation and eternal life, however. No path that denies the mediation of Jesus Christ, or which stands in conflict with any of His revealed laws and ordinances, can ever exalt a single person. All paths but the one marked by Jesus lead to Satan. Many good and honest people are wandering on these crooked paths, yet they are crooked and false paths nonetheless. This strictly exclusive doctrine was taught by the Savior Himself. He declared:

> "Enter ye in at the strait gate: for wide is the gate, and broad is the way, that leadeth to destruction, and many there be which go in thereat:
>
> "Because strait is the gate, and narrow is the way, which leadeth unto life, and few there be that find it" (Matthew 7:13-14).

In modern times, the Lord has reiterated:

> "For strait is the gate, and narrow the way that leadeth unto the exaltation and continuation of the lives, and few there be that

find it, because ye receive me not in the world neither do ye know me" (D&C 132:22).

The true doctrines of the Gospel, on the other hand, "lead the man of Christ in a strait and narrow course across that everlasting gulf of misery which is prepared to engulf the wicked – And land their souls, yea, their immortal souls, at the right hand of God in the kingdom of heaven" (Helaman 3:29-30).

Elder Milton R. Hunter explained the requirements for godhood in these terms:

> "Thus all men who ascend to the glorious status of Godhood can do so only by one method – by obedience to all the principles and ordinances of the Gospel of Jesus Christ. Fundamental in the process of obedience to truth is knowledge. We must first learn true principles before we are capable of intelligent obedience. . . .

> "Thus we do not become Godlike in this world, nor Gods in the world to come, through any miraculous or sudden gift, but only through the slow process of natural growth brought about as a result of righteous living. Some people may think that when they die they will instantaneously get rid of all their bad habits and become purified. Such is not the case. We can become purified in this world, and the same holds true in the next life, only through repentance; that is, overcoming our faults and sins and replacing them with virtues. Charles W. Penrose sustains these thoughts in the following words: "Men become like God not by some supernatural or sudden change, either in this world or another, but by the natural development of the divinity within. Time, circumstances, and the necessary intelligence are all that are required.""[192]

Obedience to the law of the Gospel of Jesus Christ is the *only* way man can become Christlike and, therefore, godlike. It cannot happen in any other way. It cannot be achieved through intensive study, Yoga, or

---

[192] Hunter, *The Gospel Through the Ages*, 115-116.

meditation. It cannot be brought about by some divine emanation from a mystical force. It does not happen through death and leaving one's physical body. There is but one "strait and narrow" path to God.

Only true converts to the discipline of salvation as taught by the Lord Jesus Christ – those who enter into His covenants and partake of His ordinances at the hands of authorized Priesthood holders – can enter into the presence of God. And this is made possible, *notwithstanding our own efforts*, through the grace and mercy of Jesus Christ. It is by His grace alone that we are saved, notwithstanding any and all of our own works.

We cannot earn, study, or pray our way into Heaven. And membership in The Church of Jesus Christ of Latter-day Saints does not guarantee it, though only in the Church are the oracles of God and the Priesthood authority found. The truth is that we are either saved by Christ's mercy, which is conditionally extended to us based on our obedience to His laws, or we are left to ourselves and devoid of His grace.

The Apostle Paul taught:

> "Knowing that a man is not justified by the works of the law, but by the faith of Jesus Christ, even we have believed in Jesus Christ, that we might be justified by the faith of Christ, and not by the works of the law; for by the works of the law shall no flesh be justified. . . .

> ". . . I live by the faith of the Son of God, who loved me, and gave himself for me.

> "I do not frustrate the grace of God: for if righteousness come by the law, then Christ is dead in vain" (Galatians 2:16, 20-21).

And to the Ephesians he wrote:

> "But God, who is rich in mercy, for his great love wherewith he loved us,

> "Even when we were dead in sins, hath quickened us together with Christ, (by grace ye are saved;). . . .

"For by grace are ye saved through faith; and that not of yourselves: it is the gift of God.

"Not of works, lest any man should boast. . . .

"But now in Christ Jesus ye who sometimes were far off are made nigh by the blood of Christ" (Ephesians 2:4-5, 8-9, 13).

Anciently, Nephi taught this harmonious doctrine and bore powerful testimony of Christ's mercy:

"For we labor diligently to write, to persuade our children, and also our brethren, to believe in Christ, and to be reconciled to God; for we know that it is by grace that we are saved, after all we can do. . . .

"And we talk of Christ, we rejoice in Christ, we preach of Christ, we prophesy of Christ, and we write according to our prophecies, that our children may know to what source they may look for a remission of their sins. . . .

". . . the right way is to believe in Christ and deny him not; for by denying him ye also deny the prophets and the law.

"And now behold, I say unto you that the right way is to believe in Christ, and deny him not; and Christ is the Holy One of Israel; wherefore ye must bow down before him, and worship him with all your might, mind, and strength, and your whole soul; and if ye do this ye shall in nowise be cast out" (2 Nephi 25:23, 26, 28-29).

Yes, after all that we can possibly do, it is by Christ's mercy alone that we are saved. Notwithstanding, or in spite, of all that we do, it is the Atonement of the Savior which saves us in the Kingdom of God. A religion or creed that denies the Savior Jesus Christ and His mercies offers no life, hope, or salvation.

There is one additional ordinance we have not mentioned yet that should be briefly noted in connection with attaining exaltation and godhood; that is the institution and ordinance of eternal marriage. Godhood cannot be achieved by individuals; it can only be achieved by a man and a woman bound together in holy matrimony. This is another crucial point in which Latter-day Saints differ from all others who believe they can become gods.

President Russell M. Nelson has taught:

> "Eternal life, or celestial glory or exaltation, is a conditional gift. . .
>
> .
>
> "No man in this Church can obtain the highest degree of celestial glory without a worthy woman who is sealed to him. This temple ordinance enables eventual exaltation for both of them. . . .
>
> "This life is the time to prepare for salvation and exaltation. In God's eternal plan, salvation is an individual matter; exaltation is a family matter."[193]

Only by entering into, and faithfully living, the covenant of celestial marriage can we be exalted. If a man or woman is to be chosen for exaltation, he or she must have a spouse by their side (D&C 131:1-4; D&C 132:19-20). Their union must be sealed by the Priesthood authority of God and ratified by the Holy Ghost. If it is not, they have *no* chance of exaltation and eventual godhood. I repeat: This point sets Latter-day Saints apart from all others who claim they can become gods of their own accord or through self-realization.

In the context of becoming gods, Elder Milton Hunter wrote this about celestial marriage:

> "The crowning Gospel ordinance requisite for Godhood is celestial marriage. . . .
>
> "Marriage is not only a righteous institution, but obedience to this law is absolutely necessary in order to obtain the highest exaltation in the Kingdom of God. . . .

---

[193] President Russell M. Nelson, "Salvation and Exaltation," General Conference, April, 2008, https://www.lds.org/general-conference/2008/04/salvation-and-exaltation?lang=eng.

> ". . . If men and women have obeyed this holy ordinance and all the other principles of the Gospel, following the resurrection and the great judgement day, *"then they shall be Gods.""*[194]

What a wonderful moment it will be when two worthy children of the Father – bound together in the unbreakable cords of celestial marriage – receive of Him their exaltation and then go on advancing in His Kingdom until they arrive at the station of gods and goddesses. Everyone has this potential because we are, truly, of the lineage of the Gods. However, this gift is dependent upon our faithfulness to Jesus Christ and our acceptance of specific Gospel ordinances, the crowning jewel of which is celestial marriage in a temple of God.

Pagan and New Age ideologies do not point man's soul to Christ as the Restored Gospel does. They do not highlight the need for the Savior Jesus Christ and His grace. They do not emphasize eternal marriage. They usually do not even promote any organized religion or specific set of rites. Instead, Satan holds out the bait of godhood in exchange for very little effort, self-discipline, and faith.

Lucifer lures people into a false sense of security by making them think *they* are God or that they don't need any Savior to redeem them. Forever and always Satan twists the everlasting Gospel in order to pervert the ways of the Lord and blind the eyes of men. It is only in the Restored Gospel of Jesus Christ, that found in The Church of Jesus Christ of Latter-day Saints, that man can access the grace of the Savior through properly-administered and eternally-binding ordinances. It is of that divine organization and the Lord whose name it proclaims that I bear solemn witness.

I wish to close this chapter with a small discussion about a Gospel principle that was mentioned above and which has been misapplied and misunderstood throughout the world. I speak of the importance of blood in religious devotion.

---

[194] Hunter, *The Gospel Through the Ages*, 118-120.

As cited above, some pagan religions and Satanic cults practice baptism by blood as well as other rituals, ceremonies, and sacrifices incorporating blood. Even the Catholic Church believes in transubstantiation or, in other words, the "preposterous" notion that the sacrament wine becomes the *literal* blood of Christ during the performing of the ordinance.[195] In these various pagan conceptions, blood usually symbolizes rebirth or cleansing. From the followers of Mithra in Persia and Rome to the believers in the Norse gods in Scandinavia, and from to the Hindus in India to the vicious Leopard Men of Africa, blood plays a central role in ritual and theology.

In this focus on blood, we see yet another kernel of Gospel truth, albeit distorted. Moses' account in *The Pearl of Great Price* informs us that Adam was originally taught the Gospel by angels. He was taught about baptism by immersion for the remission of sins and the reception of the Holy Ghost. Moses' account details the reasons for baptism and the correct mode of performing this ordinance. As you read a portion of the description, take mental note of what role blood plays and whose blood is in question. Adam was taught:

> "That by reason of transgression cometh the fall, which fall bringeth death, and inasmuch as ye were born into the world by water, and blood, and the spirit, which I have made, and so became of dust a living soul, even so ye must be born again into the kingdom of heaven, of water, and of the Spirit, and be cleansed by blood, even the blood of mine Only Begotten; that ye might be sanctified from all sin, and enjoy the words of eternal life in this world, and eternal life in the world to come, even immortal glory;

> "For by the water ye keep the commandment; by the Spirit ye are justified, and by the blood ye are sanctified. . . .

> "And now, behold, I say unto you: This is the plan of salvation unto all men, through the blood of mine Only Begotten, who shall come in the meridian of time" (Moses 6:59-60, 62).

---

[195] President Brigham Young, *Journal of Discourses*, Vol. 13, 140, July 11, 1869, http://jod.mrm.org/13/139.

After learning these doctrines and exercising faith in the still future Atonement of Jesus Christ, Adam was carried into the water by the Spirit and baptized by immersion just as Christ was baptized by immersion at the hands of John in the Jordan River. The Holy Ghost then fell upon Adam, as He also appeared at Christ's baptism, thus completing the cleansing process of baptism.

It is interesting to note that the idea of blood, mentioned five times, played such a key role in these teachings. In fact, it was the active ingredient. Adam learned that it is the *blood* of Christ, which was to be shed as a sacrifice, which sanctifies. It is Christ's blood which cleanses. Through the blood of the Lamb of God we are cleansed from our sins. Without His blood, we are not cleansed and have no place with Him in Heaven. These instructions coincide precisely with what the apostles of the New Testament taught.

The Apostle Paul expounded this crucial principle in these words:

> "But Christ being come an high priest of good things to come, by a greater and more perfect tabernacle, not made with hands, that is to say, not of this building;

> "Neither by the blood of goats and calves, but by his own blood he entered in once into the holy place, having obtained eternal redemption for us.

> "For if the blood of bulls and of goats, and the ashes of an heifer sprinkling the unclean, sanctifieth to the purifying of the flesh:

> "How much more shall the blood of Christ, who through the eternal Spirit offered himself without spot to God, purge your conscience from dead works to serve the living God? . . . .

> "And almost all things are by the law purged with blood; and without shedding of blood is no remission" (Hebrews 9:11-14, 22).

It is the blood of Christ which purges our souls of "dead works." It is His blood, and only His blood, that makes remission of sins and salvation possible. Through the voluntary sacrifice of Himself, He has "obtained eternal redemption for us." Without the Lamb's blood, there is no remission of sins. Do we appreciate the importance of the Atonement of Jesus Christ?

John also taught this principle. He said simply:

> "[I]f we walk in the light, as he is in the light, we have fellowship one with another, and the blood of Jesus Christ his Son cleanseth us from all sin" (1 John 1:7).

And *The Book of Mormon* further tutors us:

> "And again, if ye by the grace of God are perfect in Christ, and deny not his power, then are ye sanctified in Christ by the grace of God, through the shedding of the blood of Christ, which is in the covenant of the Father unto the remission of your sins, that ye become holy, without spot" (Moroni 10:33).

> "And the angel said unto me: Look! And I looked, and beheld three generations pass away in righteousness; and their garments were white even like unto the Lamb of God. And the angel said unto me: These are made white in the blood of the Lamb, because of their faith in him" (1 Nephi 12:11).

Other verses could be cited, but these demonstrate the high emphasis placed on the blood of the Redeemer Jesus Christ. Jesus was the Lamb of God, the great and last sacrifice. His blood answered the demands of the law of justice which calls for retribution against sinners. Because He paid that extraordinary price that only a God could pay, He can now extend mercy on certain conditions and overpower, as it were, justice. The scriptures teach:

> "And thus he shall bring salvation to all those who shall believe on his name; this being the intent of this last sacrifice, to bring about the bowels of mercy, which overpowereth justice, and bringeth about means unto men that they may have faith unto repentance.

> "And thus mercy can satisfy the demands of justice, and encircles them in the arms of safety, while he that exercises no faith unto repentance is exposed to the whole law of the demands

of justice; therefore only unto him that has faith unto repentance is brought about the great and eternal plan of redemption" (Alma 34:15-16).

Whether or not the "great and eternal plan of redemption" is activated in our favor depends upon our agency. Yes, all mankind will be redeemed, unconditionally, from the Fall of Adam in that they will be saved from the first death, or the death of the physical body. The Lord burst the bands of death forever that day He rose from the tomb. As a gift to the world, the Savior's Atonement unconditionally redeems all men from the grave and assures them a resurrection. But what of the second death – the spiritual death?

Elder Orson Pratt remarked:

> "You can save yourselves through the atonement, or let it alone. Jesus has done his part: he has died for us—has got the plan all laid; his blood has been shed, and he has suffered the pains of all the children of men, and in their behalf, if they will only accept the conditions."[196]

Because of our agency, "God will force no man to heav'n. He'll call, persuade, direct aright, And bless with wisdom, love, and light, In nameless ways be good and kind, But never force the human mind."[197] If man complies with Christ's conditions, he receives Christ's grace. It is Jesus Christ who saves, and who has power to save through the voluntary shedding of His blood, but we can *choose* to be saved by obeying His laws.

Abinadi told us for whom Christ shed His precious blood. Said he:

> "Behold I say unto you, that whosoever has heard the words of the prophets, yea, all the holy prophets who have prophesied concerning the coming of the Lord—I say unto you, that all those who have hearkened unto their words, and believed that the Lord

---

[196] Elder Orson Pratt, *Journal of Discourses*, Vol. 7, 258, September 11, 1859, http://jod.mrm.org/7/251.

[197] "Know This, That Every Soul Is Free," Hymn No. 240.

would redeem his people, and have looked forward to that day for a remission of their sins, I say unto you, that these are his seed, or they are the heirs of the kingdom of God.

"For these are they whose sins he has borne; these are they for whom he has died, to redeem them from their transgressions" (Mosiah 15:11-12).

If we accept Christ, have faith on His holy name, repent of our sins, follow the commandments, and endure to the end in righteousness, the Atonement of Jesus will ensure us a place on His right hand at the Judgement Day. Let us always remember, however, that it is *Jesus Christ* who saves us. Specifically, it is His redeeming blood which cleanses us and changes us in our inner being and qualifies us as heirs of salvation. The Holy Ghost can impress these truths deep into the fibers of our being and help purge us of all unrighteousness if we let Him.

We thus see that the pagan doctrine of rebirth, cleansing, or empowerment by blood is a mere echo of this true Gospel principle. However, because they lacked Priesthood authority and inspired leadership, pagan groups misapplied these principles and, over the centuries, they became blasphemous perversions. Pursuant to this belief, far too many heathen cults have practiced, and still do practice, human sacrifice or other forms of ritualistic bloodletting.

In doing all of these things, the pagans miss the most important point of it all; namely, that it is not just any blood that cleanses, but *Christ's* blood. Only the Savior's blood can cleanse and sanctify! Only Jesus Christ has the power to save. Only His Atonement justifies mankind and reconciles us with God.

The blood of a sheep, dove, or even another man, has no power whatsoever to cleanse one particle of a person from sin. The great Atonement of Christ is the only sacrifice that counts. Even ancient Israel's multitude of animal sacrifices meant nothing in and of themselves. They were simply a means of pointing people's souls toward that Messiah (Jacob 4:5) who would come to shed His own blood for the world. Abinadi taught it this way:

> "And moreover, I say unto you, that salvation does not come by the law alone; and were it not for the atonement, which God himself shall make for the sins and iniquities of his people, that they must unavoidably perish, notwithstanding the law of Moses (Mosiah 13:28).

In this example of the misapplication of blood, we confirm the great truth we have been discussing in this chapter. We verify that Satan's lie was *not* that man may become a god – for that is pure, crystal truth – but, rather, that he may do it by himself separate and apart from the Atonement of Jesus Christ. This idea is everlastingly false.

Simply, man *cannot* deify himself. He *cannot* learn how to be a god by reading about it in a book or studying with an elite organization. He *cannot* hike into the Himalayas to be taught by a Tibetan monk how to achieve enlightenment. He *cannot* sacrifice an animal or spill human blood to save himself or appease God. All of these ideas constitute a denial of the Gospel of Jesus Christ, the Lord's divinity, His exclusive claim to be the Only Begotten Son of God and Redeemer of mankind, and the very notion of a Father in Heaven who presides over a universe operated on the principles of law and order.

Yet, Satan has labored hard to persuade men that they do not need the mediation of the Savior in order to become divine, that they do not need the Atonement of Jesus Christ, and that they do not need the Gospel or any form of revealed or organized religion. Instead, they can do it on their own. As discussed, some of the methods taught by Satan and his false prophets for achieving individual "enlightenment" include meditation, obeying the teachings of advanced gurus or otherworldly Masters of Wisdom, using psychedelic drugs, indulging altered states of consciousness, communing with Lord Maitreya or some cosmic force, ruminating on the names of God, repeating mantras, becoming an aesthetic monk in a mountain cave, sacrificing children on hidden altars, leaving offerings on the shrines of so-called saints, etc. In short, the Adversary teaches man to put his trust in the arm of flesh and to reject the guidance of his Father in Heaven and the Atonement of His Son Jesus Christ (2 Nephi 28:31).

The Lord has said that "man should not counsel his fellow man, neither trust in the arm of flesh" (D&C 1:19). Perhaps this is because man is in a fallen state. The scriptures and prophets plainly teach that man is powerless and helpless without the intervention and Redemption of Jesus Christ. Jacob testified:

> "[B]ecause man became fallen they were cut off from the presence of the Lord.
>
> "Wherefore, it must needs be an infinite atonement – save it should be an infinite atonement this corruption could not put on incorruption. Wherefore, the first judgment which came upon man must needs have remained to an endless duration. And if so, this flesh must have laid down to rot and to crumble to its mother earth, to rise no more.
>
> "O the wisdom of God, his mercy and grace! For behold, if the flesh should rise no more our spirits must become subject to that angel who fell from before the presence of the Eternal God, and became the devil, to rise no more.
>
> "And our spirits must have become like unto him, and we become devils, angels to a devil, to be shut out from the presence of our God, and to remain with the father of lies, in misery, like unto himself" (2 Nephi 9:6-9).

Amulek similarly bore witness that *only* Christ's Atonement can save mankind. He said:

> "For it is expedient that an atonement should be made; for according to the great plan of the Eternal God there must be an atonement made, or else all mankind must unavoidably perish; yea, all are hardened; yea, all are fallen and are lost, and must perish except it be through the atonement which it is expedient should be made.
>
> "For it is expedient that there should be a great and last sacrifice; yea, not a sacrifice of man, neither of beast, neither of any manner of fowl; for it shall not be a human sacrifice; but it must be an infinite and eternal sacrifice.

> "Now there is not any man that can sacrifice his own blood which will atone for the sins of another. . . .
>
> ". . . therefore there can be nothing which is short of an infinite atonement which will suffice for the sins of the world" (Alma 34:9-12).

Without the Atonement of Jesus Christ, we would be lost forever; *all* of us have sinned and taken upon us corruption and physical death by entering mortality. Even children, as innocent and pure as they are, take on a fallen existence when they come into mortality, die as to the physical body, and, thus, would be lost without Christ's Redemption which stretches both directions into the eternities and rescues men not only from sin, but from physical death. We are explicitly told in scripture that "all mankind" is fallen and that little children only escape the demands of justice and the "curse of Adam" because of Christ's mercy, which comes by power of His Atonement and the shedding of His sinless blood (1 Nephi 10:6; Moroni 8:8, 12, 19; D&C 29:46; Romans 3:23-24).

Without the Lord's saving grace, we would all descend into the pit with the Devil and become his servants. Without His mercy, we, having sinned and having taken upon ourselves a fallen nature and death by coming into mortality, would be cut off from our Father and would be miserable forever. We would be deprived of a physical body, a resurrection, personal salvation, and family exaltation. When we consider this, we are compelled to exclaim what an unspeakable gift and opportunity our Elder Brother, our Savior and King, has offered us!

President Joseph Fielding Smith further illustrated man's helplessness with an astute analogy. He also emphasized the Savior's voluntary sacrifice in our behalf and how it allows us to exercise our agency to accept His Redemption. President Smith said:

> "A man walking along the road happens to fall into a pit so deep and dark that he cannot climb to the surface and regain his freedom. How can he save himself from his predicament? Not by any exertions on his part, for there is no means of escape in the pit. He calls for help and some kindly disposed soul, hearing his cries for relief, hastens to his assistance and by lowering a ladder,

gives to him the means by which he may climb again to the surface of the earth.

"This was precisely the condition that Adam placed himself and his posterity in, when he partook of the forbidden fruit. All being together in the pit, none could gain the surface and relieve the others. The pit was banishment from the presence of the Lord and temporal death, the dissolution of the body. And all being subject to death, none could provide the means of escape.

"Therefore, in his infinite mercy, the Father heard the cries of his children and sent his Only Begotten Son, who was not subject to death nor to sin, to provide the means of escape. This he did through his infinite atonement and the everlasting gospel.

"The Savior *voluntarily* laid down his life and took it up again to satisfy the demands of justice, which required an infinite atonement. His Father accepted this offering *in the stead* of the blood of all those who were under the curse, and consequently helpless. The Savior said, "I lay down my life for the sheep. . . . Therefore doth my Father love me, because I lay down my life, that I might take it up again. *No man taketh it from me, but I lay it down of myself*. I have power to lay it down, and I have power to take it again. This commandment have I received of my Father.""[198]

Fallen man sits at the bottom of a dark pit, helpless to save himself by any effort of his own. In this position, all is hopeless without intervention from above. Just as the thought occurs and doom seems certain, One from above mercifully extends a ladder to the bottom of the pit. If we choose, we may grab the rungs of the ladder and, starting from the bottom, climb gradually upward until finally we reach the safety and light. And the One we have to thank for this undeserved mercy and love is the Lord Jesus Christ, the Messiah, Emmanuel, the Morning Star, the very Son of God.

---

[198] Smith, *Doctrines of Salvation*, Vol. 1, 126-127.

Satan understands the position Jesus Christ occupies. He knows the unrivaled power of the Lord's Atonement – the power to destroy the Devil's craft forever. Therefore, Lucifer will tell any lie to achieve his goal of degrading mankind, dragging them down into the pit, and making them miserable like he is. Let us carefully avoid *all* half-truths which Satan has diluted with his lies – they have no power to save or exalt. Let us, as President Brigham Young urged, "look out for the counterfeit."

We can and should reject the falsehoods inherent in Satan's lie that we may become gods *through our own efforts* or that God is an indefinable cosmic essence that we will one day give up our individuality to merge with. These are damnable heresies (2 Peter 2:1) unworthy of acceptance by sons and daughters of God. We *need* Christ; we *cannot* do it alone. Without His mediation in our behalf, which mediation is conditional upon our repentance and faithfulness, we are everlastingly lost and cut off from the presence of our Eternal Parents and our Heavenly home.

Rather than go it alone, we must "rely upon the merits of Jesus Christ" (D&C 3:20) and give strict obedience to His laws and ordinances which lead us in an undeviating course to eternal life. We should look to our Savior in every thought without fear or doubt (D&C 6:36), apply His atoning blood in our lives (Mosiah 4:2), feast upon His love forever (Jacob 3:2), and be steadfast and immovable in our faith in Christ until the end when He will seal us His (Mosiah 5:15).

At a challenging time in the Church's early history, the Savior issued a call to His Saints. I pray that in our own times of challenge or dismay, we may heed His words and let them buoy our souls and give us confidence and hope. Let us trust in our Savior who has bought us with His holy blood (1 Corinthians 6:20) and who will not lose any who come to Him (John 6:39-40). Open your heart and receive the word of the Lord:

> "Listen to him who is the advocate with the Father, who is pleading your cause before him—
>
> "Saying: Father, behold the sufferings and death of him who did no sin, in whom thou wast well pleased; behold the blood of thy Son which was shed, the blood of him whom thou gavest that thyself might be glorified;

"Wherefore, Father, spare these my brethren that believe on my name, that they may come unto me and have everlasting life" (D&C 45:3-5).

Chapter Sixth

God Loves His Children

Anciently, when Nephi was shown an overwhelmingly glorious vision of the Savior's birth, he was asked by an angel if he understood the condescension of God. Nephi, always frank and sincere, responded:

> "I know that he loveth his children; nevertheless, I do not know the meaning of all things" (1 Nephi 11:17).

In that same vision, Nephi observed a pure tree and was asked if he knew the symbolic meaning. He replied resolutely:

> "Yea, it is the love of God, which sheddeth itself abroad in the hearts of the children of men; wherefore, it is the most desirable above all things" (1 Nephi 11:22).

The angel promptly agreed and said: "Yea, and the most joyous to the soul" (1 Nephi 11:23).

From this sacred exchange, we learn at least two very important things. The first lesson we can learn is that we don't always have the answers to life's questions. We don't know, for instance, the exact age of the earth. We don't know precisely where Kolob is, how long we lived with our Father in Heaven in pre-mortality, or what it was like to exist as intelligences. We do not remember our Father's face and we have no recollection of our Mother in Heaven. We do not now fathom how the Savior worked out His infinite Atonement for all of Heavenly Father's children. Yet, despite our finite understanding, we know the most important thing: *We know that we are God's children and that He loves us.*

Armed with this truth, we can forge ahead in faith, trusting in our Eternal Father to bring us safely back home. We can trust that our Father will protect us and defend us, like any good father protects his children. As children rely upon their parents for sustenance, shelter, and the necessities of life, so, too, can we confidently rely upon our Heavenly Father to provide all that we need and more. He wants us to have the abundant life (John 10:10).

Because He loves us so much, Elohim has blessed us with "enough and to spare" so that we will never want (D&C 104:17). In this connection, the Lord has declared: "And it is my purpose to provide for my saints, for all things are mine" (D&C 104:15). We can trust Him implicitly, for, as Peter said: "The Lord is not slack concerning his promise" (2 Peter 3:9).

The Psalmist once recited these delightful assurances:

> "The Lord is good to all: and his tender mercies are over all his works. . . .

> "The Lord is righteous in all his ways, and holy in all his works.

> "The Lord is nigh unto all them that call upon him, to all that call upon him in truth.

> "He will fulfil the desire of them that fear him: he also will hear their cry, and will save them.

> "The Lord preserveth all them that love him" (Psalm 145:9, 17-20).

Similar promises and declarations fill the pages of the holy scriptures. It seems that the Lord is eager to have us trust Him and the Father of us all. They want us to know of Their great love. They want us to feel secure, confident, and happy.

The Apostle Paul testified:

> "[W]e are more than conquerors through him that loved us.

> "For I am persuaded, that neither death, nor life, nor angels, nor principalities, nor powers, nor things present, nor things to come,

> "Nor height, nor depth, nor any other creature, shall be able to separate us from the love of God, which is in Christ Jesus our Lord" (Romans 8:37-39).

Nothing, but our own illicit actions, can separate us from God's great love! Absolutely nothing Satan or our fellow men do can detach us from the love of our Father and the love of our Elder Brother. That love is pure and binding and we have a claim on it so long as we stay within the light (D&C 95:12). We do that by loving the Savior and honoring His commandments.

To those Saints humble enough to believe in Him, Jesus has promised:

> "[T]he Father himself loveth you, because ye have loved me, and have believed that I came out from God" (John 16:27).

Yes, we have a Father who capable of love and who loves each of us dearly! We have a Father who is personal, personable, kind, meek, cheerful, charitable, and filled with the purest of love – that love which "is the most desirable above all things" and "the most joyous to the soul."

The quality that defines God more than all others is love. God *is* love. Love radiates from His Being and fills His Spirit. Because we are His children, each of us has a divine capacity to love and feel love. And because we are so loved, we ought to love one another.

The Lord affirmed: "By this shall all men know that ye are my disciples, if ye have love one to another" (John 13:35). We are in fact *commanded* to love (John 15:17). We are commanded to love the same way that Christ loves us, which is the same way the Father loves Him. He said:

> "As the Father hath loved me, so have I loved you: continue ye in my love.
>
> "If ye keep my commandments, ye shall abide in my love" (John 15:9-10).

If we keep the commandments and thereby continue in the Lord's love, we have unspeakable blessings promised to us:

> "He that hath my commandments, and keepeth them, he it is that loveth me: and he that loveth me shall be loved of my Father, and I will love him, and will manifest myself to him. . . .

". . . If a man love me, he will keep my words: and my Father will love him, and we will come unto him, and make our abode with him" (John 13:21, 23).

What incredible promises! If we keep the commandments, which is the same as continuing in Christ's love, then the Father and the Son will love us and make Their abode with us and the Savior will manifest Himself to us. What could be more satisfying and desirable than receiving the love of God and the personal manifestations of the Savior Jesus Christ?

To the fledgling band of Saints in his day, John wrote similarly encouraging words. He testified:

"Ye are of God, little children. . . .

"We are of God. . . .

"Beloved, let us love one another: for love is of God; and every one that loveth is born of God, and knoweth God.

"He that loveth not knoweth not God; for God is love.

"In this was manifested the love of God toward us, because that God sent his only begotten Son into the world, that we might live through him.

"Herein is love, not that we loved God, but that he loved us, and sent his Son to be the propitiation for our sins.

"Beloved, if God so loved us, we ought also to love one another.

". . . If we love one another, God dwelleth in us, and his love is perfected in us. . . .

"And we have known and believed the love that God hath to us. God is love; and he that dwelleth in love dwelleth in God, and God in him." (1 John 4:4, 6-12, 16).

Have you known and believed the love that God has for *you* as His special son or daughter? Do you also love others and, by so doing, allow Heavenly Father into your heart? Have you lately pondered the exceptional degree of love the Father has for you? He loved *you* so much that He sent His

Firstborn Son, Jesus Christ, to suffer unjustly at the hands of wicked men, to be beaten and spit upon, and to be nailed to a tree and killed. When you ponder that, also remember that your Elder Brother *voluntarily* suffered all of that and more *because He loves you*.

As noted earlier, President Nelson has taught that exaltation is a *family* affair. The exaltation of the entire human family – God's family – is God's business, His work, and His glory. Nothing gives Him greater satisfaction than to help His children traverse the path that leads to eternal happiness and exaltation in His mansions above.

Laboring together, our Father and Elder Brother have worked out a Plan to save the rest of us and to exalt us alongside Them in Their Heavenly Kingdom. To make this Plan active in our lives, our Elder Brother has voluntarily given His life for us because He loves us. And our Father allowed Him to do so because He also loves us.

Jesus Himself declared:

> "For God so loved the world, that he gave his only begotten Son, that whosoever believeth in him should not perish, but have everlasting life.
>
> "For God sent not his Son into the world to condemn the world; but that the world through him might be saved" (John 3:16-17).

Never was greater love shown than in the Father's sacrifice of His Son for the sins of the world and in the Son's selfless submission to the will of the Father. Because They have demonstrated Their boundless love, we can "come boldly unto the throne of grace, that we may obtain mercy, and find grace to help in time of need" (Hebrews 4:16).

Of this thing called love, President Russell M. Nelson, whom I love and sustain wholeheartedly as the Lord's current mouthpiece on earth, wrote:

> "In these latter days we who are privileged to have the Book of Mormon, to be members of the Lord's Church, to have His gospel, and to keep His commandments know something of God's infinite love. We know how to make His love our own. As we become His true disciples, we gain the power to love as He does. As we keep

His commandments, we become more like Him. We broaden our personal circle of love in reaching out to people of every nation, kindred, and tongue."[199]

We who are privileged to have the Restored Gospel of Jesus Christ do indeed know something of God's great love! We who know that we began our existence as intelligences in the pre-mortal realms know of God's love. We who understand that our pre-existent intelligence was clothed with spirit element from our Father in Heaven and that He is our *literal* Father and that we are His *literal* spirit children know of His love. We who understand the Plan of Salvation grasp the Father's love for us and His desire to see us grow, progress, and become like Him. And we who know that our Elder Brother Jesus Christ died for us certainly know of love and have been its recipients, for "greater love hath no man than this" (John 15:13).

It is impossible in our present condition to fully comprehend the extent of God's love for us and the lengths to which He and the Son have gone to care for us and provide a means of returning to Their presence to enjoy exaltation. Even so, President Dieter F. Uchtdorf expressed this thought:

> "This is a paradox of man: compared to God, man is nothing; yet we are everything to God. While against the backdrop of infinite creation we may appear to be nothing, we have a spark of eternal fire burning within our breast. We have the incomprehensible promise of exaltation—worlds without end—within our grasp. And it is God's great desire to help us reach it. . . .
>
> "God sees you not only as a mortal being on a small planet who lives for a brief season – He sees you as His child. He sees you as the being you are capable and designed to become. He wants you to know that you matter to Him."[200]

---

[199] President Russell M. Nelson, "What the Book of Mormon Teaches about the Love of God," *Ensign*, October, 2011, https://www.lds.org/ensign/2011/10/what-the-book-of-mormon-teaches-about-the-love-of-god?lang=eng.

[200] President Dieter F. Uchtdorf, "You Matter to Him," General Conference, October, 2011, https://www.lds.org/general-conference/2011/10/you-matter-to-him?lang=eng.

Perhaps it is a paradox. Perhaps the promises the Lord has extended to us are incomprehensible. Yet, notwithstanding this, we can echo Nephi who said in great faith that he did not know all things, but he absolutely knew that the Eternal Father "loveth his children." Despite all our imperfections, sins, and lack of understanding, we have a perfect knowledge that *we matter to Him*.

I bear my witness that God our Father *does* love us with a perfect love. He loves me and He loves you. He even loves those who despise Him and reject His paternal teachings. He wants them to return to Him so that He can wrap them in His loving embrace. He, and our Mother in Heaven, are cheering us on and cannot wait to embrace us once more after our long day in the university of mortality is over. He will give us all the help we need as we struggle forward and keep our eye on the prize of a happy homecoming.

And the Savior, our dear Brother, loves us enough to daily wear the wound marks from the nails in His hands and feet so that we are ever before His eyes and foremost in His heart and mind (1 Nephi 21:15-16). He cannot and will not forget us nor forsake us. He has already paid the price for our sins and He completely understands our frailties, feelings, and weaknesses. He is constantly there watching over us, struggling beside us, and bearing our burdens with us. I bear my witness of Jesus Christ, His divinity, His great love, and His rightful role as Savior of mankind.

I bear my witness of The Church of Jesus Christ of Latter-day Saints. It is the Kingdom of God on the earth. It was founded by the Lord through the Prophet Joseph Smith, whom I also love and bear testimony of. *The Book of Mormon*, as the Bible, is the word of God and testifies of Jesus Christ and His Atonement. My life would not be the same without that book of divine truth. I also have a firm testimony of the call of prophets. I undeniably know through the Holy Spirit that we are indeed led by modern prophets – men like Moses, Elijah, Peter, Nephi, and Alma. I bear witness of President Russell M. Nelson, the Lord's current prophet-president, and urge everyone to heed his counsel and to gain an independent testimony that the Lord is guiding His Church through revelation.

I love this Gospel! I love the Lord! I love my Father in Heaven! Words cannot describe the depth of my feelings. I stand in awe at the knowledge that I am a member of the family of God, that I am a son of my Eternal Father, and that I once lived in Heaven and have the opportunity to choose the correct Gospel path and make my way back to that paradise above. Stagger as I might, I am pushing forward and I know that with my Savior's help I will one day stand pure and clean before my Father in Heaven.

I pray that each of us will "treasure up these words in [our] heart. Be faithful and diligent in keeping the commandments of God, and [He] will encircle [us] in the arms of [His] love" (D&C 6:20). Let us remember that we have a loving Father and Mother in Heaven and that we are Their *literal* children. Let us remember who we are and move forward with boldness and confidence toward exaltation in our Father's Heavenly Home. Let us cherish the truth that *we are descended from the lineage of the Gods!*

In the name of Jesus Christ, my Savior, Amen.

Recommended Reading

A Century of Red, by Zack Strong

A Marvelous Work and a Wonder, by LeGrand Richards

A New Witness for the Articles of Faith, by Bruce R. McConkie

America: The Sorcerer's New Apprentice – The Rise of New Age Shamanism, by Dave Hunt and T.A. McMahon

America's Coming Crisis: Prophetic Warnings, Divine Destiny, by David N. Balmforth

An Enemy Hath Done This, by Ezra Taft Benson

Answers to Gospel Questions, by Joseph Fielding Smith

Apostasy from the Divine Church, James L. Barker

Apostasy to Restoration, by T. Edgar Lyon

Awakening to our Awful Situation: Warnings from the Nephite Prophets, by Jack Monnett

Bad Guys of the Book of Mormon, by Dennis Gaunt

Communism in Ambush: How the Scourge of the 20th Century is Preparing for Fresh Savagery, by Harun Yahya

Discourses of Brigham Young, edited by John A. Widtsoe

Doctrines of Salvation, three volumes, by Joseph Fielding Smith

Encyclopedia of New Age Beliefs, by John Ankerberg and John Weldon

Endowed from on High: Understanding the Symbols of the Endowment, by John D. Charles

Ephraim: Chosen of the Lord, by R. Wayne Shute, Monte S. Nyman, and Randy L. Bott

Exploring the Book of Mormon in the Heartland, by Rod Meldrum

Extraordinary Times, Extraordinary Beings: Experiences of an American Diplomat with Maitreya and the Masters of Wisdom, by Wayne S. Peterson

Family Leadership: Inspired Counsel for Parents, by V. Dallas Merrell

Finding Light in a Dark World, by James E. Faust

Generation Hex: Understanding the Subtle Dangers of Wicca, by Dillon Burroughs and Marla Alupoaicei

God, Family, Country: Our Three Great Loyalties, by Ezra Taft Benson

Gospel Doctrine, by Joseph F. Smith

Gospel Truth: Discourses and Writings of President George Q. Cannon, two volumes, edited by Jerreld L. Newquist

Hearing the Voice of the Lord: Principles and Patterns of Personal Revelation, by Gerald N. Lund

Hiding in Plain Sight: Unmasking the Secret Combinations of the Last Days, by Ken Bowers

His Servants Speak: Excerpts from Devotional Addresses given at Brigham Young University by General Authorities of The Church of Jesus Christ of Latter-day Saints, edited by R. Wayne Shute

If Men Were Angels: The Book of Mormon, Christ, and the Constitution, by Brad E. Hainsworth

Inside the New Age Nightmare, by Randall N. Baer

Joseph Smith: Presidential Candidate – Setting the Record Straight, by Arnold K. Garr

Just and Holy Principles: Latter-day Saint Reading on America and the Constitution, edited by Ralph C. Hancock

In Ephraim's Footsteps, by Clay McConkie

Leadership, three volumes, by Sterling W. Sill

Like Lambs to the Slaughter: Your Child and the Occult, by Johanna Michaelsen

Man – His Origin and Destiny, by Joseph Fielding Smith

Many Are Called But Few Are Chosen, by Hans Verlan Andersen

Marx & Satan, by Richard Wurmbrand

Mormon Doctrine, second edition, by Bruce R. McConkie

Motherhood: A Partnership with God, edited by Harold Lundstrom

New Age Medicine: A Christian Perspective on Holistic Health, by Paul C. Reisser, Teri K. Reisser, and John Weldon

New Age Menace: The Secret War Against the Followers of Christ, by David N. Balmforth

Occult Invasion: The Subtle Seduction of the World and Church, by Dave Hunt

On the Way to Immortality and Eternal Life, by J. Reuben Clark., Jr.

Our Destiny: The Call and Election of the House of Israel, by Robert L. Millet and Joseph Fielding McConkie

Pathways to Happiness, by David O. McKay

Principles, Promises, and Powers, by Sterling W. Sill

Prophecies and Promises – The Book of Mormon and the United States of America, by Bruce H. Porter and Rod Meldrum

Quotes from Prophets on Mothers & Families, edited by Laura M. Hawkes

Red Gadiantons: What the Prophets Have Taught about the Communist Secret Combination that Threatens Mankind, by Zack Strong

Satan's War on Free Agency, by Greg Wright

Secret Combinations Today: A Voice of Warning, by Robert E. Hales

Sermons and Missionary Services of Melvin Joseph Ballard, by Bryant S. Hinckley

Stand Fast By Our Constitution, by J. Reuben Clark, Jr.

Strategic Relocation: North American Guide to Safe Places, by Joel M. Skousen and Andrew Skousen

Take Heed to Yourselves! by Joseph Fielding Smith

Testimonies of our Leaders, edited by Forace Green

The 5,000 Year Leap: Principles of Freedom 101, by W. Cleon Skousen

The Birth We Call Death, by Paul H. Dunn

The Book of Revelation Today: The Last of the Last Days – Who, What, Where, When, Why and How, by Farley Anderson

The Elders of Israel and the Constitution, by Jerome Horowitz

The Falling Away, by B. H. Roberts

The First 2,000 Years: From Adam to Abraham, by W. Cleon Skousen

The Fourth Thousand Years: From David to Christ, by W. Cleon Skousen

The Godhead: New Scriptural Insights on the Father, the Son, and the Holy Ghost, by Duane S. Crowther

The Gospel through the Ages, by Milton R. Hunter

The Great Apostasy, by James E. Talmage

The Great Prologue, by Mark E. Petersen

The Holy Ghost, by Joseph Fielding McConkie and Robert L. Millet

The Incomparable Christ: Our Master and Model, by Vaughn J. Featherstone

The Law of the Harvest, by Sterling W. Sill

The Life Before: How Our Premortal Existence Affects Our Mortal Life, by Brent L. Top

The Majesty of God's Law, by W. Cleon Skousen

The Making of America, by W. Cleon Skousen

The Master Deceiver: Understanding Satan's Lies and How to Resist Them, by David J. Stitt

The Millennial Messiah, by Bruce R. McConkie

The Moral Basis of a Free Society, by Hans Verlan Andersen

The Mortal Messiah, three volumes, by Bruce R. McConkie

The Naked Capitalist, by W. Cleon Skousen

The Naked Communist, by W. Cleon Skousen

The New World Religion: The Spiritual Roots of Global Government, by Gary H. Kah

The Promised Messiah, by Bruce R. McConkie

The Prophet Joseph Smith's Views on the Powers and Policy of the Government of the United States, by Joseph Smith

The Spirit of America: Patriotic Addresses from America's Freedom Festival, by Bookcraft

The Third Thousand Years: From Abraham to David, by W. Cleon Skousen

The Way to Peace, by Mark E. Petersen

The World and the Prophets, by Hugh Nibley

This Day . . . And Always, by Richard L. Evans

This Land: They Came from the East, by Wayne N. May

This Nation Shall Endure, by Ezra Taft Benson

Title of Liberty: A Warning Voice, by Ezra Taft Benson

Unmasking the New Age, by Douglas R. Groothuis

Using the Book of Mormon to Combat Falsehoods in Organic Evolution, by Clark A. Peterson

Wherefore the Lord Commandeth You, by J.R. Ledkins

Woman and the Priesthood, by Rodney Turner

Yoga and the Body of Christ: What Position Should Christians Hold? by Dave Hunt

You and Your Marriage, by Hugh B. Brown

Contact Author

zackstrongbooks@outlook.com

https://amazon.com/author/zackstrong

https://theamericancitadel.com

https://libertywolf.com

https://www.facebook.com/ProphetsInTheLandAgain/

Find my previous books *A Century of Red* and *Red Gadiantons: What the Prophets Have Taught about the Communist Secret Combination that Threatens Mankind* on Amazon.

Made in the USA
Las Vegas, NV
13 April 2021